Communications
in Computer and Information Science 694

Commenced Publication in 2007
Founding and Former Series Editors:
Alfredo Cuzzocrea, Dominik Ślęzak, and Xiaokang Yang

More information about this series at http://www.springer.com/series/7899

Cyrille Artho · Peter Csaba Ölveczky (Eds.)

Formal Techniques for Safety-Critical Systems

5th International Workshop, FTSCS 2016
Tokyo, Japan, November 14, 2016
Revised Selected Papers

Springer

Editors
Cyrille Artho
KTH Royal Institute of Technology
Stockholm
Sweden

Peter Csaba Ölveczky
Department of Informatics
University of Oslo
Oslo
Norway

ISSN 1865-0929   ISSN 1865-0937   (electronic)
Communications in Computer and Information Science
ISBN 978-3-319-53945-4   ISBN 978-3-319-53946-1   (eBook)
DOI 10.1007/978-3-319-53946-1

Library of Congress Control Number: 2017931545

Printed on acid-free paper

This Springer imprint is published by Springer Nature
The registered company is Springer International Publishing AG
The registered company address is: Gewerbestrasse 11, 6330 Cham, Switzerland

Preface

This volume contains the proceedings of the Fifth International Workshop on Formal Techniques for Safety-Critical Systems (FTSCS 2016), held in Tokyo on November 14, 2016, as a satellite event of the ICFEM conference.

The aim of this workshop is to bring together researchers and engineers who are interested in the application of formal and semi-formal methods to improve the quality of safety-critical computer systems. FTSCS strives to promote research and development of formal methods and tools for industrial applications, and is particularly interested in industrial applications of formal methods. Specific topics include, but are not limited to:

- case studies and experience reports on the use of formal methods for analyzing safety-critical systems, including avionics, automotive, railway, medical, and other kinds of safety-critical and QoS-critical systems;
- methods, techniques, and tools to support automated analysis, certification, debugging, etc., of complex safety/QoS-critical systems;
- analysis methods that address the limitations of formal methods in industry (usability, scalability, etc.);
- formal analysis support for modeling languages used in industry, such as AADL, Ptolemy, SysML, SCADE, Modelica, etc.; and
- code generation from validated models.

The workshop received 23 regular paper submissions. Each submission was reviewed by at least three referees. Based on the reviews and extensive discussions, the program committee selected nine papers for presentation at the workshop and inclusion in this volume. Another highlight of the workshop was an invited talk by Naoki Kobayashi.

Many colleagues and friends have contributed to FTSCS 2016. We thank Naoki Kobayashi for giving an excellent invited talk and the authors who submitted their work to FTSCS 2016 and who, through their contributions, made the workshop an interesting event. We are particularly grateful that so many well-known researchers agreed to serve on the program committee, and that they provided timely, insightful, and detailed reviews. We also thank the editors of *Communications in Computer and Information Science* for agreeing to publish the proceedings of FTSCS 2016 as a volume in their series, and Shaoying Liu and Shin Nakajima for their help with the local arrangements.

December 2016

Cyrille Artho
Peter Csaba Ölveczky

Organization

Program Chairs

Cyrille Artho   KTH Royal Institute of Technology, Sweden
Peter Csaba Ölveczky   University of Oslo, Norway

Program Committee

Étienne André   University Paris 13, France
Toshiaki Aoki   JAIST, Japan
Cyrille Artho   KTH Royal Institute of Technology, Sweden
Kyungmin Bae   Pohang University of Science and Technology, Korea
Eun-Hye Choi   AIST, Japan
Alessandro Fantechi   University of Florence and ISTI-CNR, Pisa, Italy
Bernd Fischer   Stellenbosch University, South Africa
Osman Hasan   National University of Sciences & Technology, Pakistan
Klaus Havelund   NASA JPL, USA
Jérôme Hugues   Institute for Space and Aeronautics Engineering, France
Marieke Huisman   University of Twente, The Netherlands
Ralf Huuck   Synopsys, Australia
Fuyuki Ishikawa   National Institute of Informatics, Japan
Takashi Kitamura   AIST, Japan
Alexander Knapp   Augsburg University, Germany
Thierry Lecomte   ClearSy System Engineering, France
Yang Liu   Nanyang Technological University, Singapore
Robi Malik   University of Waikato, New Zealand
Frédéric Mallet   Université Nice Sophia Antipolis, France
Roberto Nardone   University of Naples Federico II, Italy
Vivek Nigam   Federal University of Paraíba, Brazil
Thomas Noll   RWTH Aachen University, Germany
Kazuhiro Ogata   JAIST, Japan
Peter Csaba Ölveczky   University of Oslo, Norway
Charles Pecheur   Université catholique de Louvain, Belgium
Markus Roggenbach   Swansea University, UK
Ralf Sasse   ETH Zürich, Switzerland
Martina Seidl   Johannes Kepler University Linz, Austria
Oleg Sokolsky   University of Pennsylvania, USA
Sofiène Tahar   Concordia University, Canada
Carolyn Talcott   SRI International, USA
Tatsuhiro Tsuchiya   Osaka University, Japan

András Vörös	Budapest University of Technology and Economics, Hungary
Chen-Wei Wang	State University of New York (SUNY), Korea
Mike Whalen	University of Minnesota, USA
Huibiao Zhu	East China Normal University, China

Additional Reviewers

Beillahi, Sidi Mohamed	Gillard, Xavier
Bukhari, Syed Ali Asadullah	Oortwijn, Wytse
Du, Xiaoning	Qasim, Muhammad
Fang, Huixing	Sardar, Muhammad Usama
Gentile, Ugo	Van Zijl, Lynette

On Two Higher-Order Extensions
of Model Checking
(Invited Talk)

Naoki Kobayashi

The University of Tokyo, Bunkyō, Japan
koba@is.s.u-tokyo.ac.jp

Inspired by the success of finite state model checking [2] in system verification, two kinds of its higher-order extensions have been studied since around 2000. One is model checking of higher-order recursion schemes (HORS) [3, 13], where the language for describing systems to be verified is extended to higher-order, and the other is higher-order modal fixpoint logic (HFL) model checking of finite-state systems [18], where the logic for specifying properties to be verified is extended to higher-order. Table 1 summarizes those extensions. In general, HORS model checking can be used for precisely modeling and verifying a certain class of *infinite* state systems, and HFL model checking can be used for checking *non-regular* properties of systems. HORS model checking has been successfully applied to automated verification of higher-order programs [5, 6, 8, 9, 10, 12, 14, 16, 17, 19], whereas HFL model checking has been studied for verification of concurrent systems [11, 18]. Although both HORS and HFL model checking problems are k-EXPTIME complete for the order-k fragments (where the order is the largest type-theoretic order of functions used in HORS and HFL respectively), practical model checking algorithms have been developed, which do not always suffer from the k-EXPTIME bottleneck [1, 4, 15]. We provide a brief introduction to the HORS and HFL model checking problems, their applications, and the state-of-the-art of higher-order model checkers and tools built on top of them. We also touch upon our recent result on the relationship between HORS and HFL model checking [7].

Table 1. Finite state model checking and its higher-order extensions

	Models	Logic
Finite state model checking	Finite state systems	Modal μ-calculus (or, LTL/CTL/CTL*)
HORS model checking	Higher-order recursion schemes (HORS)	Modal μ-calculus (or, tree automata)
HFL model checking	Finite state systems	Higher-order modal fixpoint logic (HFL)

References

1. Broadbent, C.H., Kobayashi, N.: Saturation-based model checking of higher-order recursion schemes. In: Proceedings of CSL 2013. LIPIcs, vol. 23, pp. 129–148 (2013)
2. Clarke, E.M., Grumberg, O., Peled, D.A.: Model Checking. The MIT Press (1999)
3. Knapik, T., Niwinski, D., Urzyczyn, P.: Higher-order pushdown trees are easy. In: Nielsen, M., Engberg, U. (eds.) FoSSaCS 2002. LNCS, vol. 2303, pp. 205–222. Springer, Heidelberg (2002)
4. Kobayashi, N.: Model-checking higher-order functions. In: Proceedings of PPDP 2009, pp. 25–36. ACM Press (2009)
5. Kobayashi, N.: Types and higher-order recursion schemes for verification of higher-order programs. In: Proceedings of POPL, pp. 416–428. ACM Press (2009)
6. Kobayashi, N.: Model checking higher-order programs. J. ACM **60**(3) (2013)
7. Kobayashi, N., Étienne Lozes, Bruse, F.: On the relationship between higher-order recursion schemes and higher-order modal fixpoint logic. In: Proceedings of POPL 2017 (2017, to appear)
8. Kobayashi, N., Sato, R., Unno, H.: Predicate abstraction and CEGAR for higher-order model checking. In: Proceedings of PLDI, pp. 222–233. ACM Press (2011)
9. Kobayashi, N., Tabuchi, N., Unno, H.: Higher-order multi-parameter tree transducers and recursion schemes for program verification. In: Proceedings of POPL, pp. 495–508. ACM Press (2010)
10. Kuwahara, T., Sato, R., Unno, H., Kobayashi, N.: Predicate abstraction and CEGAR for disproving termination of higher-order functional programs. In: Kroening, D., C.S. Păsăreanu (eds.) Proceedings of CAV 2015. LNCS, vol. 9207, pp. 287–303. Springer, Switzerland (2015)
11. Lange, M., Lozes, É., Guzmán, M.V.: Model-checking process equivalences. Theor. Comput. Sci. **560**, 326–347 (2014)
12. Murase, A., Terauchi, T., Kobayashi, N., Sato, R., Unno, H.: Temporal verification of higher-order functional programs. In: Proceedings of POPL 2016 (2016, to appear)
13. Ong, C.H.L.: On model-checking trees generated by higher-order recursion schemes. In: LICS 2006, pp. 81–90. IEEE Computer Society Press (2006)
14. Ong, C.H.L., Ramsay, S.: Verifying higher-order programs with pattern-matching algebraic data types. In: Proceedings of POPL, pp. 587–598. ACM Press (2011)
15. Ramsay, S., Neatherway, R., Ong, C.H.L.: An abstraction refinement approach to higher-order model checking. In: Proceedings of POPL 2014, pp. 61–72. ACM (2014)
16. Sato, R., Unno, H., Kobayashi, N.: Towards a scalable software model checker for higher-order programs. In: Proceedings of PEPM 2013, pp. 53–62. ACM Press (2013)
17. Unno, H., Terauchi, T., Kobayashi, N.: Automating relatively complete verification of higher-order functional programs. In: The 40th Annual ACM SIGPLAN-SIGACT Symposium on Principles of Programming Languages, POPL 2013. pp. 75–86. ACM (2013)
18. Viswanathan, M., Viswanathan, R.: A higher order modal fixed point logic. In: Gardner, P., Yoshida, N. (eds.) CONCUR. LNCS, vol. 3170, pp. 512–528. Springer, Heidelberg (2004)
19. Watanabe, K., Sato, R., Tsukada, T., Kobayashi, N.: Automatically disproving fair termination of higher-order functional programs. In: Proceedings of ICFP 2016, pp. 243–255. ACM (2016)

Contents

Specification and Verification

Automotive and Railway Systems

Circuits and Cyber-Physical Systems

Parametrized Verification

Specification and Verification

Specification and Verification of Synchronization with Condition Variables

Pedro de Carvalho Gomes[1]($\boxtimes$), Dilian Gurov[1], and Marieke Huisman[2]

[1] KTH Royal Institute of Technology, Stockholm, Sweden
pedrodcg@kth.se
[2] University of Twente, Enschede, The Netherlands

In this paper we propose a technique to specify and verify the *correct synchronization* of concurrent programs with condition variables. We define correctness as the liveness property: "every thread synchronizing under a set of condition variables eventually exits the synchronization", under the assumption that every such thread eventually reaches its synchronization block. Our technique does not avoid the combinatorial explosion of interleavings of thread behaviors. Instead, we alleviate it by abstracting away all details that are irrelevant to the *synchronization behavior* of the program, which is typically significantly smaller than its overall behavior. First, we introduce SyncTask, a simple imperative language to specify parallel computations that synchronize via condition variables. We consider a SyncTask program to have a correct synchronization iff it terminates. Further, to relieve the programmer from the burden of providing specifications in SyncTask, we introduce an economic annotation scheme for Java programs to assist the *automated extraction* of SyncTask programs capturing the synchronization behavior of the underlying program. We prove that every Java program annotated according to the scheme (and satisfying the assumption) has a correct synchronization iff its corresponding SyncTask program terminates. We show how to transform the verification of termination into a standard reachability problem over Colored Petri Nets that is efficiently solvable by existing Petri Net analysis tools. Both the SyncTask program extraction and the generation of Petri Nets are implemented in our STAVE tool. We evaluate the proposed framework on a number of test cases as a proof-of-concept.

1 Introduction

Condition variables (CV) are a commonly used synchronization mechanism to coordinate multithreaded programs. Threads *wait* on a CV, meaning they suspend their execution until another thread *notifies* the CV, causing the waiting threads to resume their execution. The signaling is asynchronous: if no thread is waiting on the CV, then the notification has no effect. CVs are used in conjunction with locks; a thread must acquire the associated lock for notifying or waiting on a CV, and if notified, must reacquire the lock.

Marieke Huisman — Supported by ERC grant 258405 for the VerCors project.

© Springer International Publishing AG 2017
C. Artho and P.C. Ölveczky (Eds.): FTSCS 2016, CCIS 694, pp. 3–19, 2017.
DOI: 10.1007/978-3-319-53946-1_1

Many widely used programming languages feature condition variables. In Java, for instance, they are provided both natively as an object's *monitor* [6], i.e., a pair of a lock and a CV, and in the concurrent API, as one-to-many `Condition` objects associated to a `Lock` object. The mechanism is typically employed when the progress of threads depends on the state of a shared variable, to avoid busy-wait loops that poll the state of this shared variable. Nevertheless, condition variables have not been addressed sufficiently with formal techniques, mainly because of the complexity of reasoning about asynchronous signaling. For instance, Leino *et al.* [14] acknowledge that verifying the absence of deadlocks when using CVs is hard because a notification is "lost" if no thread is waiting on it. Thus, one cannot verify locally whether a waiting thread will eventually be notified. Furthermore, the synchronization conditions can be quite complex, involving both control-flow and data-flow aspects as arising from method calls; their correctness thus depends on the *global thread composition*, i.e., the type and number of parallel threads. All these complexities suggest the need for *programmer-provided annotations* to assist the automated analysis, which is the approach we are following here.

In this work, we present a formal technique for specifying and verifying that "every thread synchronizing under a set of condition variables eventually exits the synchronization", under the assumption that every such thread eventually reaches its synchronization block. The assumption itself is not addressed here, as it does not pertain to correctness of the synchronization, and there already exist techniques for dealing with such properties (see e.g. [16]). Note that the above correctness notion applies to a *one-time synchronization* on a condition variable only; generalizing the notion to repeated synchronizations is left for future work. To the best of our knowledge, the present work is the first to address a *liveness* property involving CVs. As the verification of such properties is undecidable in general, we limit our technique to programs with bounded data domains and numbers of threads. Still, the verification problem is subject to a combinatorial explosion of thread interleavings. Our technique alleviates the state space explosion problem by *delimiting the relevant aspects of the synchronization*.

First, we consider correctness of synchronization in the context of a *synchronization specification language*. As we target arbitrary programming languages that feature locks and condition variables, we do not base our approach on a subset of an existing language, but instead introduce *SyncTask*, a simple concurrent programming language where all computations occur inside synchronized code blocks. We define a SyncTask program to have a correct synchronization iff it terminates. The SyncTask language has been designed to capture common patterns of CV usage, while abstracting away from irrelevant details. SyncTask has a Java-like syntax and semantics, and features the relevant constructs for synchronization, such as locks, CVs, conditional statements, and arithmetic operations. However, it is non-procedural, data types are bounded, and it does not allow dynamic thread creation. These restrictions render the state-space of SyncTask programs finite, and make the termination problem decidable.

Next, we address the problem of verifying the correct usage of CVs in real concurrent programming languages by showing how SyncTask can be used to capture the synchronization of a Java program, provided it is bounded. There is a consensus in Software Engineering that synchronization in a concurrent program must be kept to a minimum, both in the number and complexity of the synchronization actions, and in the number of places where it occurs. This avoids the latency of blocking threads, and minimizes the risk of errors, such as dead- and livelocks. As a consequence, many programs present a finite (though arbitrarily large) synchronization behavior. To assist the automated extraction of finite synchronization behavior from Java programs as SyncTask programs, we introduce an *annotation scheme*, which requires the user to (correctly) annotate, among others, the initialization of new threads (i.e., creation of `Thread` objects), and provide the initial state of the variables accessed inside the synchronized blocks. We establish that for correctly annotated, bounded Java programs, correctness of synchronization is equivalent to termination of the extracted SyncTask program.

As a proof-of-concept of the algorithmic solvability of the termination problem for SyncTask programs, we show how to transform it into a reachability problem on hierarchical Colored Petri Nets[1] (CPNs) [7]. We define how to extract CPNs automatically from SyncTask programs, following a previous technique from Westergaard [18]. Then, we establish that a SyncTask program terminates *if and only if* the extracted CPN always reaches dead markings (i.e., CPN configurations without successors) where the tokens representing the threads are in a unique *end place*. Standard CPN analysis tools can efficiently compute the reachability graphs, and check whether the termination condition holds. Also, in case that the condition does not hold, an inspection of the reachability graph easily provides the cause of non-termination.

We implement the extraction of SyncTask programs from annotated Java and the translation of SyncTasks to CPNs as the STAVE tool. We evaluate the tool on two test-cases, by generating CPNs from annotated Java programs and analyzing these with CPN Tools [8]. The first test-case evaluates the scalability of the tool w.r.t. the size of program code that does not affect the synchronization behavior of the program. The second test-case evaluates the scalability of the tool w.r.t. the number of synchronizing threads. The results show the expected exponential blow-up of the state-space, but we were still able to analyze the synchronization of several dozens of threads.

In summary, this work makes the following contributions: (i) the SyncTask language to model the synchronization behavior of programs with CVs, (ii) an annotation scheme to aid the extraction of the synchronization behavior of Java programs, (iii) an extraction scheme of SyncTask models from annotated Java programs, (iv) a reduction of the termination problem for SyncTask programs

---

[1] The choice of formalism has been mainly based on the *simplicity* of CPNs as a general model of concurrency, rather than on the existing support for efficient model checking. For the latter, model checking tools exploiting parametricity or symmetries in the models may prove more efficient in practice.

to a reachability problem on CPNs, (v) an implementation of the framework by means of STAVE, and (vi) its experimental evaluation.

The remainder of the paper is organized as follows. Section 2 introduces Sync-Task. Section 3 describes the mapping from annotated Java to SyncTask, while Sect. 4 presents the translation into CPNs, and presents test-cases. We discuss related work in Sect. 5. Section 6 concludes and suggests future work.

2   SyncTask

SyncTask abstracts from most features of full-fledged programming languages. For instance, it does not have objects, procedures, exceptions, etc. However, it features the relevant aspects of thread synchronization. We now describe the language syntax, types, and semantics.

2.1   Syntax and Types

The SyncTask syntax is presented in Fig. 1. A program has two main parts: *ThreadType**, which declares the different types of parallel execution flows, and *Main*, which contains the variable declarations and initializations and defines how the threads are composed, i.e., it statically declares how many threads of each type are spawned.

$$
\begin{array}{ll}
SyncTask ::= ThreadType^* \ Main & Block ::= \{ \ Stmt^* \ \} \\
ThreadType ::= \textbf{Thread} \ ThreadName \ \{ \ SyncBlock^* \ \} & Assign ::= VarName = Expr \ ; \\
\quad Main ::= \textbf{main} \ \{ \ VarDecl^* \ StartThread^* \ \} & Stmt ::= SyncBlock \mid Block \\
StartThread ::= \textbf{start}(\ Const\ ,\ ThreadName\ ); & \mid Assign \mid \textbf{skip}; \\
\quad Expr ::= Const \mid VarName \mid Expr \oplus Expr & \mid \textbf{while} \ Expr \ Stmt \\
\qquad \mid \textbf{min}(\ VarName\ ) \mid \textbf{max}(\ VarName\ ) & \mid \textbf{if} \ Expr \ Stmt \ \textbf{else} \ Stmt \\
VarDecl ::= VarType \ VarName(\ Expr^*\ ); & \mid \textbf{notify}(\ VarName\ ); \\
VarType ::= \textbf{Bool} \mid \textbf{Int} \mid \textbf{Lock} \mid \textbf{Cond} & \mid \textbf{notifyAll}(\ VarName\ ); \\
SyncBlock ::= \textbf{synchronized} \ (\ VarName\ ) \ Block & \mid \textbf{wait}(\ VarName\ );
\end{array}
$$

Fig. 1. SyncTask syntax

Each *ThreadType* consists of adjacent *SyncBlocks*, which are mutually exclusive code blocks, guarded by a lock. A code block is defined as a sequence of statements, which may even be another *SyncBlock*. Notice that this allows nested *SyncBlocks*, thus enabling the definition of complex synchronization schemes with more than one lock.

There are four primitive types: booleans (`Bool`), bounded integers (`Int`), reentrant locks (`Lock`), and condition variables (`Cond`). Expressions are evaluated as in Java. The boolean and integer operators are the standard ones, while `max` and `min` return a variable's bounds. Operations between integers with different bounds (overloading) are allowed. However, an out-of-bounds assignment leads the program to an error configuration.

Condition variables are manipulated by the unary operators wait, notify, and notifyAll. Currently, the language provides only two control flow constructs: while and if-else. These suffice for the illustration of our technique, while the addition of other constructs is straightforward.

The *Main* block contains the global variable declarations with initializations (*VarDecl**), and the thread composition (*StartThread**). A variable is defined by its type and name, followed by the initialization arguments. The number of parameters varies per type: Lock takes no arguments; Cond is initialized with a lock variable; Bool takes either a true or a false literal; Int takes three integer literals as arguments: the lower and upper bounds, and the initial value, which must be in the given range. Finally, start takes a positive number and a thread type, signifying the number of threads of that type it spawns.

```
1 Thread Producer {             11 Thread Consumer {            21 main {
    synchronized(m_lock){           synchronized(m_lock){          Lock m_lock();
3   while(b_els==max(b_els))    13  while((b_els==0))          23  Cond m_cond(m_lock);
      wait(m_cond);                   wait(m_cond);                 Int b_els(0,1,1);
5   if(b_els<max(b_els))       15  if((b_els>0))              25  start(1,Producer);
      b_els=(b_els+1);               b_els=(b_els-1);              start(2,Consumer);
7   else                       17  else                       27 }
      skip;                          skip;
9   notifyAll(m_cond);         19  notifyAll(m_cond);
} }                             } }
```

Fig. 2. Modelling of synchronization via a shared buffer in SyncTask

Example 1 (SyncTask program). The program in Fig. 2 models synchronization via a shared buffer. Producer and Consumer represent the synchronization behavior: threads synchronize via the CV m_cond to add or remove elements, and wait if the buffer is full or empty, respectively. Waiting threads are woken up by notifyAll after an operation is performed on the buffer, and compete for the monitor to resume execution. The main block contains variable declarations and initialization. The lock m_lock is associated to m_cond. b_els is an integer in the interval [0,1] (initially set to 1), and represents the number of elements in the buffer. One Producer and two Consumer threads are spawned with start.

2.2 Structural Operational Semantics

We now define the semantics of SyncTask, to provide the means for establishing formal correctness results.

The semantic domains are defined as follows. Booleans are represented as usual. Integer variables are triples $\mathbb{Z} \times \mathbb{Z} \times \mathbb{Z}$, where the first two elements are the lower and upper bound, and the third is the current value. A lock o is a pair $(Thread\_id \cup \{\bot\}) \times \mathbb{N}$ of the id of the thread holding the lock (or $\bot$, if none), and a counter of how many times it was acquired. A condition variable d simply stores its respective lock, which is retrieved with the auxiliary function $\overset{\smile}{lock}(d)$.

SyncTask contains global variables only and all memory operations are synchronized. Thus, we assume the memory to be sequentially consistent [11]. Let μ represent a program's memory. We write $\mu(l)$ to denote the value of variable l, and $\mu[l \mapsto v]$ to denote the update of l in μ with value v.

A *thread state* is either *running* (R) if the thread is executing, *waiting* (W) if it has suspended the execution on a CV, or *notified* (N) if another thread has woken up the suspended thread. The states W and N also contain the CV d that a thread is/was waiting on, and the number n of times it must reacquire the lock to proceed with the execution. The auxiliary function $waitset(d)$ returns the id's of all threads waiting on a CV d.

$$[\text{s1}]^a \qquad T|(\theta, \texttt{synchronized}(o)\ b, R), \mu \longrightarrow T|(\theta, \texttt{synchronized'}(o)\ b, R), \mu[o \mapsto (\theta, 1)]$$

$$[\text{s2}]^b \qquad T|(\theta, \texttt{synchronized}(o)\ b, R), \mu \longrightarrow T|(\theta, \texttt{synchronized'}(o)\ b, R), \mu[o \mapsto (\theta, n+1)]$$

$$[\text{s3}]^b \qquad \frac{T|(\theta, b_1, R), \mu \longrightarrow T|(\theta, b_2, X), \mu'}{T|(\theta, \texttt{synchronized'}(o)\ b_1, R)), \mu \longrightarrow T|(\theta, \texttt{synchronized'}(o)\ b_2, X), \mu'}$$

$$[\text{s4}]^c \qquad \frac{T|(\theta, b, R), \mu \longrightarrow T|(\theta, \epsilon, R), \mu'}{T|(\theta, \texttt{synchronized'}(o)\ b, R)), \mu \longrightarrow T|(\theta, \epsilon, R), \mu'[o \mapsto (\theta, n-1)]}$$

$$[\text{s5}]^d \qquad \frac{T|(\theta, b, R), \mu \longrightarrow T|(\theta, \epsilon, R), \mu'}{T|(\theta, \texttt{synchronized'}(o)\ b, R), \mu \longrightarrow T|(\theta, \epsilon, R), \mu'[o \mapsto (\bot, 0)]}$$

$$[\text{wt}]^e \qquad T|(\theta, \texttt{wait}(d), R), \mu \to T|(\theta, \epsilon, (W, d, n)), \mu[lock(d) \mapsto (\bot, 0)]$$

$$[\text{nf1}]^{ef} \qquad T|(\theta, \texttt{notify}(d), R), \mu \to T|(\theta, \epsilon, R), \mu$$

$$[\text{nf2}]^{eg} \qquad T|(\theta, \texttt{notify}(d), R)|(\theta', t', (W, d, n)), \mu \to T|(\theta, \epsilon, R)|(\theta', t', (N, d, n)), \mu$$

$$[\text{na1}]^{ef} \qquad T|(\theta, \texttt{notifyAll}(d), R), \mu \to T|(\theta, \epsilon, R), \mu$$

$$[\text{na2}]^{eg} \ T|(\theta, \texttt{notifyAll}(d), R)|T_W^d, \mu \to T|(\theta, \epsilon, R)|\{(\theta', t', (N, d, n))|(\theta', t', (W, d, n)) \in T_W^d\}, \mu$$

$$[\text{rd}]^h \qquad T|(\theta, t, (N, d, n)), \mu \to T|(\theta, t, R), \mu[lock(d) \mapsto (\theta, n)]$$

$^a \mu(o) = (\bot, 0) \quad ^b \mu(o) = (\theta, n) \wedge n > 0 \quad ^c \mu(o) = (\theta, n) \wedge n > 1 \quad ^d \mu(o) = (\theta, 1)$

$^e \mu(lock(d)) = (\theta, n) \wedge n > 0 \quad ^f waitset(d) = \emptyset \quad ^g waitset(d) \neq \emptyset \quad ^h \mu(lock(d)) = (\bot, 0)$

Fig. 3. Operational rules for synchronization

We represent a thread as (θ, t, X), where θ denotes its id, t the executing code, and X its state. We write $T = (\theta_i, t_i, X_i)|(\theta_j, t_j, X_j)$ for a parallel thread composition, with $\theta_i \neq \theta_j$. Also, $T|(\theta, t, X)$ denotes a thread composition, assuming that θ is not defined in T. For convenience, we abuse set notation to denote the composition of threads in the set; e.g., $T_W^d = \{(\theta, t, (W, d, n))\}$ represents the composition of all threads in the wait set of d. A *program configuration* is a pair (T, μ) of the threads' composition and its memory. A thread terminates if the program reaches a configuration where its code t is empty (ϵ); a program terminates if all its threads terminate.

The initial configuration is defined by the declarations in *Main*. As expected, the variable initializations set the initial value of μ. For example, Int i(lb,ub,v) defines a new variable such that $\mu(i) = (lb, ub, v)$, $lb \leq v \leq ub$, and Lock o() initializes a lock $\mu(o) = (\bot, 0)$. The thread composition is defined by the start declarations; e.g., start(2,t) adds two threads of type t to the thread composition: $(\theta, t, R)|(\theta', t, R)$.

Figure 3 presents the operational rules, with superscripts [a-h] denoting conditions. For readability, we just present the rules for the synchronization statements, as the rules for the remaining statements are standard (see [2, Sect. 3.4-8]).

In rule [s1], a thread acquires a lock, if available, i.e., if it is not assigned to any other thread and the counter is zero. Rule [s2] represents lock reentrancy and increases the lock counter. Both rules replace **synchronized** with a primed version to denote that the execution of synchronization block has begun. Rule [s3] applies to the computation of statements inside synchronized blocks, and requires that the thread holds the lock. Rule [s4] preserves the lock, but decreases the counter upon exiting a synchronized block. In rule [s5], a thread finishes the execution of a synchronized block, and relinquishes the lock.

In the [wt] rule, a thread changes its state to W, stores the counter of the CV's lock, and releases it. The rules [nf1] and [na1] apply when a thread notifies a CV with an empty wait set; the behavior is the same as for the skip statement. By rule [nf2], a thread notifies a CV, and one thread in its wait set is selected non-deterministically, and its state is changed to N. Rule [na2] is similar, but all threads in the wait set are awoken. By the rule [rd], a thread reacquires all the locks it had relinquished, changes the state to R, and resumes the execution after the control point where it invoked wait.

Finally, we define a SyncTask program to *have a correct synchronization* iff it terminates.

3   From Annotated Java to SyncTask

The annotation process supported by STAVE relies on the programmer's knowledge about the intended synchronization, and consists of providing hints to the tool to automatically map the synchronization to a SyncTask program. In this section we present an *annotation scheme* for writing such hints, and sketch a correctness argument for the extraction.

3.1   An Annotation Language for Java

An annotation in STAVE binds to a specific type of Java declaration (e.g., classes or methods). The annotation starts in a comment block immediately above a declaration, with additional annotations inside the declaration's body. Annotations share common keywords (though with a different semantics), and overlap in the declaration types they may bind to. The ambiguity is resolved by the first keyword (called a *switch*) found in the comment block. Comments that do not start with a keyword are ignored.

Resource annotation:

```
@resource (classes)
  @object [Id -> Id]
  @value [Id -> Id]
  @capacity [Id -> Id]
  @defaultval Int
  @defaultcap Int
  @predicate (methods)
   @inline [@maps Id->@{ Code }@]
   @code -> @{ Code }@
  @operation (methods)
   @inline [@maps Id->@{ Code }@]
   @code -> @{ Code }@
```

Synchronization annotation:

```
@syncblock [Id] (synchronized blocks)
  @threadtype Id -> Id
  @resource Id : ResourceId
  @lock Id -> Id
  @condvar Id -> Id
  @monitor Id -> Id
```

Initialization annotation:

```
@synctask [Id] (methods)
  @resource Id -> Id
  @lock Id -> Id
  @condvar Id -> Id
  @monitor Id -> Id
  @thread [Int : Id]
```

Fig. 4. Annotation language for Java programs

Figure 4 presents the annotation language. Arguments given within square brackets are optional, while text within parentheses tells which declaration types the annotation binds to. The programmer has to (correctly) provide, by means of annotations, the following *three types of information*: resources, synchronization and initialization.

A *resource* is a data type that is manipulated by the synchronization. It abstracts the state of a data structure to a bounded integer, which is potentially a *ghost variable* (as in [12]), and defines how the methods operate on it. For example, the annotation abstracts a linked list or a buffer to its size. In case a resource is mapped to a ghost variable, we say that the variable *extends* the program memory. Resources bind to classes only, and the switch @resource starts the declaration. @value and @capacity define, respectively, which class member, or ghost variable, stores the abstract state, and its maximum value. The keyword @operation binds to method declarations, and specifies that the method potentially alters the resource state. Similarly, @predicate binds to methods and specifies that the method returns a predicate about the state.

There are two ways to extract an annotated method's behavior. @code tells STAVE not to process the method, but instead to associate it to the code enclosed between @{ and }@, while @inline tells STAVE to try to infer the method declaration with the potential aid of @maps, which syntactically replaces a Java command (e.g., a method invocation) with a SyncTask code snippet.

The *synchronization* annotation defines the observation scope. It binds to synchronized blocks and methods, and the switch @syncblock starts the declaration. Nested synchronization blocks and methods are not annotated; all its information is defined in the top-level annotation. The keywords @lock and @condvar define which mutex and condition object to observe. @monitor has the combined effect of both keywords for an object's monitor, i.e., a pair of a lock and a CV. Here, @resource annotates that a local variable is a reference to a global object in the heap, which is observed and is represented by an alias.

Initialization annotations define the global pre-condition for the elements involved in the synchronization, i.e., they define the lock, condition variable and resource declarations with initial value, and the global thread composition. They bind to methods, and the switch @synctask starts the declaration. Here, @resource, @lock, @condvar and @monitor define the objects being observed, and assign global aliases to them. Finally, @thread defines that the following object corresponds to a spawned thread that synchronizes within the observed synchronization objects. The object's type must have been annotated with a synchronization annotation.

Example 2 (Annotated Java). The SyncTask program in Fig. 2 was generated from the Java program in Fig. 5. We now discuss how the annotations delimit the expected synchronization. The example also illustrates the extraction.

The @syncblock annotations (lines 5/19) add the following synchronized blocks to the observed synchronization behavior, and its arguments @monitor and @resource (lines 6/20 and 7/21, respectively) map local references to global aliases. The @resource annotation (line 29) starts the definition of a resource type. @value, @object, @capacity (lines 29/30/31) define how the abstract state

```
01 class Producer extends Thread {     29 /*@resource @capacity cap
   Buffer buffer;                             @object els->b_els
03 Producer(Buffer b){buffer=b;}       31    @value els->b_els */
   public void run() {                     class Buffer {
05 /*@syncblock                         33 int els; final int cap;
      @monitor buffer -> m                /* @operation @inline */
07    @resource buffer:Buffer */       35 void remove(){if (els>0)els--;}
   synchronized(buffer) {                  /* @operation @inline */
09  while (buffer.full())              37 void add(){if (els<cap)els++;}
      buffer.wait();                       /* @predicate @inline */
11  buffer.add();                      39 boolean full(){return els==cap;}
    buffer.notifyAll();                    /* @predicate @inline */
13 } } }                               41 boolean empty(){return els==0;}
                                          /*@synctask Buffer
15 class Consumer extends Thread {     43    @monitor b -> m
   Buffer buffer;                             @resource b->b_els */
17 Consumer(Buffer b){buffer=b;}       45 static void main(String[] s) {
   public void run() {                     Buffer b = new Buffer();
19 /*@syncblock                        47 b.els = 1; b.cap = 1;
      @monitor buffer -> m                /* @thread */
21    @resource buffer:Buffer */       49 Consumer c1 = new Consumer(b);
   synchronized(buffer) {                  /* @thread */
23  while (buffer.empty())             51 Consumer c2 = new Consumer(b);
      buffer.wait();                       /* @thread */
25  buffer.remove();                   53 Producer p = new Producer(b);
    buffer.notifyAll();                    c1.start();p.start();c2.start();
27 } } }                               55 } }
```

Fig. 5. Annotated Java program synchronizing via shared buffer

is represented by a bounded integer; in this example, the state is equivalent to `els`, which is an abstraction of the number of elements in a buffer. The `@operation` (lines 34/36) and `@predicate` (lines 38/40) annotations define how the methods operate on the state. Notice that the annotated methods have been inlined in Fig. 2, i.e., `add` is inlined in lines 5 and 6. The `@synctask` annotation above `main` starts the declaration of locks, CVs and resources, and `@thread` annotations add the underneath objects to the global thread composition.

3.2 Synchronization Correctness

The synchronization property of interest here is that "every thread synchronizing under a set of condition variables eventually exits the synchronization". We work under the assumption that every such thread eventually reaches its synchronization block. There exist techniques (such as [16]) for checking the liveness property that a given thread eventually reaches a given control point; checking validity of the above assumption is therefore out of the scope of the present work.

The following definition of correct synchronization applies to a one-time synchronization of a Java program. However, if it can be proven that if the initial conditions are the same every time the synchronization scheme is spawned, then the scheme is correct for an arbitrary number of invocations. This may be proven by showing that a Java program always resets the variables observed in the synchronization before re-spawning the threads.

Definition 1 (Synchronization Correctness). *Let P be a Java program with a one-time synchronization such that every thread eventually reaches the entry point of its synchronization block. We say that P has a correct synchronization iff every thread eventually reaches the first control point after the block.*

We defined both synchronization correctness and the termination of the corresponding SyncTask program *relative to the correctness of the annotations* provided by the programmer. Although out of the scope of the present work, the annotations can potentially be checked, or partially generated, with existing static analysis techniques. Further, we assume the memory model of synchronized actions in a Java program to be sequentially consistent.

We now connect synchronization schemes of annotated Java programs with SyncTask programs. We shall assume that the programmer has correctly annotated the program, as described in Sect. 3.1.

Theorem 1 (SyncTask Extraction). *A correctly annotated Java program has a correct synchronization iff its corresponding SyncTask terminates.*

Proof (Sketch). To prove the result, we define a binary relation R between the configurations of the Java program and its SyncTask, and show it to be a *weak bisimulation* (see [15]), implying that the SyncTask program eventually reaches a terminal configuration (i.e., all threads terminate) *if and only if* the original Java program has a correct synchronization. We refer to the accompanying technical report [5] for the full formalization, and for the most interesting cases, namely the notify and wait instructions.

The Java annotations define a bidirectional mapping between (some of) the Java program variables and ghost variables and the corresponding bounded variables in SyncTask. Thus, we define R to relate configurations that agree on *common* variables. Similarly, we define the set of *visible transitions* as the ones that update common variables, and treat all other transitions as *silent*. We argue that R is a weak bisimulation in the standard fashion: We establish that (i) the initial values of the common variables are the same for both programs, and (ii) assuming that observed variables in a Java program are only updated inside annotated synchronized blocks, we establish that any operation that updates a common variable has the same effect on it in both programs.

To prove (i) it suffices to show that the initial values in the Java program are the same as the ones provided in the initialization annotation, as described in Sect. 3.1. (Here we rely on the correctness of the annotations; however, existing techniques such as [13,14] can potentially be used for checking this.) The proof of (ii) requires to show that updates to a common variable yield the same result in both programs. It goes by case analysis on the Java instructions set. Each case shows that for any configuration pair of R, the operational rules for the given Java instruction and for the corresponding SyncTask instruction lead to a pair of configurations that again agree on the common variables. As the semantics of SyncTask presented in Sect. 2 has been designed to closely mimic the Java semantics defined in [2], the elaboration of this is straightforward. □

4 Verification of Synchronization Correctness

In this section we show how termination of SyncTask programs can be reduced to a reachability problem on Colored Petri Nets (CPN), and present an experimental evaluation of the verification with STAVE and CPN Tools.

4.1 SyncTask Programs as Colored Petri Nets

Various techniques exist to prove termination of concurrent systems. For Sync-Task, it is essential that such a technique efficiently encodes the concurrent thread interleaving, the program's control flow, synchronization primitives, and basic data manipulation. Here, we have chosen to reduce the problem of termination of SyncTask programs to a reachability problem on hierarchical CPNs extracted from the program. CPNs allow a natural translation of common language constructs into CPN components (for this we re-use results from Westergaard [18]), and are supported by analysis tools such as CPN Tools. We assume some familiarity with CPNs, and refer the reader to [7] for a detailed exposition.

The color set THREAD associates a color to each Thread type declaration, and a thread is represented by a token with a color from the set. Some components are parametrized by THREAD, meaning that they declare transitions, arcs, or places for each thread type. For illustration purposes, we present the para-metrized components in an example scenario with three thread types: blue (B), red (R), and yellow (Y).

The production rules in Fig. 1 are mapped into hierarchical CPN compo-nents, where *substitute transitions* (STs; depicted as doubly outlined rectangles) represent the non-terminals on the right-hand side. Figure 6a shows the compo-nent for the start symbol *SyncTask*. The Start place contains all thread tokens in the initial configuration, connected by arcs (one per color) to the STs denoting the thread types, and End, which collects the terminated thread tokens. It also contains the places that represent global variables.

Figure 6b shows the modelling of wait. The transition wait cond produces two tokens: one into the place modelling the CV, and one into the place modelling the lock, representing its release. The other transition models a notified thread reacquiring the lock, and resuming the execution. Figure 6c shows the modelling of notify. The Empty_cond transition is enabled if the CV is empty, and the other transitions, with one place per color, model the non-deterministic choice of which thread to notify. The component for notifyAll (not shown) is similar.

The initialization in *Main* declares the initial set of tokens for the places representing variables, and the number and colors of thread tokens. A Lock creates a place containing a single token; it being empty represents that some thread holds the lock. The color set CPOINT represents the control points of wait statements. A Condition variable gives rise to an empty place representing the waiting set, with color set CONDITION. Here, colors are pairs of THREAD and CPOINT. Both data are necessary to route correctly notified threads to the correct place where they resume execution.

4.2   SyncTask Termination as CPN Reachability

We now enunciate the result that reduces termination of a SyncTask program to a reachability problem on its corresponding CPN.

Theorem 2 (SyncTask Termination). *A SyncTask program terminates iff its corresponding CPN unavoidably reaches a dead configuration in which the End place has the same marking as the Start place in the initial configuration.*

Proof (Sketch). A CPN declares a place for each SyncTask variable. Moreover, there is a clear correspondence between the operational semantics of a SyncTask construct and its corresponding CPN component. It can be shown by means of weak bisimulation that every configuration of a SyncTask program is matched by a unique sequence of consecutive CPN configurations. Therefore, if the End place in a dead configuration has the same marking as the Start place in the initial configuration, then every thread in the SyncTask program terminates its execution, for every possible scheduling (note that the non-deterministic thread scheduler is simulated by the non-deterministic firing of transitions).   □

CPN termination itself can be verified algorithmically by computing the reachability graph of the generated CPN and checking that: (*i*) the graph has

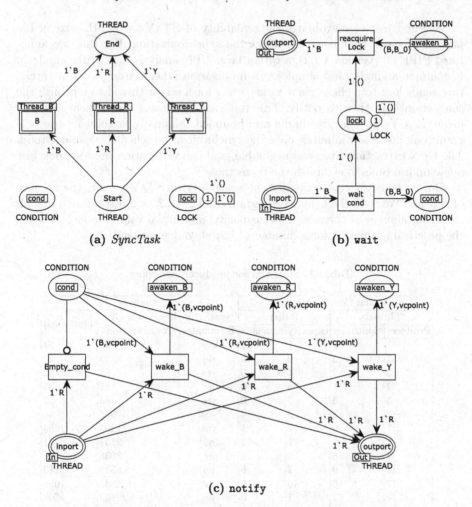

(a) *SyncTask*

(b) wait

(c) notify

Fig. 6. Top-level component and condition variables operations

no cycles, and (*ii*) the only reachable dead configurations are the ones where the marking in the End place is the same as the marking in the Start place in the initial configuration.

4.3   The STaVe Tool

We have implemented the parsing of annotated Java programs to generate Sync-Task programs, and the extraction of hierarchical CPNs from SyncTask, as the STAVE [4] tool. We now describe the experimental evaluation of our framework. This includes the process of annotating Java programs, extraction of the corresponding CPNs, and the analysis of the nets using CPN Tools.

Our first test case evaluates the scalability of STAVE w.r.t. the size of the part of program that does *not* affect the synchronization. For this, we annotated PIPE [3] (version 4.3.2), a rather large CPN analysis tool written in Java. It contains a single (and simple) synchronization scheme using CVs: a thread that sends logs to a client via a socket waits for a server thread to establish the connection, and then to notify. This test case illustrates that synchronization involving CVs is typically simple and bounded. Manually annotating the program took just a few minutes, once the synchronization scheme was understood. The CPN extraction time was negligible, and the verification process took just a few milliseconds to establish the correctness.

Our second test case evaluates the scalability of STAVE w.r.t. the number of threads. We took the example program from Sect. 2, and instantiated it with a varying number of threads, buffer capacity, and initial value. Table 1 presents the practical evaluation for a number of initial configurations.

Table 1. Statistics for producer/consumer

Initial Configuration					Analysis	
Threads		Buffer		SyncTask	Reachable CPN	Time (ms)
Producer	Consumer	capacity	elements	Terminates	Configurations	
1	2	1	1	yes	42	31
1	2	2	0	no	43	28
2	2	1	0	yes	91	32
7	1	5	0	no	157	33
3	3	1	0	yes	283	32
6	5	5	4	yes	968	40
7	6	7	1	yes	1395	54
6	5	1	1	no	2131	71
7	6	1	1	no	3938	112
11	9	7	6	no	6573	183
17	16	16	16	no	24883	1097
11	11	1	0	yes	29143	1308
14	13	7	1	yes	29573	1331
14	13	1	1	no	64075	2867
26	24	25	24	no	78191	4524
18	18	5	1	yes	133824	7917
16	21	5	5	yes	164921	9952
18	18	1	1	yes	197563	70614
20	18	2	1	no	211702	131226

We observe an expected correlation between the number of tokens representing threads, the size of the state space, and the verification time. Less expected for us was the observed influence of the buffer capacities and initial states. We conjecture that the initial configurations that model high contention, i.e., many threads waiting on CVs, induce a larger state space. The experiments also show how termination depends on the thread composition and the initial state. Hence, a single change in any parameter may affect the verification result.

5   Related Work

Leino *et al.* [14] propose a compositional technique to verify the absence of deadlocks in concurrent systems with both locks and channels. They use deductive reasoning to define which locks a thread may acquire, or to impose an obligation for a thread to send a message. The authors acknowledge that their quantitative approach to channels does not apply to CVs, as messages passed through a channel are received synchronously, while a notification on a condition variable is either received, or else is lost.

Popeea and Rybalchenko [16] present a compositional technique to prove termination of multi-threaded programs, which combines predicate abstraction and refinement with *rely-guarantee* reasoning. The technique is only defined for programs that synchronize with locks, and it cannot be easily generalized to support CVs. The reason for this is that the thread termination criterion is the absence of infinite computations; however, a finite computation where a waiting thread is never notified is incorrectly characterized as terminating.

Wang and Hoang [17] propose a technique that permutes actions of execution traces to verify the absence of synchronization bugs. Their program model considers locks and condition variables. However, they cannot verify the property considered here, since their method does not permute matching pairs of *wait-notify*. For instance, it will not reorder a trace where, first, a thread waits, and then, another thread notifies. Thus, their method cannot detect the case where the notifying thread is scheduled first, and the waiting thread suspends the execution indefinitely.

Kaiser and Pradat-Peyre [9] propose the modelling of Java monitors in Ada, and the extraction of CPNs from Ada programs. However, they do not precisely describe how the CPNs are verified, nor provide a correctness argument about their technique. Also, they only validate their tool on toy examples with few threads. Our tool is validated on larger test cases, and on a real program.

Kavi *et al.* [10] present PN components for the synchronization primitives in the Pthread library for C/C++, including condition variables. However, their modelling of CVs just allows the synchronization between two threads, and no argument is presented on how to use it with more threads.

Westergaard [18] presents a technique to extract CPNs for programs in a toy concurrent language, with locks as the only synchronization primitive. Our work borrows much from this work w.r.t. the CPN modelling and analysis. However, we analyze full-fledged programming languages, and address the complications of analyzing programs with condition variables.

Finally, Van der Aalst *et al.* [1] present strategies for modelling complex parallel applications as CPNs. We borrow many ideas from this work, especially the modelling of hierarchical CPNs. However, their formalism is over-complicated for our needs, and we therefore simplify it to produce more manageable CPNs.

6   Conclusion

We presented a technique to prove the correct synchronization of Java programs using condition variables. Correctness here means that if all threads reach their synchronization blocks, then all will eventually terminate the synchronization. Our technique does not avoid the exponential blow-up of the state space caused by the interleaving of threads; instead, it alleviates the problem by isolating the synchronization behavior.

We introduced SyncTask, a simple language to capture the relevant aspects of synchronization using condition variables. Also, we define an annotation scheme for programmers to map the expected synchronization in a Java program to a SyncTask program. We establish that the synchronization is correct w.r.t. the above-mentioned property *iff* the corresponding SyncTask terminates. As a proof-of-concept, to check termination we define a translation from SyncTask programs into Colored Petri Nets such that the program terminates *iff* the net invariably reaches a special configuration. The extraction of SyncTask from annotated Java programs, and the translation to CPNs, is implemented as the STAVE tool. We validate our technique on some test-cases using CPN Tools.

Our current results hold for a number of *restrictions* on the analyzed programs. In future work we plan to address and relax these restrictions, integrate special-purpose static analyzers for the separate types of required annotations, incorporate more sophisticated model checkers for checking termination of SyncTask programs, and perform a more diverse experimental evaluation and comparison with other verification techniques.

References

1. Aalst, W.M.P., Stahl, C., Westergaard, M.: Strategies for modeling complex processes using colored petri nets. In: Jensen, K., Aalst, W.M.P., Balbo, G., Koutny, M., Wolf, K. (eds.) Transactions on Petri Nets and Other Models of Concurrency VII. LNCS, vol. 7480, pp. 6–55. Springer, Heidelberg (2013). doi:10.1007/978-3-642-38143-0_2

2. Cenciarelli, P., Knapp, A., Reus, B., Wirsing, M.: An event-based structural operational semantics of multi-threaded java. In: Alves-Foss, J. (ed.) Formal Syntax and Semantics of Java. LNCS, vol. 1523, pp. 157–200. Springer, Heidelberg (1999). doi:10.1007/3-540-48737-9_5

3. Dingle, N.J., Knottenbelt, W.J., Suto, T.: PIPE2: A tool for the performance evaluation of generalised stochastic Petri nets. SIGMETRICS 36(4), 34–39 (2009)

4. de Carvalho Gomes, P.: SyncTAsk VErifier (2015). http://www.csc.kth.se/~pedrodcg/stave

5. de Carvalho Gomes, P., Gurov, D., Huisman, M.: Algorithmic verification of multithreaded programs with condition variables. Technical report, KTH Royal Institute of Technology, October 2015. http://urn.kb.se/resolve?urn=urn:nbn:se:kth:diva-176006

6. Hoare, C.A.R.: Monitors: An operating system structuring concept. Commun. ACM 17(10), 549–557 (1974)

7. Jensen, K., Kristensen, L.M.: Coloured Petri Nets: Modelling and Validation of Concurrent Systems, 1st edn. Springer, Heidelberg (2009)
8. Jensen, K., Kristensen, L., Wells, L.: Coloured petri nets and CPN tools for modelling and validation of concurrent systems. Int. J. Softw. Tools Technol. Transfer 9(3–4), 213–254 (2007)
9. Kaiser, C., Pradat-Peyre, J.-F.: Weak fairness semantic drawbacks in java multithreading. In: Kordon, F., Kermarrec, Y. (eds.) Ada-Europe 2009. LNCS, vol. 5570, pp. 90–104. Springer, Heidelberg (2009). doi:10.1007/978-3-642-01924-1_7
10. Kavi, K., Moshtaghi, A., Chen, D.J.: Modeling multithreaded applications using petri nets. Int. J. Parallel Prog. 30(5), 353–371 (2002)
11. Lamport, L.: How to make a multiprocessor computer that correctly executes multiprocess programs. IEEE Trans. Comput. 28(9), 690–691 (1979)
12. Leavens, G., Baker, A., Ruby, C.: JML: A notation for detailed design. In: Kilov, H., Rumpe, B., Simmonds, I. (eds.) Behavioral Specifications of Businesses and Systems. The Springer International Series in Engineering and Computer Science, vol. 523, pp. 175–188. Springer, US (1999)
13. Leino, K.R.M., Müller, P.: A basis for verifying multi-threaded programs. In: Castagna, G. (ed.) ESOP 2009. LNCS, vol. 5502, pp. 378–393. Springer, Heidelberg (2009). doi:10.1007/978-3-642-00590-9_27
14. Leino, K.R.M., Müller, P., Smans, J.: Deadlock-free channels and locks. In: Gordon, A.D. (ed.) ESOP 2010. LNCS, vol. 6012, pp. 407–426. Springer, Heidelberg (2010). doi:10.1007/978-3-642-11957-6_22
15. Milner, R.: Communicating and Mobile Systems: the π-Calculus, pp. 52–53. Cambridge University Press, New York (1999). Chap. 6
16. Popeea, C., Rybalchenko, A.: Compositional termination proofs for multi-threaded programs. In: Flanagan, C., König, B. (eds.) TACAS 2012. LNCS, vol. 7214, pp. 237–251. Springer, Heidelberg (2012). doi:10.1007/978-3-642-28756-5_17
17. Wang, C., Hoang, K.: Precisely deciding control state reachability in concurrent traces with limited observability. In: McMillan, K.L., Rival, X. (eds.) VMCAI 2014. LNCS, vol. 8318, pp. 376–394. Springer, Heidelberg (2014). doi:10.1007/978-3-642-54013-4_21
18. Westergaard, M.: Verifying parallel algorithms and programs using coloured petri nets. In: Jensen, K., Aalst, W.M., Ajmone Marsan, M., Franceschinis, G., Kleijn, J., Kristensen, L.M. (eds.) Transactions on Petri Nets and Other Models of Concurrency VI. LNCS, vol. 7400, pp. 146–168. Springer, Heidelberg (2012). doi:10.1007/978-3-642-35179-2_7

An Interval Logic
for Stream-Processing Functions:
A Convolution-Based Construction

Brijesh Dongol[✉]

Department of Computer Science, Brunel University, London, UK
Brijesh.Dongol@brunel.ac.uk

Abstract. We develop an interval-based logic for reasoning about systems consisting of components specified using stream-processing functions, which map streams of inputs to streams of outputs. The construction is algebraic and builds on a theory of convolution from formal power series. Using these algebraic foundations, we uniformly (and systematically) define operators for time- and space-based (de)composition. We also show that Banach's fixed point theory can be incorporated into the framework, building on an existing theory of partially ordered monoids, which enables a feedback operator to be defined algebraically.

1 Introduction

Many systems (e.g., hybrid systems) require logics that are capable of reasoning about both discrete and continuous behaviours; scalability in reasoning methods for such systems has long been an open challenge. Especially difficult is a logic that enables reasoning about time- and space-based properties, including feedback, to be (de-)composed in a uniform manner. From a uniformity perspective, one way forward is the development of logics and reasoning frameworks from algebraic foundations [12].

In this paper, we build on our previous work on *convolution* [8], which is a concept taken from *formal power series* [2,9]. Essentially, convolution defines multiplication for functions of type $Q^M = M \to Q$, where M is a partial monoid (see Sect. 3) and Q is a quantale (see Sect. 5). For any $x \in M$, the convolution of $f, g \in Q^M$ is given by

$$(f \cdot g)\,x = \sum_{x = y \circ z} f\,y \odot g\,z.$$

That is, multiplication · at the level of the functions f and g is defined as the sum of all possible decompositions of the argument x into components y and z, where $x = y \circ z$ and each term in the sum is obtained by applying f to y and g to z, then multiplying the results of the function applications using $\odot$.

There are many possible instantiations of M and Q, which allows the algebra to capture many different models of computation (see [8] for details). As we shall

© Springer International Publishing AG 2017
C. Artho and P.C. Ölveczky (Eds.): FTSCS 2016, CCIS 694, pp. 20–35, 2017.
DOI: 10.1007/978-3-319-53946-1_2

see, in this paper, the quantale Q that we consider is a boolean quantale, and M itself has a richer algebraic structure. In particular, we use a monoidal structure M consisting of three different multiplication operators: one for (de)composing time, and two for different types of functional (de)composition. We show that by lifting each of these multiplications using convolution results in a tri-quantale over Q^M.

From these algebraic foundations, we construct a new logic for a computation model, suited for reasoning about stream-based systems (e.g., hybrid systems). The logic combines *interval-based reasoning* [14,16,19] with *stream-processing functions* [3,17], where components are modelled by functions from streams of inputs to streams of outputs (see Fig. 1). A basic form of this logic has already been described [8,14], but this existing treatment does not distinguish between inputs and outputs. As such, the basic form is unable to cope with functional composition and feedback. The extended logic in this paper copes with both in a straightforward manner, while retaining the generality of the previous approach [8]. We discuss possible variations of our logic throughout this paper.

This paper is structured as follows. Section 2 introduces our target computation model of stream-processing functions and Sect. 3 discusses the algebraic structure, which is used to define pipelined and parallel composition. Section 4 presents a method for reasoning about feedback, adapting Cataldo et al.'s algebraic constructions [4]. Section 5 provides further algebraic background (quantales and convolution), which we use in Sect. 6 to develop our full logic, consisting of both intervals and stream-processing functions. Section 7 describes method for reasoning about modalities and Sect. 8 concludes and discusses future work.

2   Stream-Processing Functions

We aim to reason about systems that evolve over time. These may be modelled by *streams*, which are total functions of type $T \to X$, where X denotes the (potentially infinite) set of values and $(T, \le)$ is a linearly ordered set, denoting times. It is well known that T can be instantiated to, for instance, $\mathbb{Z}$ to reason about discrete systems and $\mathbb{R}$ to reason about hybrid systems [4,5,10].

Systems may take more than one input stream and produce multiple output streams. If $X_i \subseteq X$ is a set of values, we let $X^{T,m}$ denote $X_1^T \times X_2^T \times \cdots \times X_m^T$. Thus, each $x \in X^{T,m}$ is an m-tuple and each x_i is a stream over type X_i. An (m, n)-ary *stream-processing function* with m input and n output streams is a function $f : X^{T,m} \to Y^{T,n}$. Note that streams (and hence stream-processing functions) do not contain variables; stream-processing functions simply take an m-tuple of input values and transform them into an n-tuple of output values.

Although a stream-processing function (of type X^T) defines values over all time in T, reasoning typically only takes place after initialisation. For convenience, we assume $0 \in T$ and that stream-processing functions are initialised at time 0.

One of the benefits of using stream-processing functions (which naturally distinguish between input/output streams) is that they simplify reasoning about

Fig. 1. (m, n)-ary stream-processing function

feedback. In order to ensure feedback is well defined, we require that the streams are κ-causal, with some delay κ. A stream-processing function is *causal* iff its input until time $t \geq 0$ completely determines its output until time t, and is κ-*causal* iff its input until time $t \geq 0$ completely determines its output until time $t + \kappa$ (where $\kappa > 0$). (Delayed) causality imposes the basic requirement that a system cannot anticipate the future values of its inputs. These concepts are formalised below. We use notation $f =_t g$ to denote $\forall u \in T . u \leq t \Rightarrow f u = g u$, where, following algebraic conventions, we write $f x$ for function application $f(x)$.

Definition 1. *Let f be an (m, n)-ary stream-processing function. We say f is* causal *iff*

$$\forall x, x' \in X^{T,m}, t \in T_{\geq 0} . (x =_t x') \Rightarrow (f x =_t f x')$$

*and that f is κ-*causal *with delay $\kappa > 0$ iff*

$$\forall x, x' \in X^{T,m}, t \in T_{\geq 0} . (x =_t x') \Rightarrow (f x =_{t+\kappa} f x').$$

We will refer to a causal stream-processing function as a *behaviour* and a κ-causal stream-processing function as a *delayed behaviour*.

Example 2. Suppose the temperature of a fridge is given by a stream *temp* (whose behaviour is unspecified for now). A controller that turns the motor on/off to keep the temperature between K_{max} and K_{min} can be modelled by a delayed behaviour:

$$C(temp) = \lambda t : T . \begin{cases} on & \text{if } temp\,(t - \kappa) > K_{max} \wedge t \geq \kappa \\ off & \text{if } temp\,(t - \kappa) < K_{min} \vee 0 \leq t < \kappa \\ C\,temp\,(t - \kappa) & \text{otherwise} \end{cases}$$

The disjunct $0 \leq t < \kappa$ in the second case defines the initial value of the motor (upto time κ). □

A possible behaviour of the system from Example 2 is given below.

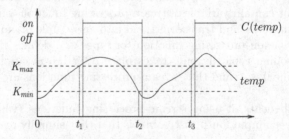

The temperature *temp* fluctuates between K_{max} an K_{min}. The stream processing function C takes *temp* as input and transforms it into some output $C(temp)$ resulting in the values *on* or *off*. Note the delay κ between the value of *temp* rising above K_{max} (e.g., at t_1) and the output *on*, as well as the value of *temp* dipping below K_{min} (e.g., at t_2) and the output *off*.

3 Composition Algebraically

It is straightforward to see that various composition operators can be defined for stream-processing functions [3,17], e.g., pipelined composition (see Fig. 2) as well as parallel composition (see Fig. 3). This section describes an algebraic construction, where compositions are defined at the level of partial monoids, and later instantiated to obtain compositions for our computation model of stream-processing functions. In Sect. 6, we show how our algebraic theory (based on convolution), can be used to lift these structure to the level of specifications. First, we recap our algebraic theory.

Partial Monoids and Bi-Monoids. A *partial monoid* is a structure $(M, \circ, D, E)$ such that M is a set (known as the *carrier set* of the algebra), $D \subseteq M \times M$ the domain of composition, and $\circ : D \to M$ a partial operation of composition. Composition is associative, $x \circ (y \circ z) = (x \circ y) \circ z$, in the sense that if either side of the equation is defined then so is the other and both sides are equal. Furthermore, $E \subseteq M$ is a set of (generalised) units, where for each $x \in M$ there exist $e, e' \in E$ such that $e \circ x = x = x \circ e'$. We follow the convention of leaving out the D from the signature of the partial monoids under consideration, where possible.

Example 3 (Ordered Pairs). Consider the Cartesian product $A \times A$ over a set A. Define

$$D_{OP} = \{(p, q) \in (A \times A) \times (A \times A) \mid \pi_2\, p = \pi_1\, q\}$$

where π_i is the projection onto the ith component of the given tuple. Let $E_{OP} = \{(a, a) \mid a \in A\}$. Define the *cartesian fusion product* $p \gg q = (\pi_1\, p, \pi_2\, q)$. In the presence of D_{OP}, the operator $\gg$ composes two ordered pairs whenever the second coordinate of the first one is equal to the first coordinate of the second one. This turns $(A \times A, \gg, D_{OP}, E_{OP})$ into a partial monoid. □

The definitions of monoids generalise to n operations. For example, for $n = 2$, a partial *bi-monoid* is a structure $(M, \circ_1, \circ_2, E_1, E_2)$ such that $(M, \circ_1, E_1)$ and $(M, \circ_2, E_2)$ are partial monoids.

Pipeline and parallel composition. To use this algebraic theory, it is simpler to view each stream-processing function as sets of input/output pairs, where a function $f : X \to Y$ is represented by a set of pairs $\{(x, y) : X \times Y \mid x \in dom\, f \wedge y = f\, x\}$. The carrier set F for our algebra is defined as follows. Let $F_{m,n} = X^{T,m} \times Y^{T,n}$ be the set of all (m, n)-ary input/output tuples and let

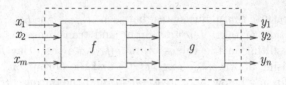

Fig. 2. Pipelined composition $f \gg g$

$F = \bigcup_{m,n:\mathbb{N}} F_{m,n}$ be the set of all input/output tuples. Also let id be the identity function.

Pipeline composition takes all output messages from the first component and uses them as inputs to the second (see Fig. 2).

Lemma 4 (Pipeline composition). $(F, \gg, id)$ *is a partial monoid with definedness relation* D_{OP}.

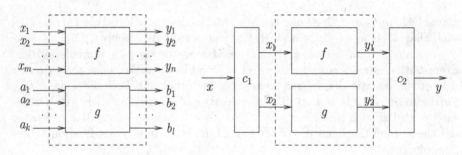

Fig. 3. Parallel composition $f \otimes g$ **Fig. 4.** Duplicating/combining inputs/outputs

Parallel composition (see Fig. 3) of stream-processing functions simply constructs a new tuple, combining the first and second arguments to the multiplication. The proof of this lemma is straightforward. We use notation $x \frown y$ to denote concatenation for tuples x and y and $\langle \rangle$ to denote the empty tuple.

Lemma 5 (Parallel composition). $(F, \otimes, \{(\langle \rangle, \langle \rangle)\})$ *is a (total) monoid, where multiplication is defined by* $((x, y) \otimes (a, b)) = (x \frown a, y \frown b)$.

The following corollary combines these two results.

Corollary 6. $(F, \gg, \otimes, id, \{(\langle \rangle, \langle \rangle)\})$ *is a partial bi-monoid.*

Note that because we view stream-processing functions as tuples of inputs to tuples of outputs, $f(x_1, x_2)$ may not have the same meaning as $f(x_2, x_1)$, i.e., the parallel composition operator is not necessarily commutative. Commutativity can be regained by using streams of type $T \to V \to X$, mapping variable names

V to values X. We leave the study of the (more complicated) stream processing functions that result from these as a topic of future study.

Clearly, it should be possible for two components operating in parallel to share inputs, or produce an output that combines the outputs of the two components. Such situations can be easily modelled by defining for instance, a duplicator that splits some shared input stream into two disjoint outputs. Similarly, outputs can be combined by a stream-processing function that collates, combines and processes outputs from several parallel sources. An example is given in Fig. 4, which defines the component $c_1 \gg (f \otimes g) \gg c_2$.

4 Feedback

The streams under consideration are over a linear order T. For such models, the use of Banach's theory to ensure the existence of a unique fixed point is well known [4,17]. This includes constructive fixed-point theorems that enable calculation of this unique fixed point [4]. We recap Cataldo et al.'s main result (and the background needed to understand this result); then apply it to our setting of (m, n)-ary stream-processing functions.

Feedback algebraically. Following Cataldo et al., the generalisation of Banach's fixed-point theory is given in terms of a *pomonoid* (as in *p*artially *o*rdered *monoid*), which is a structure $(\Gamma, \sqsubseteq, \oplus, \bot)$ such that $(\Gamma, \oplus, \bot)$ is a monoid and $(\Gamma, \sqsubseteq)$ is a partial order with minimum element $\bot$. Given a set X and a pomonoid $(\Gamma, \sqsubseteq, \oplus, \bot)$, we define a *petric* (as in *p*omonoid m*etric*) to be any $d : X \times X \to \Gamma$ such that for all $x, y, z \in X$:

1. $d\,x\,y = \bot$ iff $x = y$,
2. $d\,x\,y = d\,y\,x$, and
3. $d\,x\,z \sqsubseteq d\,x\,y \oplus d\,y\,z$

For example, any metric is a petric over the pomonoid $(R_{\geq 0}, \leq, +, 0)$.

An infinite sequence $G = (\gamma_0, \gamma_1, \dots) \in \Gamma^\omega$ is *decaying* iff for all $\gamma \in \Gamma \backslash \{\bot\}$ there exists an $n \in N$ such that for all $k \geq n$, $\gamma_k \sqsubset \gamma$, i.e., for any non-zero value γ, there is a point in G where the elements from that point onwards are below γ. An infinite sequence $X_s = (x_0, x_1, \dots) \in X^\omega$ is *Cauchy* iff for all $\gamma \in \Gamma \backslash \{\bot\}$, there exists an $n \in N$ such that for all $k, m \geq n$, $(d\,x_k\,x_m) \sqsubset \gamma$. We say that X_s *converges* to $x \in X$ iff the sequence $((d\,x_0\,x), (d\,x_1\,x), \dots) \in \Gamma^\omega$ is decaying. The set X is *Cauchy complete* iff for all Cauchy sequences $(x_0, x_1, \dots) \in X^\omega$, there exists a unique $x \in X$ such that the sequence $(x_0, x_1, \dots)$ converges to x.

These definitions are used to define a scheme for constructing the fixed point of a function $f : X \to X$, given by the following recursion, where $i \geq 0$:

$$f^0\,x = x \qquad\qquad f^{i+1}\,x = f(f^i\,x)$$

We say f is a *strict contraction* iff $\forall x, y \in X$. $x \neq y \Rightarrow d\,(f\,x)\,(f\,y) \sqsubset d\,x\,y$ for some petric d. For a discrete time domain, a *strict contraction* is enough to ensure a fixed-point is reached. Given $x, y \in X$ and $n \in \mathbb{N}$, let

$$B_n\,x\,y = \left\{ \bigoplus_{i=n}^{k} d\,(f^i\,x)\,(f^i\,y) \mid k \in \mathbb{N} \wedge k \geq n \right\}$$

A strict contraction f is a *decaying contraction* iff for all $x, y \in X$, there exists a decaying sequence $(\gamma_0, \gamma_1, ...) \in \Gamma^\omega$ where γ_n is an upper bound for $B_n\,x\,y$.

Theorem 7 ([4])**.** *If X is Cauchy complete with respect to petric d, and if $f : X \to X$ is a decaying contraction, then f has a unique fixed point $\mathit{fix}(f) \in X$. Moreover, for any $x \in X$, the sequence $((f^0\,x), (f^1\,x), ...)$ converges to $\mathit{fix}(f)$.*

Feedback for stream-processing functions. We now define feedback for stream-processing functions, which feeds k outputs of an $(m + k, n + k)$-ary delayed behaviour back to k inputs (see Fig. 5). Notation $\pi_{[i,j]}(x_1, x_2, \ldots, x_n)$ denotes the projection $\pi_{[i,j]}(x_i, x_{i+1}, \ldots, x_j)$ for $1 \leq i \leq j \leq n$.

Definition 8. *Let $f : X^{T,m} \times Z^{T,k} \to Y^{T,n} \times Z^{T,k}$ be an $(m + k, n + k)$-ary stream-processing function. Then $\mu^k f$ is a (m, n)-ary stream-processing function such that the value $(y_1, \ldots, y_n)$ of $(\mu^k f)(x_1, \ldots, x_m)$ is given by*

$$(y_1, \ldots, y_n, z_1, \ldots, z_k) = f\,(x_1, \ldots, x_m, z_1, \ldots, z_k)$$

where $(z_1, \ldots, z_k)$ is the solution of the equation

$$(z_1, \ldots, z_k) = \pi_{[n+1,n+k]}\,f\,(x_1, \ldots, x_m, z_1, \ldots, z_k). \tag{1}$$

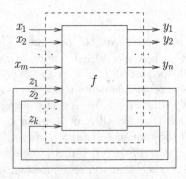

Fig. 5. Feedback composition $\mu^k f$

The theorem below follows immediately via an application of Cataldo et al's result for *eventually decaying* contractions. We elide the definition of eventually decaying, simply noting that every decaying contraction is eventually decaying.

Theorem 9. *If $f : X \to X$ is κ-causal, then f is a decaying contraction and has a unique fixed point.*

Corollary 10. *If $f : X^{T,m} \times Z^{T,k} \to Y^{T,n} \times Z^{T,k}$ is κ-causal, then $\pi_{[n+1,n+k]} f$ is a decaying contraction and has a unique fixed point.*

Example 11. Consider the controller in Example 2 operating in parallel with an environment (which modifies *temp*) depending on the value of the motor. We define

$$C_E(motor) = \lambda t : T . \text{ if } motor\ t = on \text{ then } lower\ t \text{ else } raise\ t$$

where we assume *lower* (respectively, *raise*) is a continuous monotonically decreasing (increasing) function describing the rate of change of *temp*. The overall system is described by the composition: $\mu^1(C \gg C_E)$. This function is well-defined since its fixed point is uniquely determined. $C \gg C_E$ is contractive with delay κ, and hence, Corollary 10 can be applied.

5   Quantales and Power Series

The framework we have defined thus far enables reasoning about and composing stream-processing functions. We wish to extend this into a reasoning framework, and to this end, incorporate an interval temporal logic [5,10,16,19], which may be used to reason about the safety, liveness, and real-time properties that a system possesses. It turns out that this extension can be constructed using an algebraic approach, by lifting the notion of a stream-processing function to a behaviour, which is a predicate over a stream-processing function and an interval.

This section presents the algebraic underpinnings to make the above aims possible. A *quantale* is a structure $(Q, \leq, \cdot, 1)$ such that $(Q, \leq)$ is a complete lattice, $(Q, \cdot, 1)$ is a monoid and the distributivity axioms

$$\left(\sum_{i \in I} x_i\right) \cdot y = \sum_{i \in I} (x_i \cdot y), \qquad x \cdot \left(\sum_{i \in I} y_i\right) = \sum_{i \in I} (x \cdot y_i)$$

hold, where $\sum X$ denotes the supremum of a set $X \subseteq Q$. We write 0 and U for the least and the greatest elements of the quantale with respect to $\leq$. The two annihilation laws $x \cdot 0 = 0 = 0 \cdot x$ hold in any quantale.

Example 12. The quantale of booleans $\mathbb{B} = \{0, 1\}$ with $0 \leq 1$, binary supremum or join $\sqcup$ and composition as binary infimum or meet $x \cdot y = x \sqcap y$ plays an important role for interval logics. It also satisfies distributivity laws with respect to join and meet and every element is complemented.

Convolution. The algebraic foundations for this paper is based on power series from formal languages, which provides mechanisms for lifting properties of the underlying algebraic structures to the level of functions over these structures. More formally, a *power series* is a function $f : M \to Q$ from a partial monoid M

into a quantale Q. Operators on f are defined by lifting operators on M and Q as follows. For $f, g : M \to Q$, an index set I, a family of functions $f_i : M \to Q$ and $i \in I$, we define

$$\left(\sum_{i \in I} f_i\right) x = \sum_{i \in I} f_i\, x \qquad\qquad (f \cdot g)\, x = \sum_{x = y \circ z} (f\, y) \odot (g\, z)$$

Note that the first operation is just pointwise lifting with $(f + g)\, x = f\, x + g\, x$ as a special case. The composition $f \cdot g$ is called *convolution*. The variables y and z underneath the sum are implicitly existentially quantified. A more precise but less convenient notation is $(f \cdot g)\, x = \sum \{q \in Q \mid \exists y, z.\, x = y \circ z \wedge q = f\, y \odot g\, z\}$. The sum is lifted pointwise; $(f + g)\, x = f\, x + g\, x$ arises as a special case. In addition, we define the $\mathbb{0} : M \to Q$ and $\mathbb{1} : M \to Q$ by

$$\mathbb{0}\, x = 0, \qquad\qquad \mathbb{1}\, x = \text{if } x \in E \text{ then } 1 \text{ else } 0.$$

Hence $\mathbb{0}$ is the constant function that returns value 0 and $\mathbb{1}$ is the subobject classifier for E. The quantale structure lifts from Q to the function space Q^M of power series.

Theorem 13 ([8]). *Let* $(M, \circ, D, E)$ *be a partial monoid. If* $(Q, \leq, \odot, 1)$ *is a unital quantale, then so is* $(Q^S, \leq, \cdot, \mathbb{1})$.

The order $\leq$ on Q^M is obtained from that on Q by pointwise lifting: $f \leq g$ iff $f\, x \leq g\, x$ holds for all $x \in M$.

There are a variety of instantiations for quantale Q^M. Here, we are mainly interested in the quantale $\mathbb{B}^M \cong \mathcal{P} M$ of power series of type $M \to \mathbb{B}$ into the quantale of booleans, which is the power set quantale of the partial monoid M. In this instance, convolution becomes

$$(p \cdot q)\, x = \sum_{x = y \circ z} p\, y \sqcap q\, z.$$

Moreover, $\mathbb{1} = E$ is a boolean-valued function, hence $\mathbb{1}\, x$ holds iff $x \in E$. The boolean algebra structure of $\mathbb{B}$ is preserved by the lifting to $\mathbb{B}^M$. Hence distributive laws between join and meet hold and boolean complements of predicates can be defined.

As with monoids, it is possible to extend quantales with more than one multiplication operator. For example, a *bi-quantale* is a structure $(Q, \leq, \cdot_1, \cdot_2)$ such that $(Q, \leq, \cdot_1)$ and $(Q, \leq, \cdot_2)$ are quantales. A bi-quantale is *unital* iff both its multiplications have units.

6   Interval-Stream Specifications

With the necessary algebraic background in place, we develop our interval-based reasoning framework. The basis for this work is a specification construct that defines behaviours of system components using *interval-stream predicates*, which are predicates over an interval and an (m, n)-ary stream-processing function.

Formally, we assume $I(T) = \{[a, b] \mid a, b \in T \wedge a \leq b\}$ denotes the set of all (closed) intervals over the linear poset $(T, \leq)$. An interval-stream predicate has type $I(T) \times F \to \mathbb{B}$, mapping a given interval and stream-processing function to a boolean. Interval stream predicates can be understood as expressing properties of a stream-processing function f applied to an interval φ. They are similar to higher-order functions such as maps or folds in functional programming.

Example 14. Consider the specification of a system that controls a *motor* depending on the input value of the *temp*. Suppose we wish to specify that the *motor* is on at the end of any interval φ in which *temp* stays above K_{max}. This may be formalised by the interval-stream predicate *React*, where:

$$React\ \varphi\ (temp, motor) = (\forall t : \varphi\ .\ temp\ t > K_{max}) \Rightarrow motor\ (max\ \varphi) = on$$

Now recall the controller C from Example 2. Clearly, $React\ \varphi\ (temp, C\ temp)$ does not necessarily hold because ϕ may refer to a time prior to system initialisation, or C may not have enough time to react within ϕ. However, it is possible to show that, for any φ such that $min\ \varphi \geq 0$ and $max\ \varphi - min\ \overline{\varphi} > \kappa$, we have $React\ \varphi\ (temp, C\ temp)$. $\square$

Combining intervals and stream-processing functions algebraically. We develop an algebraic construction of interval-stream predicates using our convolution-based liftings. First, we must understand the algebraic structure of intervals. It is straightforward to show that intervals form a partial monoid. Let

$$D_{CI} = \{(a, b) \in I(T) \times I(T) \mid max\ a = min\ b\} \qquad E_{CI} = \{[t, t] \mid t \in T\}$$

be the domain of composition and set of all point intervals, respectively. Define the *interval fusion product* $a\ ;\ b = a \cup b$ that composes two intervals $[t_1, t_2]$ and $[u_1, u_2]$ by taking their union $[t_1, t_2]$ whenever $t_2 = u_1$. This turns $(I(T), ;, D_{CI}, E_{CI})$ into a partial monoid.

Note 15. An algebraic treatment of semi-open intervals can also be given [8], which leads to an alternative interval logic [5] that simplifies reasoning about discontinuities when discrete values change. However, because such a logic is more complex, we leave out this variation in this paper, and consider full development of such a framework to be future work.

Recall that we have already established that partial stream-processing functions form a bi-monoid (Corollary 6). Combining this result with the interval monoid results in a carrier set of type $\mathbf{M} = I(T) \times F$ and three partial multiplication operators:

- ; that operates as chop on the intervals;
- $\gg$ that operates as pipeline on the stream-processing functions; and
- $\otimes$ that operates as parallel composition on the stream-processing functions.

This results in a partial tri-monoid $(\mathbf{M}, ;, \gg, \otimes, E_;, E_\gg, E_\otimes)$, where:

$$(z_1, f) ; (z_2, f) = (z_1 ; z_2, f)$$
$$(z, f_1) \gg (z, f_2) = (z, f_1 \gg f_2)$$
$$(z, f_1) \otimes (z, f_2) = (z, f_1 \otimes f_2)$$

define the three monoidal operations. The chop operates on the interval component, leaving the stream-processing function unchanged, while the pipeline and parallel composition operators are applied to the functional component, leaving the interval component unchanged.

The definedness relation for the partial relations are given by lifting the definedness relations to the level of the cross product:

$$D_; = \{(x_1, f_1) \times (x_2, f_2) \mid (x_1, x_2) \in D_{CI} \wedge f_2 = f_2\}$$
$$D_\gg = \{(x_1, f_1) \times (x_2, f_2) \mid x_1 = x_2 \wedge (f_1, f_2) \in D_{OP}\}$$
$$D_\otimes = \{(x_1, f_1) \times (x_2, f_2) \mid x_1 = x_2\}$$

The unit sets for the three operators are $E_; = \{(i, f) \mid i \in E_{CI} \wedge f \in F\}$, $E_\gg = \{(i, f) \mid i \in I(T) \wedge f \in \mathrm{id}\}$ and $E_\otimes = \{(i, (\langle\rangle, \langle\rangle)) \mid i \in I(T)\}$.

Tri-quantales. Our aim is to lift these monoidal operations to the level of the interval-stream predicates using convolution. First we define the generic theory over the structure $Q^{M_1 \times M_2}$, where M_1 is a monoid, M_2 is a bimonoid and Q is quantale.

Theorem 16 below shows that this lifting gives us a tri-quantale structure in the generic case when the target algebra is a quantale. Later, we will instantiate this theorem and obtain our theory of interval predicates. Suppose $(M_1, \circ_1, E_1)$ is a partial monoid, and $(M_2, \circ_2, \circ_3, E_2, E_3)$ a partial bi-monoid. Define a structure

$$\mathcal{Q} = (Q^{M_1 \times M_2}, \leq, \cdot_1, \cdot_2, \cdot_3, \mathbb{1}_1, \mathbb{1}_2, \mathbb{1}_3)$$

where the three multiplication operators over $Q^{M_1 \times M_2}$ are defined using convolution as follows for $p, q \in Q^{M_1 \times M_2}$:

$$(p \cdot_1 q)(\varphi, f) = \sum_{\varphi = \varphi_1 \circ_1 \varphi_2} p(\varphi_1, f) \circ q(\varphi_2, f)$$

$$(p \cdot_2 q)(\varphi, f) = \sum_{f = f_1 \circ_2 f_2} p(\varphi, f_1) \circ q(\varphi, f_2)$$

$$(p \cdot_3 q)(\varphi, f) = \sum_{f = f_1 \circ_3 f_2} p(\varphi, f_1) \circ q(\varphi, f_2)$$

Theorem 16. *If $(M_1, \circ_1, E_1)$ is a partial monoid, $(M_2, \circ_2, \circ_3, E_2, E_3)$ is a partial bi-monoid and $(Q, \leq, \circ)$ is a unital quantale, then $\mathcal{Q}$ is a tri-quantale. Furthermore, if $(Q, \leq, \circ)$ is distributive, then so is $\mathcal{Q}$.*

As an example, we verify the unit law for the first multiplication operator.

$$(\mathbb{1}_1 \cdot_1 q)(\varphi, f)$$

$$= \sum_{\varphi = \varphi_1 \circ_1 \varphi_2} \mathbb{1}_1(\varphi_1, f) \circ q(\varphi_2, f)$$

$$= (\sum_{\substack{(\varphi = e \circ_1 \varphi) \\ e \in E_1}} \mathbb{1}_1(e, f) \circ q(\varphi, f)) + (\sum_{\substack{\varphi = \varphi_1 \circ_1 \varphi_2 \\ \varphi_1 \notin E_1}} \mathbb{1}_1(\varphi_1, f) \circ q(\varphi_2, f))$$

$$= (\sum_{\substack{(\varphi = e \circ_1 \varphi) \\ e \in E_1}} \top \circ q(\varphi, f)) + (\sum_{\substack{\varphi = \varphi_1 \circ_1 \varphi_2 \\ \varphi_1 \notin E_1}} 0 \circ q(\varphi_2, f))$$

$$= (\top \circ q(\varphi, f)) + 0$$

$$= q(\varphi, f).$$

Power series over $\mathbf{M}$. To apply Theorem 16 to our setting of interval-stream predicates, we instantiate the monoidal structure to $\mathbf{M}$ and the quantale to the boolean quantale $\mathbb{B}$. Thus we obtain the following corollary.

Corollary 17. $(\mathbb{B}^{\mathbf{M}}, \leq, ;, \gg, \otimes, \mathbb{1}_;, \mathbb{1}_\gg, \mathbb{1}_\otimes)$ *is a unital distributive tri-quantale.*

Although these operators have a similar algebraic structure, they manipulate their arguments in different ways, which highlights the uniformity and power of our approach. The predicate $p \, ; \, q$ holds for a function f and interval $[a, b]$, if that interval can be split into two subintervals $[a, c]$ and $[c, b]$ such that p holds for f and $[a, c]$ and q holds for f and $[c, b]$. Predicate $p \gg q$ holds for a function f and interval φ if f consists of the composition f_1 of f_2 such that p holds for f_1 and φ and q holds for f_2 and φ. Predicate $p \otimes q$ is similar to $p \gg q$, except f must be split using $\otimes$.

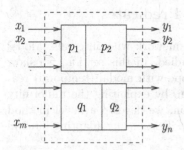

Fig. 6. $(p_1 \, ; \, p_2) \otimes (q_1 \, ; \, q_2)$

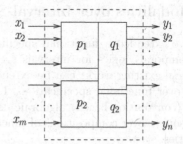

Fig. 7. $(p_1 \otimes p_2) \, ; \, (q_1 \otimes q_2)$

The differences are most apparent when we consider interval-stream predicates containing combinations of these operations. For instance, consider the differences between $(p_1 \, ; \, p_2) \otimes (q_1 \, ; \, q_2)$ and $(p_1 \otimes p_2) \, ; \, (q_1 \otimes q_2)$, which are depicted in Figs. 6 and 7, respectively. In Fig. 6, the initial component is first split into two parallel subcomponents, then, using ;, the intervals in which these subcomponents operate are split. Note that the two splittings of the intervals are independent, because the parallel composition guarantees this. On the other hand, in Fig. 7, the interval split occurs first, and for each of the subintervals, the parallel composition operator splits the stream functions into two disjoint subsets.

It is possible to perform a similar exercise using $\gg$ in place of $\otimes$, i.e., consider the difference between $(p_1 ; p_2) \gg (q_1 ; q_2)$ and $(p_1 \gg p_2) ; (q_1 \gg q_2)$, as depicted in Figs. 8 and 9, respectively. In Fig. 8, the initial component is first split using pipelined composition, which requires that we find a set of outputs of $(p_1 ; p_2)$ that can be used as inputs to $(q_1 ; q_2)$. The intervals arguments to $p_1 ; p_2$ and $q_1 ; q_2$ can be split independently. On the other hand, in Fig. 9, the interval split occurs first, and for each of these subintervals, it must be possible to find a intermediate set of outputs of p_i that can be used as inputs to q_i.

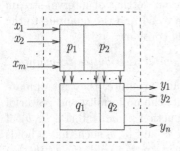

Fig. 8. $(p_1 ; p_2) \gg (q_1 ; q_2)$

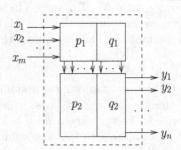

Fig. 9. $(p_1 \gg p_2) ; (q_1 \gg q_2)$

7 Modalities over Interval-Stream Predicates

We have extended a functional specification framework with intervals. Modal (and temporal) logics for intervals are well studied. In this section, we show how these existing works can be extended to cope with modal (temporal) reasoning over functional specifications. In addition, by exploiting the uniformity of our (convolution-based) algebraic construction, we develop a novel method for reasoning over compositions of functional specifications by adapting interval modalities.

A negation operator $\neg$ is available for every boolean quantale, which can be lifted point-wise to the level of our interval-stream tri-quantale $\mathbb{B}^M$. The chop operator can be used to define eventually p $(\Diamond p)$ and combined with $\neg$ to define $(\Box p)$ as follows:

$$\Diamond p = \top ; p ; \top \qquad \Box p = \neg \Diamond \neg p$$

Thus $(\Diamond p)(\varphi, f)$ holds iff the interval component there is some subinterval of φ' of φ such that $p(\varphi', f)$ holds. In other words, if $\varphi = [a, b]$, then $(\Diamond p)(\varphi, f)$ holds iff $p([a', b'], f)$ where $a \le a' \le b' \le b$. On the other hand, $(\Box p)(\varphi, f)$ holds iff $p(\varphi', f)$ holds for every subinterval φ' of φ.

Note 18. The definition for $\Diamond p$ must be modified if infinite intervals are considered. Namely, the first $\top$ within $\Diamond p$ must be replaced by an element *fin*, which is a predicate that returns $\top$ iff the given interval is finite. For an algebraic treatment, see for example [8,14].

The example below shows how one can use these modalities to develop specifications as predicates over interval stream-processing functions.

Example 19. Suppose we wish to specify a component f that satisfies the property for an input interval φ:

"if the input temperature *temp* is ever above K_{max} for k time units, then the output *motor* is set to *on* sometime within φ".

We construct the interval-stream predicate bottom up to demonstrate how the logic works. First we define a predicate for the first part of the antecedent:

$$\mathsf{higher}\, \varphi\, (temp, motor) = (max\, \varphi - min\, \varphi \ge k) \wedge (\forall t \in \varphi \,.\, (temp\, t) > K_{max})$$

The first conjunct states that the length of φ is at least k and the second states that the value *temp* within for each time t in φ is above K_{max}. Note that the output component *motor* is ignored on the right hand side of the equation above, but is present to enable the functions below to be defined using lifting constructs. We are now able to express the property that the temperature eventually rises above K_{max} using the $\Diamond$ operator:

$$\mathsf{ev\_higher}\, \varphi\, (temp, motor) = (\Diamond \mathsf{higher})\, \varphi\, (temp, motor)$$

Thus $\mathsf{ev\_higher}\, \varphi\, (temp, motor)$ holds iff there is some subinterval φ' of φ such that $\mathsf{higher}\, \varphi'\, (temp, motor)$ holds. In particular, $\Diamond$ is defined in terms of ;, which only splits the interval argument. Next, we define an interval-stream predicate for the consequent:

$$\mathsf{motor\_on}\, \varphi\, (temp, motor) = \exists t : \varphi \,.\, (motor\, t) = on$$

With this, we arrive at an interval-stream predicate that formalises the requirement above:

$$\mathsf{Spec} = \mathsf{ev\_higher} \Rightarrow \mathsf{motor\_on}$$

Returning to our component C from Example 2, it is straightforward to show $\mathsf{Spec}\, \varphi\, (temp, C\, temp)$ holds for any interval φ such that $min\, \varphi \ge 0$.

Modalities over stream-processing functions. The modalities over intervals as defined above are standard; the difference here is that they are applied to stream-processing functions. Our algebraic construction highlights the structural similarities between chop ; defined for intervals, and pipeline $\gg$ and parallel $\otimes$ composition defined for stream-processing functions, which provides us with an opportunity to define new modalities over the input/output pairs. In particular, we define modalities analogous to $\Diamond$ as follows:

$$\Diamond_{\gg} p = \top \gg p \gg \top \qquad\qquad \Box_{\gg} p = \neg \Diamond_{\gg} \neg p$$
$$\Diamond_{\otimes} p = \top \otimes p \otimes \top \qquad\qquad \Box_{\otimes} p = \neg \Diamond_{\otimes} \neg p$$

Thus $(\Diamond_{\gg} p)\,\varphi f$ holds iff f is of the form $f_1 \gg f_2 \gg f_3$ such that $p\,\varphi f_2$ holds. Similarly, $(\Diamond_{\otimes} p)\,\varphi f$ holds iff f is of the form $f_1 \otimes f_2 \otimes f_3$ and $p\,\varphi f_2$ holds. Both operators $\Diamond_{\gg}$ and $\Diamond_{\otimes}$ are useful for stating the existence of a subcomponent that satisfies property p over the given interval φ. Dually, $\Box_{\gg} p$ iff for any pipelined decomposition p holds for that decomposition ($\Box_{\otimes}$ is similar). We leave full development of such a theory as future work.

8   Conclusion and Future Work

We have algebraically constructed a logic for reasoning about stream-based systems. Applying these constructions to hybrid systems, we obtain a flexible computation model, in contrast to existing model-theoretic approaches [11,15,18] that are defined using automata (or similar transition-system-like model), which are somewhat rigid in their structure. Our constructions unify reasoning whenever possible; the theoretical underpinnings are provided by convolution [8], which enables operators to be lifted to the level of functions. Our work is distinguished from other algebras for hybrid systems [7,8,14], which do not distinguish between inputs and outputs using stream-processing functions.

This work is still in its initial stages, but presents a method for bringing algebraic reasoning into hybrid systems [8]. Areas such as network theory have already benefitted from the generality, conciseness and uniformity that algebraic reasoning enables [1]. Future work will include development of neighbourhood logics [10,13], Hoare logics [8] and mechanisation [6]. Due to the quantale-like structure of our algebra, the mathematical foundations are already available, and hence, these planned future works can be rapidly developed.

Acknowledgements. This research is supported by EPSRC Grant EP/N016661/1. The author thanks Ian Hayes and Georg Struth for helpful discussions, as well as the anonymous reviewers for their comments.

References

1. Anderson, C.J., Foster, N., Guha, A., Jeannin, J.-B., Kozen, D., Schlesinger, C., Walker, D.: NetKAT: semantic foundations for networks. In: POPL, pp. 113–126. ACM (2014)

2. Berstel, J., Reutenauer, C.: Les Séries Rationnelles et Leurs Langagues. Masson (1984)
3. Broy, M.: Refinement of time. Theor. Comput. Sci. **253**(1), 3–26 (2001)
4. Cataldo, A., Lee, E., Liu, X., Matsikoudis, E., Zheng, H.: A constructive fixed-point theorem and the feedback semantics of timed systems. In: Discrete Event Systems, pp. 27–32, July 2006
5. Dongol, B., Derrick, J.: Interval-based data refinement: a uniform approach to true concurrency in discrete and real-time systems. Sci. Comput. Program. **111**, 214–247 (2015)
6. Dongol, B., Gomes, V.B.F., Struth, G.: A Program Construction and Verification Tool for Separation Logic. In: Hinze, R., Voigtländer, J. (eds.) MPC 2015. LNCS, vol. 9129, pp. 137–158. Springer, Heidelberg (2015). doi:10.1007/978-3-319-19797-5_7
7. Dongol, B., Hayes, I.J., Meinicke, L., Solin, K.: Towards an Algebra for Real-Time Programs. In: Kahl, W., Griffin, T.G. (eds.) RAMICS 2012. LNCS, vol. 7560, pp. 50–65. Springer, Heidelberg (2012). doi:10.1007/978-3-642-33314-9_4
8. Dongol, B., Hayes, I.J., Struth, G.: Convolution as a unifying concept: applications in separation logic, interval calculi, and concurrency. ACM Trans. Comput. Log. **17**(3), 15 (2016)
9. Droste, M., Kuich, W., Vogler, H. (eds.): Handbook of Weighted Automata. Springer, Heidelberg (2009)
10. Goranko, V., Montanari, A., Sciavicco, G.: A road map of interval temporal logics and duration calculi. J. Appl. Non-Classical Logics **14**(1–2), 9–54 (2004)
11. Henzinger, T.A.: The theory of hybrid automata. In: LICS 1996, pp. 278–292. IEEE Computer Society, Washington, DC (1996)
12. Hoare, T., van Staden, S.: In praise of algebra. Formal Asp. Comput. **24**(4–6), 423–431 (2012)
13. Höfner, P., Möller, B.: Algebraic neighbourhood logic. J. Log. Algebr. Program. **76**(1), 35–59 (2008)
14. Höfner, P., Möller, B.: An algebra of hybrid systems. J. Log. Algebr. Program. **78**(2), 74–97 (2009)
15. Lynch, N., Segala, R., Vaandraager, F.: Hybrid I/O automata. Inf. Comput. **185**(1), 105–157 (2003)
16. Moszkowski, B.C.: A complete axiomatization of interval temporal logic with infinite time. In: LICS, pp. 241–252 (2000)
17. Müller, O., Scholz, P.: Functional specification of real-time and hybrid systems. In: Maler, O. (ed.) HART 1997. LNCS, vol. 1201, pp. 273–285. Springer, Heidelberg (1997). doi:10.1007/BFb0014732
18. Rönkkö, M., Ravn, A.P., Sere, K.: Hybrid action systems. Theor. Comput. Sci. **290**, 937–973 (2003)
19. Zhou, C., Hansen, M.R.: Duration Calculus: A Formal Approach to Real-Time Systems. Monographs in Theoretical Computer Science. An EATCS Series. Springer, Heidelberg (2004)

Automotive and Railway Systems

Automating Time Series Safety Analysis for Automotive Control Systems in STPA Using Weighted Partial Max-SMT

Shuichi Sato[1,2(✉)], Shogo Hattori[2], Hiroyuki Seki[2], Yutaka Inamori[1], and Shoji Yuen[2]

[1] Data Analytics Research-Domain, Toyota Central R&D Labs., Inc., Nagakute, Japan
{shuichi-sato,inamori}@mosk.tytlabs.co.jp
[2] Graduate School of Information Science, Nagoya University, Nagoya, Japan
{hatsutori,seki,yuen}@sqlab.jp
http://www.tytlabs.com/

Abstract. Recently, Systems-Theoretic Process Analysis (STPA) has been studied for automobile safety analysis. When STPA is used later in the design phase, significant effort is required to detect causal scenarios of unsafe control actions (UCAs), especially those related to intermittent disturbances in multiple signals. We propose a method to automate this disturbance detection by checking the satisfiability of trace formulas extended with *cushion variables*. At a state transition, cushion variable values are used instead of original variable values to determine the next state. A signal disturbance is regarded as assigning different values to variables and corresponding cushion variables. Specifying the equality between variables and cushion variables as *soft* clauses, a Weighted Partial Max-SMT solver mechanically searches an assignment for a trace to satisfy the UCA property. We applied the proposed technique to a simplified automotive control system to demonstrate some examples of automatic detections of reasonable intermittent multi-signal disturbances.

Keywords: Safety analysis · Time series analysis · Automotive control systems · STPA · State transition systems · Trace formula

1 Introduction

In a variety of fields, such as the aerospace, medicine, and automotive industries, system architectures and functionality are becoming increasingly complicated. Systems-Theoretic Process Analysis (STPA) [1,2] has been proposed as a new safety analysis technique based on a new accident causation model, System-Theoretic Accident Model and Process (STAMP), for analyzing hazard and safety issues in complex systems. Some works [3,4] have demonstrated the advantages of STPA over existing safety analysis techniques such as Fault Tree Analysis (FTA) [5], Failure Mode and Effects Analysis (FMEA) [6], and Hazards

© Springer International Publishing AG 2017
C. Artho and P.C. Ölveczky (Eds.): FTSCS 2016, CCIS 694, pp. 39–54, 2017.
DOI: 10.1007/978-3-319-53946-1_3

Preparation (Step 0)
    - Identify Accidents and Hazards
    - Construct Control Structure
Step 1: Identify Unsafe Control Actions
Step 2: Identify Causes of Unsafe Control Actions

Fig. 1. STPA procedure

and Operability Analysis (HAZOP) [7]. STPA has been applied in different areas, such as aerospace [8], railroad transportation [9], and medical research [10]. In the automotive field, Hommes [11] proposes to apply STPA to safety analysis compliant with ISO26262, a functional safety standard for road vehicles.

STPA is a top-down systems engineering approach and incorporates control system theory. It considers both component failures and system interactions and treats accidents as a control, not a failure, problem. STPA can be applied during concept development and throughout the design process. Figure 1 outlines the steps of the STPA procedure. The *Control Structure* in Fig. 1 comprises the components and paths of a control and feedback system. An *unsafe control action* (*UCA*) is a control action, such as an operation command to an actuator, that leads to a hazard.

Steps 1 and 2 are carried out with the consideration of a safety engineer, based on guidewords from STPA. Some works point out that examining the controller and assessing each feedback in the control path to see whether a path can cause UCAs in Step 2 requires effort, time, and in-depth knowledge [12]. It is especially difficult to deal with intermittent multi-signal disturbances arising from some undesired factors such as temporal wire disconnections, when we use STPA in later design phases, because there are an enormous number of time series patterns in multiple signals to consider for the thorough STPA application.

In this paper, we focus on the intermittent multi-signal disturbances that cause UCAs in automobiles. Generally, intermittent signal disturbances are subtle; thus, we consider it very useful to automate the analysis on those disturbances. For this purpose, we present an automating method to check the property for traces of an automotive control system with bounded length. We reduce the reachability (to undesirable states) to the satisfiability problem (abbreviated as SAT) by encoding a given state transition system into a logical formula. This approach is promising because it allows for the utilization of efficient algorithms and tools (e.g., SAT solver) for judging satisfiability. To this end, we first characterize the system as a trace formula [13,14], whose model is a set of traces, and define the UCA property as a constraint over state variables. In normal situations, the system is supposed to work correctly, where the trace formula with the UCA property is not satisfied. In the case that an error occurs, some values are altered such that they do not satisfy the trace formula but do satisfy the UCA property. Thus, we must describe both the normal and abnormal behavior of the system and use abnormal behavior caused by multi-signal disturbances as a constraint.

An automotive control system reaches hazardous states when control actions with incorrect values are provided over a certain period of time. From those experiences, we consider that a UCA expression is required to address time series. To efficiently derive the UCAs caused by fewer incorrect values, we introduce an encoding of the model into a formula for acquiring intermittent multi-signal UCA-causing disturbances by limiting the number of failures in the constraints.

We adopt a method for describing the constraints underlying problems and detecting the corresponding signal disturbances automatically. We introduce new variables, called *cushion variables*, that correspond to the original variables and allow a different value assignment from those of the original variables. We define a signal disturbance as the assignment of a different value to a system variable. The faulty values of cushion variables cause undesignated transitions, which we model as UCAs. Considering that the values of an original variable and its cushion are equal in a normal behavior, we explicitly add the equalities between original and cushion variables. By defining a UCA over the cushion variables, assigning faulty values to cushion variables may satisfy the UCA violating the equality between variables and cushion variables. The violated equality is regarded as the signal disturbance that causes the UCA. To obtain the concrete value assignment, we make the cushion variable equations as soft clauses in the Weighted Partial Max-SMT problem. By adding blocking clauses we obtain a new assignment with a signal disturbance. By repeating this, we can enumerate all signal disturbances to cause the UCA.

The main contribution of this paper is the proposal of a method for reducing the problem of finding UCA-causing multi-signal disturbances in STPA to the problem of checking the satisfiability of the trace formula extended with cushion variables. The proposed method can automate the process of obtaining intermittent multi-signal disturbances using a Weighted Partial Max-SMT solver and provide detailed design support to STPA safety analysis.

The remainder of this paper is organized as follows. Section 2 explains how to model the problem of acquiring UCA-causing multi-signal patterns. Section 3 presents a method for acquiring intermittent multi-signal disturbances using a Weighted Partial Max-SMT. Section 4 describes case studies that apply our method to a simplified automotive control system with cruise control, and Sect. 5 discusses our conclusions and outlines future work.

2   Behavioral Constraints

In this section, we describe the construction of a system model for finding the intermittent multi-signal disturbance set that causes UCAs with Weighted Partial Max-SMT. The model consists of four parts: a trace formula expressing system behavior, the UCA property, signal disturbance possibilities, and intermittent signal disturbance constraints. These parts are modeled as constraints in the Weighted Partial Max-SMT, which will be explained in the following sections.

2.1   Trace Formulas

We model an automotive control system as a finite state transition system where a state is an assignment of values to variables and a state transition is a value update of variables. Since an automotive control is usually designed by a deterministic discrete event system, the behavior of the transition system is the set of state traces. A *trace formula* [13,14] is a Boolean formula satisfied by value assignments for the traces which are obtained by unrolling cycles in the transition system for a fixed number of times. A trace formula is satisfied only when the assignment of an indexed variable in the trace formula shows a concrete execution. In a trace formula, a state is regarded as a conjunction of equalities between variables and expressions, where variables are indexed by execution steps. States other than the initial state are determined by the preceding states. We convert a finite state transition system to a loop-free program for given k and construct the trace formula for the program.

Let $M = (S, X, s_0, W)$ be given where $S = \{s_1, \cdots, s_m\}$ is the set of control states, X is the set of variables, $s_0 \in S$ is the initial control state and W is the set of transitions. $w \in W$ is given as a triple (s, ρ, s') where $s, s' \in S$ and ρ is a set of constraints over X in s and s'. A state of M is (s, ν_X) where $s \in S$ and ν_X is a value assignment for X. For a state (s, ν_X) and a transition $w = (s, \rho, s')$, a state transition of M is given as $(s, \nu_X) \to (s', \nu'_X)$ when $\nu_X, \nu'_X \models \rho(X, X')$ meaning that ν_X for X and ν'_X for X' satisfy the constraint $\rho(X, X')$.

We give a loop-free program with bound k in the following way. st and x_i for $x_i \in X$ are declared where st ranging over 1 to m keeps the current state. The program is constructed by a series of switch statements whose bodies describe the transitions in general. Let $\{(s_i, \rho_{i1}, s_{i1}), \cdots, (s_i, \rho_{in_i}, s_{in_i})\}$ be the all transitions from s_i in W and $\#(s_i) = i$. Since ρ_i specifies the constraints for a transition from s_i to s_j, ρ_{ij} can be expressed as the conjunction of a guard $g_{ij}(X)$ in s_i and an update relation $X' = f_{ij}(X)$ in s_j. The statement for a transition $\mathsf{trans}_W(s_i)$ from s_i is defined as follows:

```
if g_{i1}(X) then X := f_{i1}(X) ; st :=#(s_{i1});
else if g_{i2}(X) then X := f_{i2}(X) ; st :=#(s_{i2});
        ...
else if g_{in_i}(X) then X := f_{in_i}(X) ; st :=#(s_{in_i});
```

One step of the program denoted as $\mathsf{step}(W)$ is:

```
switch( st ) {
  case #(s_1):  trans_W(s_1)
        ...
  case #(s_m):  trans_W(s_m)
}
```

The whole loop-free program is given as the declaration of st and x_i for X followed by the repetition of $\mathsf{step}(W)$ for k times.

$$\text{int } st, x_1, \cdots x_1; \underbrace{\mathsf{step}(W); \quad \cdots \quad \mathsf{step}(W);}_{k-\text{times}}$$

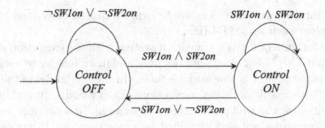

Fig. 2. State transition system

```
int st := 0;
// st represents the state.
// 0: ControlOFF, 1: ControlON
bool sw1on := false;
bool sw2on := false;

// Transition at execution step 1
switch(st) {
    case 0:
        if (sw1on = true && sw2on = true) { st := 1; }
        else { st := 0; }
    case 1:
        if (sw1on = false || sw2on = false) { st := 0; }
        else { st := 1; }
}
                    ...
// Transition at execution step 10
switch(st) {
    case 0:
        if (sw1on = true && sw2on = true) { st := 1; }
        else { st := 0; }
    case 1:
        if (sw1on = false || sw2on = false) { st := 0; }
        else { st := 1; }
}
```

Fig. 3. Pseudocode of loop-free program

Clearly, executing the program above traces the original transition system with deterministic transitions. For instance, consider the state transition system in Fig. 2, with two states labeled *ControlON* and *ControlOFF*. In this system, the transition from *ControlOFF* to *ControlON* occurs only when both *SW1on* and *SW2on* are *true*. Figure 3 shows the loop-free program for Fig. 2 with $k = 10$. Here $st = 0, 1$ means that a state of a system is *ControlOFF*/*ControlON*. As shown in [14], the loop free program is converted to a logical formula. While all variables are boolean in [14], we extend the variables to integer, allowing the equalities to integer constants. The trace formula can be converted to the form for a SMT solver such as SMT-LIB.

The trace formula of a given transition system with the execution step bound of K is denoted $\mathsf{TF}^{\leq K}$. For simplicity, we only assign an integer to each variable. (For a Boolean variable, 1 is *true* and 0 is *false*.) In the remainder of the paper, we use the following variable notation conventions. Each variable should be uniquely identified by its index as well as its name. We write u_i for a variable identified by index i in X; variables are also identified by name (e.g., y). When the variable with index of i and also with the name of y appears in a trace formula at step j, it is written as $u_{i,j}$ or y_j, where $u_{i,j}$ or y_j belongs to x_j in a trace formula.

2.2   UCA Property

An automotive control system is designed to never reach a hazardous state when a control action with an incorrect value is provided over a very short time period (due to, e.g., electrical noise). In contrast, an automotive control system may reach hazardous states when a control action with an incorrect value continues to be provided for a certain period of time. For example, a vehicle in cruise control mode can reach a hazardous state, in the case that it outputs 0 as the acceleration command value for a few consecutive clock cycles (e.g., 5) although the leading vehicle moves away from it. Thus, a UCA is reasonably expressed as a time series of the assignment of improper values to n-consecutive variables in traces. For this n, we introduce $n\text{-}UCA_F^{\leq K}$ as the UCA property over a trace as follows:

$$n\text{-}UCA_F^{\leq K} \equiv \exists i.\ i \leq K - n + 1 \wedge (\bigwedge_{\ell=0}^{n-1} F(\overrightarrow{U}(i+\ell)))$$

where K is the trace bound length, F is a predicate defined over variables, and $\overrightarrow{U}(j)$ is a vector of variables at the jth execution step, $(u_{1,j}, \cdots, u_{n,j})$. In the example of the vehicle in cruise control mode as mentioned above, F consists of the variables indicating an acceleration command and a distance to the leading vehicle, and n is the number of a certain consecutive clock cycles, e.g., 5. In automotive control systems, some variables are the signals that direct upcoming actions. We assume that UCAs can be detected by observing these values.

2.3   Signal Disturbance via Cushion Variables

Provided that the system is properly designed, we assume that no assignments satisfy both a trace formula and $n\text{-}UCA_F^{\leq K}$. If some variables are unexpectedly altered at some steps in the trace, the UCA property $n\text{-}UCA_F^{\leq K}$ with the trace formula becomes satisfiable. We describe this value alteration as a *signal disturbance*. Signal disturbances are regarded as mismatches among variables in the execution fragments. In our setting, to present signal disturbances, we need to explicitly assign a value different from the original value to cause some UCAs. For this purpose, we introduce an extra variable called a *cushion variable* for each variable. The cushion variable corresponding to $u_{i,j}$ is written as $u'_{i,j}$. In normal situations, the same value is assigned both to a variable and its cushion. If a signal value is altered, we assign a different value to its cushion variable. By preparing the extra variable, it is possible to trace failure points by checking for equality between original and cushion variables. The equality between variables and their cushions in $\mathsf{TF}^{\leq K}$ is expressed as Ω_U^K:

$$\Omega_U^K \equiv \forall i, j. \bigwedge_{u_i \in U} \bigwedge_{j \leq K} u_{i,j} = u'_{i,j}.$$

A value assignment that does not satisfy Ω_U^K contains a disturbed signal pattern.

Definition 1 (Disturbed signal pattern). *Given a set of variables* $U = \{u_{i_1}, \cdots, u_{i_m}\}$, *a disturbed signal pattern for an assignment* σ, $DSP_U(\sigma)$, *is the set of equations:*

$$DSP_U(\sigma) = \{u_{i,j} = u'_{i,j} | \sigma(u_{i,j}) \neq \sigma(u'_{i,j}), i \in I, j \leq K\}$$

where I *is the set of variable indexes of* U.

The trace formula with signal disturbances of U is obtained by replacing all $u_{i,j}$ on the right-hand side of the $\mathsf{TF}^{\leq K}$ equations with $u'_{i,j}$, for $i \in I$. This modified trace formula is written as $\mathsf{TF}_U'^{\leq K}$. For example, assume a transition system has a variable, $Speed_i$, which is an element of the transition condition and the update of the variable $Speed_i$ is specified as $Speed_i := Speed_{i-1} + Accel_{i-1} - Brake_{i-1}$ in the trace formula. In this case we replace $Speed_{i-1}$, $Accel_{i-1}$, and $Brake_{i-1}$ with their corresponding cushion variables. As a result, the example is rewritten as: $Speed_i := Speed'_{i-1} + Accel'_{i-1} - Brake'_{i-1}$. The clause $u_{i,j} = u'_{i,j}$ represents the passing of data from the part updating $u_{i,j}$ to the part referring to it. If the clause $u_{i,j} = u'_{i,j}$ is *false*, $u_{i,j}$ is considered to be disturbed.

$\mathsf{TF}_U'^{\leq K} \wedge \Omega_U^K \wedge n\text{-}UCA_F^{\leq K}$ is not satisfiable, since $\mathsf{TF}_U'^{\leq K} \wedge \Omega_U^K \Leftrightarrow \mathsf{TF}^{\leq K}$, whereas there may be an assignment σ that satisfies $\mathsf{TF}_U'^{\leq K} \wedge (\Omega_U^K - DSP_U(\sigma)) \wedge n\text{-}UCA_F^{\leq K}$. This shows that a UCA occurs if a signal disturbance happens at $DSP_U(\sigma)$.

2.4   Intermittent Signal Disturbance

We are the most interested in *intermittent signal disturbances*. In general, a disturbance with fewer signal alterations is difficult to find. In order to adjust the scope of signal disturbances, it is useful to limit the number of value alterations at a signal disturbance within a certain period of execution fragments. We add the following constraints Ψ.

$$\Psi \equiv \forall i, j, \ 1 \leq i \leq N, \ 1 \leq j \leq K - p + 1. \ \sum_{r=0}^{p-1} R(u_{i,j+r}, u'_{i,j+r}) \leq L. \quad (1)$$

$$R(u_{i,j}, u'_{i,j}) = \begin{cases} 0 & \text{if } u_{i,j} = u'_{i,j} \\ 1 & \text{if } u_{i,j} \neq u'_{i,j}. \end{cases}$$

Ψ restricts traces so that the signal disturbance occurs no more than L times in p execution steps.

3   Detecting Signal Disturbances by Satisfiability Using Weighted Partial Max-SMT Solvers

Once the system behavior and UCAs are formalized as in Sect. 2, intermittent signal disturbances are automatically detected using the encoded model described there. Our method consists of two phases in Fig. 4; the repetition of the phases enables the enumeration of UCA-causing signal disturbances. Phase 1 constructs a formula from target system behavior with bound K, cushion variables for possible signal disturbances, and a UCA property. In Phase 2, UCA-causing disturbed signal patterns are automatically extracted by a Weighted Partial Max-SMT solver. Each phase is described in detail below.

In Phase 1, given a state transition system, the UCA property, and the set of possibly disturbed variables U, formula Φ is constructed as follows:

$$\Phi \equiv \mathsf{TF}'^{\leq K}_{U} \wedge n\text{-}UCA^{\leq K}_{F} \wedge \Psi \wedge \Omega^{K}_{U}. \tag{2}$$

When passing Φ to Phase 2, we define Ω^{K}_{U} as soft clauses and the remainder of Φ as hard clauses. We also specify *weights* for each equation in Ω^{K}_{U}. The weights control the order in which signal disturbances are obtained. Specifying weights requires a heuristic that depends upon the particular disturbed signal patterns expected. In the following experiment, we uniformly weigh all soft clauses. This minimizes the number of signal alterations, since a Weighted Partial Max-SMT solver tries to minimize the sum of the weights of soft clauses that are not satisfied. According to our objectives, we can change the weighting policy.

In Phase 2, we apply a Weighted Partial Max-SMT solver to Φ. The solver attempts to find a variable assignment that satisfies all hard constraints and soft clauses with minimum weight sums. If the solver finds such an assignment, the value of each variable and the soft clauses not satisfied are returned. These soft clauses show a disturbed signal pattern.

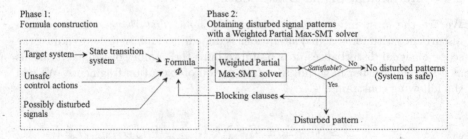

Fig. 4. Method for obtaining a disturbed signal pattern

Blocking clauses. To acquire additional patterns, we add the hard clauses, denying the disturbed signal patterns as blocking clauses, in Φ and repeat Phase 2. For example, if we get $DSP_U(\sigma) = \{(u_{1,1} = u'_{1,1}), (u_{4,3} = u'_{4,3})\}$, the following clauses are added to hard clauses:

$$u_{1,1} = u'_{1,1} \lor u_{4,3} = u'_{4,3}.$$

As these hard clauses force $u_{1,1} = u'_{1,1} \lor u_{4,3} = u'_{4,3}$, the solver tries to find out a different variable assignment that satisfies $u_{1,1} = u'_{1,1}$ or $u_{4,3} = u'_{4,3}$. New disturbed signal patterns are enumerated by adding blocking clauses to Φ and applying the Weighted Partial Max-SMT solver to the modified Φ. We repeat the loop until Φ can no longer be satisfied to enumerate all disturbed signal patterns for the UCA. In practice, if Φ can still be satisfied after a certain number of repetitions, it would be reasonable to start redesigning the system or to add some new component or mechanism to avoid the UCA.

The strategy to add blocking clauses varies depending on the system characteristics. For example, assuming that value alterations by signal disturbances can be amended by protecting the variables, all equations of the variables are blocking clauses regardless of their indices. The values passed over the network can be checked by the lower level of the platform. This increases execution costs, but is sometimes very effective when the suitable variable is protected.

4   Case Study

4.1   Target System

The target system in our case study is a simplified automotive control system consisting of three electronic control units (ECUs): adaptive cruise control (ACC), neutral transmission control (TC), and arbiter (ABT). The system is designed to control vehicle speed according to the driver's gas and brake pedal operations and the cruise control function provided by the ACC ECU. When we operate the car in "Drive" using the ACC, if no brake pedal operations occur and the leading vehicle moves further away from our car, the ACC function outputs an acceleration command. In response to that command, the car can accelerate if the transmission gears are properly engaged.

Figure 5 shows an overview of signal flows in the target system. Table 1 enumerates the signals used in this system. The functionality of each ECU is shown in Table 2. The ACC ECU controls acceleration and deceleration by generating *ACC_AccelControlData* and *ACC_BrakeControlData*. The values of these signals are calculated based on *Distance* and the difference between *VehicleSpeed* and *LeadingVehicleSpeed*, which are usually observed by sensors in a real-world automotive control system. The TC ECU shifts into neutral gear by outputting *TC_NeutralControlData* when *VehicleMoving* is *false* and *BrakeControlOn* is *true*, in order to improve gas mileage. The ABT ECU generates *ABT_Accel*.

ControlData and *ABT_BrakeControlData* based on output from the ACC ECU and the driver's pedal operation. This ECU assigns a value larger than

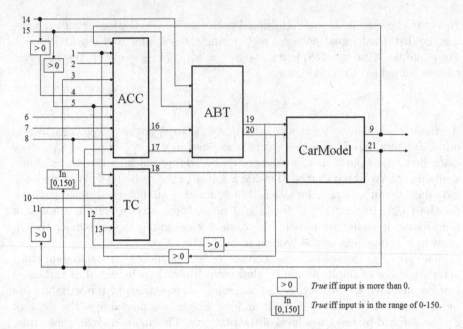

Fig. 5. Overview of simplified automotive control system. Each number refers to an explanatory entry in Table 1.

the values of *ACC_AccelControlData* and *AccelPedal* to *ABT_AccelControlData*. It also assigns a value larger than the values of *ACC_BrakeControlData* and *BrakePedal* to *ABT_BrakeControlData*. Each ECU is executed periodically by processing signals shown in Table 1.

The CarModel in Fig. 5 shows the physical behavior of the vehicle. It generates *VehicleSpeed* based on *ABT_AccelControlData*, *ABT_BrakeControlData*, *TC_ NeutralControlData*, previous *VehicleSpeed*, etc. It also outputs *Distance* simultaneously calculated based on previous *Distance*, *LeadingVehicleSpeed*, and *Vehicle Speed*. Linear arithmetic, comparison, and conditional branch operations are included in this model. The control logic in the ACC ECU includes the comparison between *VehicleSpeed* and *LeadingVehicleSpeed*. The CarModel has linear arithmetic functions to calculate *VehicleSpeed*. ACC and TC ECUs contain state transitions with Boolean guard conditions.

4.2   Experimental Result

All signals in Table 1 are regarded as possibly being disturbed in this experiment. Here, we focus on a hazard; the vehicle does not accelerate in cruise control mode although the leading vehicle moves away from it. Applying STPA to the system with the hazard, Step 1 derives a UCA: an acceleration command is not provided

Table 1. Target system signals

No.	Name	Type	Meaning
1	*IGSWOn*	bool	*True* iff Ignition switch is on
2	*RadarCruiseSWOn*	bool	*True* iff ACC main switch is on
3	*VehicleSpeedOK*	bool	*True* iff vehicle speed is in [0, 150]
4	*AccelPedalOn*	bool	*True* iff gas pedal is stepped on
5	*BrakePedalOn*	bool	*True* iff brake pedal is stepped on
6	*ShiftRange*	int	Shift range(-2:P -1:R 0:N 1–5:D)
7	*Fail_ACC*	bool	*True* iff ACC fails
8	*LeadingVehicleSpeed*	int	Speed of leading vehicle
9	*Distance*	int	Distance to leading vehicle
10	*Fail_TC*	bool	*True* iff the TC fails
11	*VehicleMoving*	bool	*True* iff vehicle is moving
12	*ABT_AccelControlOn*	bool	*True* iff *ABT_AccelControlData* > 0
13	*ABT_BrakeControlOn*	bool	*True* iff *ABT_BrakeControlData* > 0
14	*AccelPedal*	int	Amount by which gas pedal is depressed
15	*BrakePedal*	int	Amount by which brake pedal is depressed
16	*ACC_AccelControlData*	int	Acceleration control value from ACC ECU
17	*ACC_BrakeControlData*	int	Braking control value from ACC ECU
18	*TC_NeutralControlData*	bool	Neutral control value from TC ECU
19	*ABT_AccelControlData*	int	Integrated acceleration control value
20	*ABT_BrakeControlData*	int	Integrated braking control value
21	*VehicleSpeed*	int	Speed of vehicle

Table 2. ECUs in target system

Name	Function
ACC	Controls acceleration and deceleration in accordance with leading vehicle
TC	Shifts into neutral gear during brief stops in order to improve gas mileage
ABT	Arbitrates multiple control requests

for five consecutive clock cycles in cruise control mode, even though the leading vehicle moves further away. Let F be defined as follows:

$$LeadingVehicleSpeed = 0 \land \quad Distance > C_d \quad \land BrakePedal = 0$$
$$\land \ AccelPedal = 0 \land \ RadarCruiseSW \ \land \ ABT\_AccelControlData = 0.$$

Then the UCA definition is as follows:

$$n\text{-}UCA_F^{\leq K} \equiv \exists j.\ 1 \leq j \leq K - n + 1 \ \wedge$$

$$\bigwedge_{r=0}^{n-1} (Leading VehicleSpeed_{j+r} = 0 \wedge Distance_{j+r} > C_d$$

$$\wedge\ BrakePedal_{j+r} = 0 \wedge AccelPedal_{j+r} = 0$$

$$\wedge\ RadarCruiseSW_{j+r}$$

$$\wedge\ ABT\_AccelControlData_{j+r} = 0).$$

Here K, n, and C_d are set to 10, 5, and 70 respectively. L in Eq. (1) is set to 1. Values are assigned to the variables as follows:

- $IGSW_j = true$
- $RadarCruiseSW_j = true$
- $ShiftRange_j = 4$
- $BrakePedal_j = 0$
- $FailACC_j = false$
- $LeadingVehicleSpeed_j$ changes as: 30, 60, 90, 90, 120, 120, ...
- $VehicleSpeed_0 = 0$

We used the Yices SMT solver v.1.0.29 [15]. The weight for each equation in Ω_U^K is set to 10. The following section describes our experimental result. Section 4.2.1 presents the result of attempting to obtain UCA-causing disturbed signal patterns consisting of two signals. Section 4.2.2 provides experimental results that show the effect when some signals cannot be disturbed with a certain protection mechanism.

4.2.1   Disturbed Signal Patterns Consisting of Two Signals

We have obtained UCA-causing disturbed signal patterns consisting of two signals. Each pattern makes intuitive sense for the automotive control system model. Table 3 lists the names of the signals in each pattern. The disturbance of signals such as *ShiftRange*, *VehicleSpeed*, *VehicleSpeedOK* and *BrakePedalOn* indirectly affects the satisfiability of $n\text{-}UCA_F^{\leq K}$, with a delay that comes from the state transition system characteristics representing the automotive control system. Table 4 shows the pattern corresponding to the top row in Table 3. *VehicleSpeed* becomes 151 with a disturbance (0 if not disturbed) at the execution step $t = 2$, and *ShiftRange* becomes 3 with a disturbance (4 if not disturbed) at $t = 4$. These disturbances can cause a situation in which the system does not provide an acceleration command at $t = 1$-5 in cruise mode, despite the distance to the leading vehicle increasing. We can easily obtain other patterns consisting of *VehicleSpeed* and *ShiftRange* by adding blocking clauses that refrain from outputting the same pattern in Table 4.

Table 3. Signals in each disturbed pattern

Signal names	
ShiftRange	*VehicleSpeed*
RadarCruiseSW	*VehicleSpeed*
VehicleSpeedOK	*VehicleSpeed*
BrakePedalOn	*VehicleSpeed*

Table 4. Example of disturbed signal pattern

t	*VehicleSpeed*		*ShiftRange*	
	Normal value	Disturbed result	Normal value	Disturbed result
1	0	0	4	4
2	0	151	4	4
3	0	0	4	4
4	0	0	4	3
5	0	0	4	4

4.2.2 Disturbed Signal Patterns Under Signal Protection

From Table 3, we know that *VehicleSpeed* is involved in all four patterns. From this, we expect that no two-signal disturbances can cause UCAs if we refrain from disturbing *VehicleSpeed* in some way.[1] Under the condition that *VehicleSpeed* is not disturbed, we obtained ten disturbed signal patterns consisting of three signals, as shown in Table 5. The variables in each row of Table 5 can generate a UCA-causing disturbance pattern and Table 6 shows the actual signal disturbance pattern for the top row of Table 5. Our method detects more complicated time series patterns than those with two signals. The computation time to obtain the pattern in Table 6 is 1.83 s on a machine with an Intel Core i5-3470 3.20 GHz CPU, 6.00 GB RAM, and Microsoft Windows 7 Professional. Per Table 5, *LeadingVehicleSpeed* is a key in patterns consisting of three signals. Any three-signal disturbance cannot cause UCAs if we refrain from disturbing of *VehicleSpeed* and *LeadingVehicleSpeed*. This fact was verified by adding a blocking clause preventing disturbances to *VehicleSpeed* and *LeadingVehicleSpeed*.

Note that for two-signal disturbances, the total possible number of value pairs for two signals is 840, even if each signal is binary; for three-signal disturbances, the total number is greater than 10,000. Hence, it is difficult to enumerate UCAs by hand, even for short time series.

---

[1] It is a design decision whether a certain mechanism is introduced in the system to protect a critical signal (*VehicleSpeed*, in this example) from disturbance, though protecting all signals against disturbance is unrealistic.

Table 5. Signals in each disturbed signal pattern

Signal names		
RadarCruiseSW	*LeadingVehicleSpeed*	*ACC_AccelControlData*
RadarCruiseSW	*ShiftRange*	*LeadingVehicleSpeed*
ShiftRange	*LeadingVehicleSpeed*	*ACC_AccelControlData*
RadarCruiseSW	*VehicleSpeedOK*	*LeadingVehicleSpeed*
VehicleSpeedOK	*LeadingVehicleSpeed*	*ACC_AccelControlData*
RadarCruiseSW	*BrakePedalOn*	*LeadingVehicleSpeed*
VehicleSpeedOK	*ShiftRange*	*LeadingVehicleSpeed*
VehicleSpeedOK	*BrakePedalOn*	*LeadingVehicleSpeed*
BrakePedalOn	*LeadingVehicleSpeed*	*ACC_AccelControlData*
BrakePedalOn	*ShiftRange*	*LeadingVehicleSpeed*

Table 6. Example of disturbed signal pattern

t	*RadarCruiseSW*		*LeadingVehicleSpeed*		*ACC_AccelControlData*	
	Normal value	Disturbed result	Normal value	Disturbed result	Normal value	Disturbed result
1	On	On	30	30	0	0
2	On	On	60	−21	0	0
3	On	Off	90	90	0	0
4	On	On	90	90	0	0
5	On	On	120	120	280	−1

5   Conclusion

We focused on STPA safety analysis and presented an automating method to identify the faulty behavior by signal disturbances that causes UCAs in automotive control systems using Weighted Partial Max-SMT solvers. Our method is useful especially when dealing with an intermittent multi-signal disturbance that is difficult to find by hand. By checking the satisfiability of a trace formula extended with cushion variables, we modeled possible traces with multi-signal disturbances. We have shown that such value assignments can be found using a Weighted Partial Max-SMT solver. We applied our method to a simplified virtual automotive control system with three ECUs, including cruise control. Our method succeeded in detecting intermittent multi-signal disturbances that were difficult to be enumerated by hand within a reasonable time period. By observing the signal patterns obtained by the proposed method, it is often possible to point out which signals are essential to avoid an occurrence of UCAs, as demonstrated in Sect. 4.2. By focusing on those important signals, time series safety information is obtained for each disturbed signal pattern. Such information is expected to be utilized for high-level countermeasures, i.e., a real-time monitoring that checks states of a system at all times and defends a system before a signal disturbance matches a UCA-causing pattern. Furthermore, in actual automotive control systems, the probability that each signal is disturbed is not the same. Our method can handle these probabilities by controlling the weights of soft clauses in Eq. (2).

The following challenges to our method remain unresolved. The appropriate boundary K of unrolling loops can be thought as a scalability parameter. For periodic behavior, it is possible to find appropriate values of K. In addition, although the computation time to obtain the disturbed patterns is rather small in the experiment, we need a compositional extension of our analysis for a whole automotive control system.

Similar to this study, a STPA with formal methods has been proposed and its use evaluated with an automated automotive system in [16]. Their method is applied to identify hazards and support reasoning about completeness in Step 1 of STPA. [14] provides a tool for the formal verification of ANSI-C programs using Bounded Model Checking (BMC). Their tool checks safety properties such as the correctness of pointer constructs. [17] proposed a method for automatically identifying the root cause of a program that shows faulty behavior with the combination of SAT-based formal verification and model-based diagnosis theory. The techniques in [14,17] do not provide the way to describe signal disturbances that might occur while the program runs. All both techniques can address are bugs included in programs under the assumption that no signal disturbances arise. We provided the method to obtain the patterns of signals with unexpected data failures that lead to erroneous states in automotive control systems in [18]. This technique did not deal with UCAs which were expressed as a time series and was not capable of acquiring intermittent patterns.

Finally, in the future, we wish to extend the proposed technique to the analysis of actual countermeasures to safety issues. The countermeasures ensuring $u_{i,j} = u'_{i,j}(\exists i, \forall j)$ are difficult to be actually implemented, due to uncontrollable factors such as sensor noise. We will consider the design of countermeasures by adding more relaxed hard constraints such as $|u_{i,j} - u'_{i,j}| < \epsilon$ repeatedly into Φ. In addition, we plan to investigate a way of using the time series information of disturbed signal patterns for designing sophisticated UCA prevention countermeasures.

References

1. Leveson, N.G.: Engineering a Safer World: Systems Thinking Applied to Safety. MIT Press, Cambridge (2011)
2. Leveson, N.G.: A systems-theoretic approach to safety in software intensive systems. IEEE Trans. Dependable Secure Comput. 1, 66–86 (2004)
3. Sotomayor, R.: Comparing STPA and FMEA on an automotive electric power steering system. In: STAMP Workshop, Boston (2015)
4. Balgos, Y.: A systems theoretic application to design for the safety of medical diagnostic devices. Master Dissertation, Boston (2012)
5. Ericson, C.: Fault tree analysis - a history. In: Proceedings of the International System Safety Conference (1999)
6. Procedure for Performing a Failure Mode Effect and Criticality Analysis. In: United States Military Procedure, MIL-P-1629 (1949)

7. Troyan, J.E., Vine, L.Y.L.: HAZOP. Loss Prev. **2**, 125 (1968)
8. Owens, B., Herring, M., Dulac, N., Leveson, N., Ingham, M., Weiss, K.: Application of a safety-driven design methodology to an outer planet exploration mission. In: IEEE Aerospace Conference, pp. 1–24. Big Sky, USA (2008)
9. Dong, A.: Applicaton of CAST and STPA to railroad safety in China. Master's thesis, Massachusetts Institute of Technology (2012)
10. Thomas, J., Ang, Y.H., Chung, K., Gao, O.Q.: STPA analysis of intravenous patient-controlled analgesia. In: STAMP Workshop (2016)
11. Hommes, Q.V.E.: Safety analysis approaches for automotive electronic control systems. In: Society of Automotive Engineers' Meeting (2015)
12. Abdulkhaleq, A., Wagner, S.: Experiences with applying STPA to software-intensive systems in the automotive domain. In: STAMP Workshop, Boston (2013). http://www.iste.unistuttgart.de/fileadmin/user_upload/iste/se/publ/Application_of_STPA_to_Automative_Domain.pdf
13. Jose, M., Majumdar, R.: Cause clue clauses: error localization using maximum satisfiability. ACM SIGPLAN Not. **46**(6), 437–446 (2011)
14. Clarke, E., Kroening, D., Lerda, F.: A tool for checking ANSI-C programs. In: Jensen, K., Podelski, A. (eds.) TACAS 2004. LNCS, vol. 2988, pp. 168–176. Springer, Heidelberg (2004). doi:10.1007/978-3-540-24730-2_15
15. Dutertre, B., Moura, L.D.: The YICES SMT solver. http://yices.csl.sri.com/
16. Thomas, J., Suo, D.: STPA-based method to identify and control feature interactions in large complex systems. In: Proceedings of the 3rd European STAMP, Amsterdam (2015)
17. Lamraoui, S.-M., Nakajima, S.: A formula-based approach for automatic fault localization of imperative programs. In: Merz, S., Pang, J. (eds.) ICFEM 2014. LNCS, vol. 8829, pp. 251–266. Springer, Heidelberg (2014). doi:10.1007/978-3-319-11737-9_17
18. Hattori, S., Yuen, S., Seki, H., Sato, S.: Automated hazard analysis with pMAX-SMT for automobile systems. In: Pre-proceedings of the International Workshop on Automated Verification of Critical Systems, Edinburgh (2015)

Uniform Modeling of Railway Operations

Eduard Kamburjan[✉] and Reiner Hähnle

Department of Computer Science, TU Darmstadt, Darmstadt, Germany
{kamburjan,haehnle}@cs.tu-darmstadt.de

Abstract. We present a comprehensive model of railway operations written in the abstract behavioral specification (ABS) language. The model is based on specifications taken from the rulebooks of Deutsche Bahn AG. It is statically analyzable and executable, hence allows to use static and dynamic analysis within one and the same formalism. We are able to combine aspects of micro- and macroscopic modeling and provide a way to inspect changes in the rulebooks. We illustrate the static analysis capability by a safety analysis based on invariant reasoning that only relies on assumptions about the underlying railway infrastructure instead of explicitly exploring the state space. A concrete infrastructure layout and train schedule can be used as input to the model to examine dynamic properties such as delays. We illustrate the capability for dynamic analysis by demonstrating the effect that different ways of dealing with faulty signals have on delays.

1 Introduction

Railway systems are a domain where formal modeling of systems and formal analysis methods are generally accepted by industry and partially required by certification authorities [3]. Therefore, the railway domain is an active and important area of applied research in formal methods.

Models of railways can be classified according to their level of abstraction and their intended degree of analyzability. Regarding the *abstraction level*, modeling approaches tend to be either *microscopic* or *macroscopic*. The former focus on modeling a local part of a railway network, e.g., a few train station to be as precise enough to examine local and detailed properties. On the other hand, macroscopic models aim to be sufficiently abstract to cover a large part of the whole network to analyze global or coarse properties. Regarding *analyzability*, current models concentrate on a single aspect only, e.g., the safety of interlocking and signaling systems or the network throughput.

Railways are complex systems whose global properties such as safety or capacity are determined by low-level structural components as well as by communication protocols between stations at a high abstraction level. Failures of the infrastructure happen at the component (i.e., low) level, but they have global impact, e.g., a faulty signal introduces delays that are not analyzable in a model that abstracts away from individual signals.

© Springer International Publishing AG 2017
C. Artho and P.C. Ölveczky (Eds.): FTSCS 2016, CCIS 694, pp. 55–71, 2017.
DOI: 10.1007/978-3-319-53946-1_4

To reconcile different levels of abstraction, we propose a uniform modeling approach that is flexible enough to capture and analyze a wide range of properties. This uniformity has important advantages:

1. The overall effort of modeling is reduced, because each aspect needs to be modeled only once.
2. Aspects from macro- and microscopic modeling can be represented in a single model.
3. Hence, it is possible to analyze the effects that perturbations at a low abstraction level have on the global, system-wide behavior.

Our modeling method is based on the ABS language [18], which was originally designed to model and analyze concurrent/distributed *software* systems. We argue that its concurrency and object model are a good match for railway systems, too. We substantiate our claim by performing two complementary kinds of analysis carried out with one and the same model:

Dynamic analysis of runtime behavior. ABS models are executable. We demonstrate how a change in the rules for handling faulty signals influences the travel time of a train passing this signal. To do so, we simulate the scenario and compare the generated event traces. The example is based on a fault in a single signal, but the rules to handle this case involve up to three different train stations and two trains. The fault is only observable at a microscopic modeling level, but its effects have a global impact.

Static analysis of a global safety property. We prove that on a single line between two stations it is never the case that there are two trains announced in opposing direction. Our analysis is based on *deductive* invariant reasoning and not on model checking. We analyze the *communication structure* between trains, infrastructure and station, so we are able to state safety *independently* of a concrete track plan, as long as that is well-formed.

We do not verify implementation details of the structural components such as correctness of interlocking tables, but assume other, well-established methods have checked these. We concentrate on procedures and communication, and how a fault is handled *on the operational level*. E.g., we do not model the internal behavior of the signal once it broke, but we model precisely, how the mitigating communication between stations and trains in the signal's proximity ensure safety. Such procedures are described in detail in the *Fahrdienstvorschrift* [6] for all railways in Germany operated by Deutsche Bahn AG. Our model is a partial formalization of the description of ETCS 1LS within that rulebook. Our main contributions are:

1. A novel, uniform modeling approach of railways in the concurrent, executable language ABS that allows static and dynamic analysis.
2. A deductive invariant-based analysis of safety of railway communication.

The paper is organized as follows: In Sect. 2 we present the ABS language and in Sect. 3 our model of railway operations. In Sect. 4 we show how changes in procedures can be analyzed by simulation. In Sect. 5 we show a safety property and show how ABS admits its formal proof. Related work is in Sect. 6 and we conclude in Sect. 7.

2 ABS

ABS is an object-oriented, executable modeling language designed to model concurrent and distributed software systems [18]. Its syntax is loosely based on Java and most concepts of ABS are (intentionally, to ease its usage) standard. We refrain from introducing the whole language, instead we focus on three of its distinguishing features that are relevant in the present context: The concurrency model based on asynchronous method calls, explicit modeling of time, and formal semantics. A full introduction can be found in [11,18].

ABS models can be compiled into executable Erlang, Java, Maude, ProActive or Haskell code. In this case an *initialization block* must be provided (not necessary for deductive static analysis). This is a special ABS statement that serves as the entry point of a model. While ABS classes describe general behavior, the initialization block sets up a scenario.

2.1 Concurrency Model

ABS extends the actor [14] paradigm: Objects on different processors do not share memory. Each processor may host several objects from different classes. Even though ABS permits objects on the same processor to access shared memory, we carefully avoid this possibility in our model to render verification easier.

ABS objects are strictly encapsulated and have neither public nor static fields. Any inter-object communication is accomplished by asynchronous[1] method calls: The caller invokes a method and continues its own execution without waiting for the call to terminate. Instead, the caller has a *future* as a handle, which is used to wait for the called method (if necessary) and to read its return value.

Example 1. The following code calls method m on the object stored in o and saves the future in local variable f (line 1); it waits for m to terminate (line 3) and reads the return value into local variable i (line 4).

```
1  Fut<Int> f = o!m();
2  ... do something else ...
3  await f?;
4  Int i = f.get;
```

---

[1] For abstraction of sequential computations there are synchronous calls as well.

If there is no code between lines 1 and 3, then there is a shorthand notation for this idiom that avoids creation of an explicit future: Int i = **await** a!m(). □

Upon receiving the call, the callee object creates a new process and puts it into its process pool. For a process to become active, the currently active process on its processor must *explicitly* release control by termination or waiting. The statement **await** g releases control by the active process and waits for the guard g to become true. The guard g has one of the following forms:

- a future query f?, where the process can be reactivated after the process corresponding to this future has terminated;
- a side-effect free boolean expression (including future queries), where the process can be reactivated whenever the expression evaluates to true, e.g., **await this**.counter > 5;
- a time advancing expression as introduced in the next section.

The explicit release of control allows to reduce the number of interleavings between processes, since between the **await** statements, a process has exclusive control over the object memory and can be regarded as sequential.

The scheduler is non-deterministic, i.e., whenever more than one process can be reactivated, one of them is chosen non-deterministically.

2.2 Modeling Time

ABS allows to advance time explicitly [2] in processes. There are two statements to let time pass:

- duration(t1,t2); blocks the active process between t1 and t2 time units. ABS leaves open how long a time unit is—in this work we use seconds.
- **await** duration(t1,t2); suspends the active process between t1 and t2 time units. At runtime a number between t1 and t2 is randomly chosen. The process can be activated earliest after this time, but if other processes are active and consume time, it may take longer.

There is no global clock, each object has a local clock. The clock of an object is advanced if (1) it is the earliest local clock and (2) no process in any other object can advance its clock. The local time can be accessed with now().

2.3 Four Event Semantics

The formal semantics of ABS can be described with the help of communication events, each describing a communication action of a process [8]. We use four different events, one for each possible action of a process that is visible to the outside: activation of the process, starting its execution, termination, and obtaining a value from a future. Whenever such an action occurs, the process appends the corresponding event to the global history. Note that when executing the model in a runtime environment, there is no such history, it is only used to define the semantics and reason about possible behaviors.

Definition 1 (Events). *Let O, O' range over object IDs, f over futures, e over expressions and m over method names. The symbol e^* denotes a possibly empty sequence of expressions and represents the parameters of a method call. Events Ev are defined by the following grammar:*

$$
\begin{aligned}
\text{Ev::} = \quad & \text{invEv}(O, O', f, m, e^*) && \textit{(Invocation Event)} \\
| \; & \text{invREv}(O, O', f, m, e^*) && \textit{(Invocation Reaction Event)} \\
| \; & \text{futEv}(O', f, m, e) && \textit{(Resolution Event)} \\
| \; & \text{futREv}(O, f, e) && \textit{(Resolution Reaction Event)}
\end{aligned}
$$

An invocation event is added when O calls $O'.m(e^*)$ with future f as a handle. The invocation reaction event is added once O' starts the execution of this call. ABS assumes that the call is received at the same timepoint as the invocation, but not that it is immediately executed. The resolution event is added once the process which has f as its handle terminates with the return value e in object O'. The resolution reaction event is added once object O reads the value e from future f. Note that O is not necessarily the caller object, because f can be passed as an argument.

Every history h an ABS system produces is *well-formed*, satisfying certain conditions on the ordering of events. For example, if there is an $i \in \mathbb{N}$ with $h[i] = \text{invREv}(O, O', f, m, e^*)$, then there must be a $j < i$ with $h[j] = \text{invEv}(O, O', f, m, e^*)$. This condition expresses that every process starts its execution only after it was called. The well-formedness conditions for all event types are in [8].

Example 2. Assume that histories are axiomatized as a theory of finite sequences. Then we can express invariant properties over histories as formulas in first-order logic. For example, the property that for each object, between any two calls of method m there is a call of method m' can be written as the following formula:

$\forall\, \textsf{Object}\; O;\; \forall\, \textsf{Int}\; i, j;\; i < j \rightarrow$

$\Big((\exists\, \textsf{Object}\; O', O'';\; \exists\, \textsf{Fut}\; f, f';\; \exists\, \textsf{Expr}^*\; e, e';$

$\qquad history[i] \doteq \textsf{invocEv}(O', O, f, m, e) \land history[j] \doteq \textsf{invocEv}(O'', O, f', m, e'))$

$\quad \rightarrow (\exists\, \textsf{Int}\; k;\; i < k < j \land \exists\, \textsf{Object}\; O';\; \exists\, \textsf{Fut}\; f;\; \exists\, \textsf{Expr}^*\; e;$

$\qquad history[k] \doteq \textsf{invocEv}(O', O, f', m', e)) \Big)$ □

Global history invariants can capture system properties and may reference the fields of any object in the system. An invariant must hold at each point when a process terminates or is suspended, hence it is sufficient to create proof obligations that are local to methods: Because of strong encapsulation, methods on one object have no direct access to the fields of other objects—to verify global invariants, these are split into local invariants that specify the object-local history. The KeY-ABS tool [7] is then able to statically and formally verify that each method in a class preserves its local history.

With invariant-based reasoning we are able to state properties of *all* histories realized by a system, while the execution of the ABS model generates only one history. However, the four event semantics in [8] does not include the timed semantics of ABS and is thus not able to express properties concerning time. This is the subject of future work.

3   The Railway Operation Model

Our model is focused on operations and is derived from rulebooks. Not all components are described in the rulebooks, but also in requirement specifications or technical documents. For instance, the communication between stations is in part described in *Ril 408* [6] and in part by documents specifying the mechanisms for route blocks. We consider participating infrastructure elements as black boxes and only describe their behavior to extent that it is specified in the rules. If the rules do not fully specify component behavior, then we complete the behavior from the descriptions found in technical documents, but without implementation details. For example, we do not distinguish between mechanical and electronic interlocking systems.

We model physical behavior, including vehicle dynamics, with sufficient precision to establish capacity and safety properties. On the other hand, we simplify some scenarios which are either forbidden in the rulebooks or that have a negligible effect on the properties to be shown. For example, we compute braking distances using the track gradient, but we do not model how trains roll back a short distance after releasing their brakes.

Our model uses *instantaneous communication*—communication has no delay and is processed immediately, state changes take no time. In the future we plan to model such delays, but we expect this to be straightforward.

3.1   Infrastructure

We model the rail track plan as a graph, where nodes are fixed *points of information flow* and edges are tracks between these points.

Definition 2 (Point of Information Flow). *A point of information flow (PIF) is a position on a track where one of the following criteria applies:*

- *There is a structural element allowing a train to receive information, for example, a signal or a data transmission point of a train protection system.*
- *It has a critical distance in the direction of a signal: At this point the signal is seen at the latest (for example, according to* Ril 819.0203, Chap. 3 *this occurs at 300 m if $v_{max} > 120$ km/h).*
- *There is a structural element allowing a train to send information, for example, a track clearance detection device (axle counter), or the end points of switches that transfer information when passed over.*

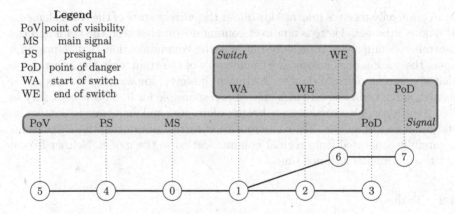

Fig. 1. Structure of a station entry

We also model the change of gradient on a track as a PIF, as this information is needed to compute breaking distances correctly. PIFs are an abstraction that assume that all these elements have no length, or can be represented by *multiple* PIFs modeling their beginning and end (for example, switches). This simplification reduces the accuracy of the simulation of physical properties, such as the exact position of a train. Our model, however, is designed for the precise analysis of communications and operational protocols. Information about the exact physical behavior could be obtained from tools for cyber-physical simulations, if so desired.

Each graph node in a rail track plan is modeled as an object of class `NodeImpl` and has a list of objects of subclasses of `TrackElement`. The latter represent different kinds of PIFs and we refer to them as *track elements*.

Track elements are grouped into *logical elements*. For example, a main signal, a presignal, the points of earliest visibility of the presignal, and the points of danger covered by the main signal are grouped as a *Signal*. Figure 1 shows the entry to a train station with one entry signal and one switch. A signal can have multiple points of danger or visibility and two signals can share one presignal.

We refer to edges between two nodes as *tracks*, to the set of tracks between two signals as *section* and to the set of tracks between the exit signal of one station and the entry signal of another as *line*. The track lengths are modelled as an attribute of edges. There may be multiple lines between two stations.

Nodes, edges, logical and track elements forward information, but do not initialize or delay communication. When a train passes a node, the method `trainLeaves` or `trainEnters` is called (depending on which part of the train passes the node). To model the communication protocol, then either method `triggeredFront` or `triggeredBack` of all track elements on the node is called. Its return value is propagated back to the train and, eventually, the information is also propagated to the station. In this manner a train can read, for example, the state of a signal. Also the station can call state changing methods on all logical elements in its area.

A train only receives information about the current state of the track elements at a node it passes. There is no direct communication between the train and the controller. Similarly, a train only initiates the communication that it passed a node, the station does not receive the identity of the train, only the information that it passed a point of danger. A station, however, knows which trains are in its area and a train knows which station is responsible for it. This is necessary so that a station can issue emergency break orders, etc., and for a train to contact its station in case of a fault. The communication carried out during those situations is carefully separated from regular communication in the model. Neither logical nor track elements advance time.

3.2   Trains

Trains have two positions, front and end, each modeled as the distance on a track relative to the most recent node. For example, if the front of a train is on track e, 5 m behind a node n, then this position is described as $(e, n, 5)$. A train has a speed, an acceleration state (stable/braking/accelerating) and a length (the distance between its front and its end) as well as attributes such as maximal acceleration and brake retardation that depend on the production series.

Edges maintain a pointer to the trains that pass them, so if a train occupies more than two edges the information that it occupies the edges in between the first and last is not lost.

Trains are modeled to drive on *simulation events*. At every PIF where the train is active, it computes its next event and the time until this event must be processed. There are three kinds of simulation events:

- The front of a train reaches the next node
- The end of a train reaches the next node
- A train stops accelerating/braking

When a train stops, it does not compute a new event. It can, however, receive a command, directly from the station or by observing a signal, set its state to accelerating and continue driving.

Consider the simulation event when a train reaches a node n with its front. It receives information from all track elements at this node and changes its state according to that information. Figure 2 displays the method to process such an event. Line 7 changes the state to an emergency brake when passing a "Stop" at the main signal, unless *Order 2* (pass the next "Stop" at a signal) was issued.

Not all events are computed by trains. A station can issue an order at any time by calling method Train.command. In this case the train computes (i) its current state, based on the current time and the most recent state, (ii) changes its state according to the issued order, (iii) computes, based on the state change, the next event. The process that waits for the old (now invalid order) cannot be canceled in ABS. Instead a counter of the number of orders the train received is increased. When the process of the defunct event is reactivated it checks this counter and immediately terminates if it has advanced.

```
 1 await duration(t,t); //wait
 2 List<Information> li = await n!triggerFront(this, now(), posFront);
 3 while (j < length(li)) {
 4   Information i = nth(li,j);
 5   case i {
 6     Info(STOP) => //passing main signal
 7       if (!listContains(orders, Ord2)) {accelState = Emergency;}
 8     StartPrepare(STOP) => //passing presignal
 9       if (!listContains(orders, Ord2)) {accelState = Break(0);}
10     ... //other branches
11     _ => skip;
12   }
13   j = j+1;
14 }
15 ... //updating location
16 this.detNext(); //compute next event
```

Fig. 2. Train front arrives at a node **n**

Currently the trains in our model always accelerate and break with maximal force and drive with the maximal permitted speed at each point. In future work we want to model different driving profiles as well as phenomena such as roll out. We expect this to be straightforward.

3.3 Stations

The German railway system has different modes of operation for driving trains outside and inside of stations. Here we focus on operation outside of stations. We differentiate between two kinds of stations: *Blockstellen* which operate block signals and only divide a track line into two parts to increase the possible number of trains on the line and *Zugmeldestellen* (Zmst, simply called "station" for short) which are able to "store" trains and rearrange their sequence. The generalization of both is *Zugfolgestelle* (Zfst).

Each signal is assigned to exactly one Zfst managing it and every switch is assigned to exactly one Zmst. The Zmst is responsible to set the switches and signals correctly when a train passes.

Each Zmst A has a schedule consisting of a list of tuples: time t, train number z, outgoing signal S and target Zmst B (by convention, trains go from A to B). For each schedule item, the Zmst launches a process that waits for t seconds and then attempts to set signal S to "Go" to let z pass. Entry signals are set to "Go" when a train was announced to arrive at this signal, exit signals are set to "Go" when a train is issued to leave on this signal, is accepted and the signal is not locked. To let a train drive from Zmst A to Zmst B on a line L, the following conditions must be fulfilled:

– It is possible to set the signal at A covering the first section S of L to "Go", i.e., S is not locked by A and A has the permit token for S.
– B accepts the train and is notified about its departure.

There are three communication protocols to ensure this:

Locking sections. Each Zfst is responsible for several logical elements such as switches and signals. In addition to the internal state of the signals, the interlocking system itself has a state that depends on the neighboring Zfst. Each section has an additional Boolean state *locked*.

Consider a signal covering a section leading out of the Zfst. After a signal is set to "Go" and a train passes it, the section it covers is automatically *locked* and the electronic message "*preblock*" is sent to the subsequent signal. A signal cannot be set to "Go" again, as long as the section it covers is locked. It must be unlocked by receiving the "*backlock*" message from the subsequent signal. That signal in turn can only send "*backlock*" after the train passed. This is one of the measures preventing a track section being occupied by more than one train.

Permit token. For each line there is one token that allows a station to admit trains on this line. Without the token the signal that covers the track cannot be set to "Go". There are various safety protocols to acquire a token. Here we consider the following: To acquire a token, station A must request it from its counterpart B. The request is granted when all trains that left B in direction of A have arrived.

Upon initialization the token is given to exactly one station on each line.

Accepting and reporting back trains. Before a train leaves a station A with destination B, A *offers* the train and waits for B to accept. This ensures that B has (or will have) a track to park the train. Before the train departs, the departure is *announced* to B. Once the train arrives, B may report back to A that the train arrives. This is not obligatory in modern systems, as long as no fault occurs. For modeling purposes we assume that all trains are reported back.

The code in the upper part of Fig. 3 shows part of the code modeling the protocol from station A's side: Lines 2–5 ensure that A has the permission to use S. The method `reqPermit` terminates after B granted the request for the token. Line 7 ensures that A does not lose the permit while waiting for B to accept the train, by explicitly forbidding it (allowing it again in 12). Line 8 offers the train to B and line 9 notifies about the impending departure. Line 11 suspends the process until the next section is unlocked. The code in the lower part of Fig. 3 is the method modeling the request for the permit token from B's side: The first conjunct in the guard waits until there are no more trains on S from B to A and the second one waits until B has the token.

Only trains and Zmst advance time, trains by waiting for their next event, Zmst by waiting for the next item in their schedule.

```
1  // ... extract correct signals and sections
2  if (!lookupUnsafe(permit, S)) { //Zmst does not have permission
3      await nextM!reqPermit(this, S); //acquire permit token
4      permit = put(permit, S, True);
5  }
6
7  permitLock = put(permitLock, S, True); //lock token
8  await nextM!offer(train, this); // offer
9  nextM!notify(n, lookupUnsafe(duration, nextM), this, A); // register
10
11 await !lookupUnsafe(outLocked, S); // wait until next section is free
12 permitLock = put(permitLock, S, False);
13 // ... set train as departed and set signal to "Go"
```

```
1  Unit reqPermit(TrainNotify sw, Route rtNotify){
2      Route rt = getOther(inNotify, rtNotify);
3      await lookupUnsafe(expectOut, rt) == Nil &&
4          lookupUnsafe(permit, rt);
5      permit = put(permit, rt, False);
6  }
```

Fig. 3. Protocol of the offering station and for releasing the token

4   Dynamic Analysis

ABS models with initialization blocks are executable and can be compiled into Java 8, Haskell, Maude, ProActive, and Erlang. The concurrency model described in Sect. 2 is implemented as a runtime environment. In this section we show it can be used to analyze dynamic behavior of a concrete track plan. The object-oriented paradigm of ABS allows to vary the behavior and to perform comparisons between different versions without the need to make global changes to the model.

The *Fahrdienstvorschrift* regulates not merely the behavior of trains and stations during normal operation, but also in case of errors and incidents. As an example, we modeled the behavior for the case when a signal cannot be set back to "Stop". In the terminology of safety-critical systems, this would be called a "single stuck-at-Go fault". We describe the scenario with the following diagram:

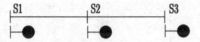

A train passed signal S2 which cannot be set back to "Stop". As a consequence, S1 cannot be set to "Go". Additional communication and explicit orders are required to mitigate this situation, such that trains may continue using this

part of the line. According to *Ril 408.0611* and *Ril 408.0411*, the following communication protocol applies:

1. The train dispatcher T2 responsible for signal S2 communicates to the train dispatcher T1 responsible for signal S1 that signal S2 cannot be set to "Stop".
2. When a train arrives at Signal S1, then T1 requests a *Gleisfreiprüfung* (clearance check) for the track section between S1 and S2, as well as the section between S2 and S3.
3. After clearance is confirmed the train receives two orders:
   Order 2: Pass signal S1, despite S1 signaling "Stop"
   Order 14.4: Stop at signal S2, despite S2 signaling "Go"
4. Once the train arrives at signal S2, T2 issues an *Order 2* to pass signal S2.

The communication protocol has four endpoints (including the train dispatcher responsible for S3 who ensures that the track between S2 and S3 is clear). It cannot be represented and, therefore, is not analyzable in a model that is focussed on a single interlocking station. According to *Ril 408.0411*, the train must always halt before it can receive orders directly from the train dispatcher: *one* broken signal causes *two* stops for each train passing this network section.

The train is always ordered to stop at signal S2, even though it is has been checked that the next section is clear. The reason is that signal S2 might cover a switch. The *Gleisfreiprüfung* only ensures that the section is clear, but not that the switches are set correctly. Hence the train must halt to give the dispatcher an opportunity to set the *Fahrstraße* (train route) correctly.

To optimize capacity one could consider to refine the rulebook such that there are two rules—one for signals covering switches, as described above, and one for signals not covering switches. In the latter, *Order 14.4* in item 3 and item 4 in the communication protocol is not given. Changes in rulebooks incur considerable

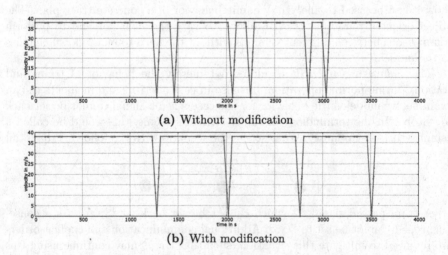

(a) Without modification

(b) With modification

Fig. 4. Comparison of train behaviors in case of a faulty signal

```
1 TrainI train = await s!getObserver();
2 await train!acqStop();
3 train!order(list[Order2, Order144]);
```

```
1 TrainI train = await s!getObserver();
2 await train!acqStop();
3 train!order(list[Order2]);
```

Fig. 5. ABS model of original and alternative rule at Zfst for faulty signal .

expenses caused by safety analysis, training, certification, etc. To decide whether this is justified, one has to estimate the expected capacity increase.

Capacity is hard to determine and always requires a concrete track plan and schedule [15]. As a proof of concept for our approach, we modeled a simple track plan with five Zfst arranged in a circle having a circumference of 22.5 km, where one signal has the stuck-at-Go fault described above.[2]

We simulated how one train runs on this track for 3600 s. The resulting v-t diagram is shown in Fig. 4. It can be seen that requiring one stop less decreases delays—the train needs 787 s for a round with the original rule and 744 s for a round with the changed rule, a decrease of 5%.

The original and the changed ABS model are illustrated in Fig. 5: in the method that models a Zfst setting its signal to "Go", we simply issue one order less to the train than before.[3] In this example, the fault itself is deterministic. It is part of the input, which signal breaks at what point in time. The simulation takes less than one second with the Erlang backend of ABS.

The modeled scenario is, of course, a mere approximation of actual railway operations: the train is assumed to always drive with maximal speed and acceleration, the track plan is not realistic. However, it demonstrates that our modeling approach can be employed to analyse the effect of rule changes. In the future we intend to enrich our model with realistic speed parameters, simulating the average behavior of train drivers. As explained in Sect. 3.1, the track plan in our ABS model is encapsulated in a graph. It is possible to generate this graph automatically from actual track plans available in digital form.

5 Static Analysis

The EN 50128 [3] standard recommends the usage of formal methods in software development for railway control systems. Our approach is a model on the *architectural level*, i.e., we abstract away from the concrete software and hardware.

---

[2] Model available at formbar.raillab.de/index.php/en/publications-and-tools/demo.

[3] This model transformation is not a behavioral refinement, therefore, it cannot be captured in refinement-based formalisms. ABS offers *software product lines* as an effective method to manage and track changes, see [12] for a detailed discussion.

For distributed software services and, in particular, cloud-based applications, for which ABS was originally developed, the usage of formal methods at the architectural level is established [21]. In this section we argue that railway systems benefit as well from using formal methods at a high level of abstraction.

As pointed out in the previous section, some safety properties can only be established at the global level and cannot be analyzed by local verification of a subsystem. This does not imply that local verification at the implementation level is useless or unnecessary: its results can be imported into an abstract model in the form of guarantees or assertions.

As described at the end of Sect. 2.3, the strength of ABS's concurrency model is that it allows to decompose global invariants into local ones which are then checked separately for each method. That is possible, because of a rely-guarantee argument where guarantees are justified by strong data encapsulation (all fields are strictly private): this implies that any ABS code between two release points behaves atomically and, hence, can be verified like sequential code. It greatly simplifies reasoning about concurrent systems.

Formal verification rests on *invariants* that are assumed when code is started or resumed and must be established when it suspends or terminates, in other words, they must hold whenever communication takes place in the modeled system. In concrete terms, each method is proven separately to preserve its local class invariant. It is not necessary to explore the global state space of a system and invariants are established without reference to an initial state. In the railway context this means we are able to reason about behavior *without a concrete track plan*. As an example we consider the following property:

"Let S be a section between two Zmst A, B. If A releases the permit token for S, then there are no trains on S in the direction of B."   (1)

This means that, if B requests the token and A releases it, then all trains in the direction from A to B have already arrived in B.

Depending on the interlocking systems in the station, different mechanisms to ensure this property are in place. Here we consider a variant of an older interlocking system, where the permit token is not secured technically, but transferred by a phone call between train dispatchers. To transfer the token, the dispatcher of that station which currently does not have it calls his counterpart and requests transfer. The other dispatcher may only release the token when all trains that departed from his side have been reported back.

In this paper we present our modeling approach and provide a proof-of-concept, hence a full-fledged case study that includes verification of the complete interaction between nodes, track elements, logical elements, Zmst and trains, is out of scope. In particular, we make some assumptions:

A.1 Lines are encoded correctly, i.e., a line L from A to B is encoded with its first section on A and its last on B and there are tracks that connect A and B using the correct in- and outsignal.

A.2 Tracks have length strictly greater than 0.

Property (1) can be expressed as a history invariant which is formalized in first-order logic and can be verified with KeY-ABS [7]. In the following formula let A, B be two Zmst and $S, \hat{S}$ two sections of a line L such hat S is the first section of L from A and $\hat{S}$ the first section of L from B. It expresses that when A releases the permit token to B, every train that was announced from A to B was reported back by B to A.

$$\forall\, \mathsf{Int}\ i;\ \big(\exists\, \mathsf{Fut}\ f;\ h[i] \doteq \mathsf{futEv}(A, f, \mathsf{reqErlaubnis}, (B, S))\big) \rightarrow$$
$$\forall\, \mathsf{Train}\ T,\ \mathsf{Int}\ j;\ j < i \rightarrow$$
$$\Big(\big(\exists\, \mathsf{Fut}\ F;\ h[j] \doteq \mathsf{invREv}(A, B, f, \mathsf{anmelden}, (T, t, A, S))\big) \rightarrow \tag{2}$$
$$\exists\, \mathsf{Int}\ k,\ \mathsf{Fut}\ f;\ h[k] \doteq \mathsf{invREv}(B, A, f, \mathsf{rueckmeldung}, (B, T, \hat{S})) \wedge j < k < i\Big)$$

Theorem 1. *Invariant* (2) *holds for method* `reqErlaubnis` *in Fig. 3 (and all other methods in its class), i.e., if it holds at the start of the method, then it is reestablished after termination.*

This does not yet show that there are never two trains on one line in opposing directions. To show that one must additionally establish that if a train enters a line, then it was offered, accepted and announced and that when a train is reported back, then the train left the line. A proof sketch of Theorem 1 is in the Appendix. It has also been proven mechanically with the help of KeY-ABS.

6   Related Work

The work closest to ours is by James et al. [17], who presented a formalization of ETCS level 2 in Real-Time Maude and analyze the communication between trains and one station. Like ours, their approach is set at the design level and encompasses all components needed for driving trains. However, it is restricted to one specific rail yard, necessitated by the use of model checking instead of deductive invariant reasoning. A further difference is that our work concentrates on ETCS level 1LS, which is the most relevant within the network of Deutsche Bahn AG. Maude is an object-oriented language based on term rewriting and one of the backends supported by ABS. Therefore, potentially both modeling approaches might be combined.

Individual rail yard components such as interlocking systems have been analyzed by multiple approaches, for example, recently in SystemC [13], OCRA [19] and CSP||B [20]. An overview over approaches for interlocking systems, the most frequently analyzed component, can be found in the survey of Fantechi et al. [9] and a comparison of ABS with these approaches in [12].

There are two main approaches to combine micro- and macroscopic models:

– Relating several models of increasing abstraction level and using the appropriate one for a given use case. This is either done by generating more abstract models on demand from a microscopic model or annotating the relation between a micro- and a macroscopic model [4,16].

– Mesoscopic modeling, which aims to be a middle ground in terms of abstraction, tailored for a given use case. A recent application of this approach was generating timetables by de Fabris et al. [5].

Our approach leans towards mesoscopic modeling, but achieves simplification not by summarizing multiple elements, but by abstracting from certain aspects. For example, we do model each magnet of the train protection system PZB, but assume these as having no length. Similarly, established mesoscopic models do not consider the communication layer, which is the main focus of our work.

7   Conclusion and Future Work

We presented an approach to modeling and analysis of railway systems based on an object-oriented, concurrent, executable modeling language. The modeling formalism is able to unify aspects from micro- and macroscopic modeling and allows to analyze static (for example, safety) as well as dynamic (for example, delays) properties of a rail yard based on a single model. For static analysis we use deductive invariant reasoning which allows to prove properties for any valid track plan and initial configuration.

As the next step, we plan to calibrate and validate our model with real data on a part of the actual railway network of Deutsche Bahn AG. This includes establishing realistic driving profiles regaring acceleration and speed as well as to determine the precision of our approach in terms of train positions. On the safety side, we plan to provide a formalization of all incident scenarios described in the rulebooks [6] and to prove a suitable safety property for this model. Furthermore, we plan to use analysis tools developed for ABS *software* models, such as complexity and deadlock analysis [1,10], to examine the properties of the rulebook and for carrying out a capacity analysis.

Acknowledgements. We thank Sebastian Schön for his insights into train operations and the anonymous reviewers for helpful comments. This work is supported by FormbaR, 'Formalisierung von betrieblichen und anderen Regelwerken', part of AG Signalling/DB RailLab in the Innovation Alliance of Deutsche Bahn AG and TU Darmstadt.

References

1. Albert, E., Arenas, P., Flores-Montoya, A., Genaim, S., Gómez-Zamalloa, M., Martin-Martin, E., Puebla, G., Román-Díez, G.: SACO: static analyzer for concurrent objects. In: Ábrahám, E., Havelund, K. (eds.) TACAS 2014. LNCS, vol. 8413, pp. 562–567. Springer, Heidelberg (2014). doi:10.1007/978-3-642-54862-8_46
2. Bjørk, J., de Boer, F.S., Johnsen, E.B., Schlatte, R., Tarifa, S.L.T.: User-defined schedulers for real-time concurrent objects. ISSE **9**(1), 29–43 (2013)
3. CENELEC. DIN EN 50128:2011, Railway applications - Communication, Signalling and Processing Signals
4. Cui, Y., Martin, U.: Multi-scale simulation in railway planning and operation. Promet Traffic Transp. **23**(6), 511–517 (2011)

5. de Fabris, S., Longo, G., Medeossi, G., Pesenti, R.: Automatic generation of railway timetables based on a mesoscopic infrastructure model. J. Rail Transp. Planning Manage. **4**(1–2), 2–13 (2014)
6. Deutsche Bahn Netz AG, Frankfurt, Germany. Fahrdienstvorschrift Richtlinie 408. August 2016: http://fahrweg.dbnetze.com/fahrweg-de/nutzungsbedingungen/regelwerke/betriebl_technisch/eiu_interne_regeln_ril_408.html
7. Din, C.C., Bubel, R., Hähnle, R.: KeY-ABS: a deductive verification tool for the concurrent modelling language ABS. In: Felty, A.P., Middeldorp, A. (eds.) CADE 2015. LNCS (LNAI), vol. 9195, pp. 517–526. Springer, Cham (2015). doi:10.1007/978-3-319-21401-6_35
8. Din, C.C., Owe, O.: Compositional reasoning about active objects with shared futures. Formal Aspects Comput. **27**(3), 551–572 (2015)
9. Fantechi, A., Flammini, F., Gnesi, S.: Formal methods for railway control systems. STTT **16**(6), 643–646 (2014)
10. Giachino, E., Laneve, C., Lienhardt, M.: A framework for deadlock detection in core abs. Softw. Syst. Model. **15**(4), 1013–1048 (2016)
11. Hähnle, R.: The abstract behavioral specification language: a tutorial introduction. In: Giachino, E., Hähnle, R., de Boer, F.S., Bonsangue, M.M. (eds.) Proceeding Formal Methods for Component-Based Systems FMCO, pp. 1–37 (2012)
12. Hähnle, R., Muschevici, R.: Towards incremental validation of railway systems. In: Margaria, T., Steffen, B. (eds.) ISoLA 2016. LNCS, vol. 9953, pp. 433–446. Springer, Cham (2016). doi:10.1007/978-3-319-47169-3_36
13. Haxthausen, A.E., Peleska, J., Kinder, S.: A formal approach for the construction and verification of railway control systems. Formal Aspects Comput. **23**(2), 191–219 (2011)
14. Hewitt, C., Bishop, P., Steiger, R.: A universal modular ACTOR formalism for artificial intelligence. In: Nilsson, N.J. (ed.) Proceedings of the 3rd International Joint Conference on Artificial Intelligence, Standford, CA, USA, 20–23 August 1973, pp. 235–245. William Kaufmann (1973)
15. International Union of Railways (UIC). Capacity (UIC code 406) (2004)
16. International Union of Railways (UIC). IRS 30100 - RailTopoModel - Railway Infrastructuretopological Model (2016)
17. James, P., Lawrence, A., Roggenbach, M., Seisenberger, M.: Towards safety analysis of ERTMS/ETCS level 2 in real-time Maude. In: Artho, C., Ölveczky, P.C. (eds.) FTSCS 2015. CCIS, vol. 596, pp. 103–120. Springer, Cham (2016). doi:10.1007/978-3-319-29510-7_6
18. Johnsen, E.B., Hähnle, R., Schäfer, J., Schlatte, R., Steffen, M.: ABS: a core language for abstract behavioral specification. In: Aichernig, B.K., Boer, F.S., Bonsangue, M.M. (eds.) FMCO 2010. LNCS, vol. 6957, pp. 142–164. Springer, Heidelberg (2011). doi:10.1007/978-3-642-25271-6_8
19. Limbrée, C., Cappart, Q., Pecheur, C., Tonetta, S.: Verification of railway interlocking - compositional approach with OCRA. In: Lecomte, T., Pinger, R., Romanovsky, A. (eds.) RSSRail 2016. LNCS, vol. 9707, pp. 134–149. Springer, Cham (2016). doi:10.1007/978-3-319-33951-1_10
20. Moller, F., Nguyen, H.N., Roggenbach, M., Schneider, S., Treharne, H.: Defining and model checking abstractions of complex railway models using CSP||B. In: Biere, A., Nahir, A., Vos, T. (eds.) HVC 2012. LNCS, vol. 7857, pp. 193–208. Springer, Heidelberg (2013). doi:10.1007/978-3-642-39611-3_20
21. Newcombe, C., Rath, T., Zhang, F., Munteanu, B., Brooker, M., Deardeuff, M.: How Amazon web services uses formal methods. CACM **58**(4), 66–73 (2015)

Circuits and Cyber-Physical Systems

Formal Verification of Gate-Level Multiple Side Channel Parameters to Detect Hardware Trojans

Imran Hafeez Abbasi[✉], Faiq Khalid Lodhi, Awais Mehmood Kamboh,
and Osman Hasan

School of Electrical Engineering and Computer Science (SEECS),
National University of Sciences and Technology (NUST), Islamabad, Pakistan
{imran.abbasi,faiq.khalid,awais.kamboh,osman.hasan}@seecs.nust.edu.pk

Abstract. The enhancements in functionality, performance, and complexity in modern electronics systems have ensued the involvement of various entities, around the globe, in different phases of integrated circuit (IC) manufacturing. This environment has exposed the ICs to malicious intrusions also referred as Hardware Trojans (HTs). The detection of malicious intrusions in ICs with exhaustive simulations and testing is computationally intensive, and it takes substantial effort and time for all-encompassing verification. In order to overcome this limitation, in this paper, we propose a framework to formally model and analyze the gate-level side channel parameters, i.e., dynamic power and delay, for Hardware Trojan detection. We used the nuXmv model checker for the formal modeling and analysis of integrated circuits due to its inherent capability of handling real numbers and support of scalable SMT-based bounded model checking. The experimental results show that the proposed methodology is able to detect the intrusions by analyzing the failure of the specified linear temporal logic (LTL) properties, which are subsequently rendered into behavioural traces, indicating the potential attack paths in integrated circuits.

Keywords: Model checking · Hardware Trojans · Formal verification · Side channel analysis · nuXmv · Gate level modeling

1 Introduction

The rapid scale growth of semiconductor design and fabrication technology has raised serious concerns about integrated circuits trustworthiness and security, particularly in the military and industrial applications [3,14,28]. The issue of hardware trust has become prominent in the recent years due to large scale outsourcing of IC fabrication to untrusted foundries, making them vulnerable to Hardware Trojans insertion [6]. Malicious intrusion in ICs may result in change of specifications or functionality, unreliability and degraded performance, and leakage of confidential information, such as encryption keys. The effects can be

© Springer International Publishing AG 2017
C. Artho and P.C. Ölveczky (Eds.): FTSCS 2016, CCIS 694, pp. 75–92, 2017.
DOI: 10.1007/978-3-319-53946-1_5

catastrophic, such as failure of critical avionics system, leakage of secret encryption keys, failing of defense satellite system [1, 21] and compromise of heterogeneous network of Internet of Things (IoTs) [24]. Hardware Trojans are generally of two types: (i) functional Trojans change the system functionality by addition or deletion of functional units in a circuit with malicious purpose and (ii) parametric Trojans reduce reliability of the IC to increase the likelihood of system failure by modifying physical parameters, such as modifying the power consumption resulting in faster aging than expected.

Hardware Trojan detection schemes are broadly classified into logic based testing, side channel analysis and reverse engineering [5]. Logic based testing techniques uses generation of random test vectors and implementation of different methods to trigger the Trojan circuits and observe their effects at the output [9]. Side channel analysis is based on measuring the variations in observable physical parameters, such as delay, power, electromagnetic (EM) signal analysis and current sensing in order to detect any alteration with the structural characterization of the integrated circuit design [12]. Side channel analysis techniques are more commonly used because of their higher performance, relatively lower costs and nondestructive testing capabilities. Agarwal et al. proposed a power analysis based technique by applying random patterns at inputs of ICs under test and comparing their measurements with the power signature of a golden model [2]. The golden IC model is obtained from reverse engineering of limited number of ICs. Similarly, Wang et al. proposed an approach to generate average and covariance based power traces [29] employing the singular value decomposition (SVD) algorithm and eigenvector projection analysis, respectively, to detect the malicious intrusions. The focus of delay based detection techniques [15, 18, 26] is on the delay measurements of individual paths of the circuit due to activation of Hardware Trojans and their comparison with of delay fingerprints from golden ICs. These above-mentioned delay and power signature analysis techniques are based on extensive simulations or by testing on real hardware systems, which requires immense time, cost and resources. Moreover, the measurements acquired through sensors cannot encompass all the possible input conditions for larger ICs and result in an extensive amount of data, which is difficult to handle with conventional automation techniques [17].

Formal verification [13] can overcome the above stated limitations of simulation based techniques for Hardware Trojan detection by virtue of its inherent soundness and completeness. The formal verification based methods, such as SAT solving and Model Checking, have been used with the soft intellectual property (IP) of the IC to detect Hardware Trojans, provided that user has access to a hardware description language code or netlist of the IC. In the recent past, researchers have presented different frameworks for the formalization and verification of IP core security properties. Xuehui et al. proposed an approach that applies multistage assertion based verification, equivalence and code coverage analysis, redundant circuit removal for isolation of suspicious signals, and sequential automatic test pattern generations (ATPG) [33]. Lodhi et al. have proposed to utilize model checking for analyzing the delay based vulnerabilities in integrated circuits [19]. In this approach, the timing behaviour and functionalities of IC are translated into the corresponding state-space model and LTL properties, respectively. Rathmair et al. have presented a property checking based method which verifies functional properties deduced from system specification using a model checker. The counterexample is subsequently analyzed to detect potential attack paths [27]. Ngo et al. have presented a methodology to use assertions derived from temporal logic and converting them into a synthesizable checker [23]. This method involves identification and verification of critical behavioral invariants using assertion based property specification language (PSL). The verified behavioral invariants are used to design the hardware property checker (HPC) which is subsequently integrated in ICs to verify the properties. However, to the best of our knowledge, so far no work is being reported, which considers the formal verification of performance properties to detect intentional malicious enhancement of hardware design. Moreover, the above-mentioned assertion based property checking methods are vulnerable to Trojan insertions at netlist and layout levels, and will only be able to detect functional Trojans.

In this paper, we present a generic framework based on the behavioral model of the IC to detect malicious hardware intrusions. We assume the attack model B [32], in which we have a netlist available in the form of trusted design, but the foundry is considered untrusted to which the design is outsourced for manufacturing. The attacker in the foundry can insert Hardware Trojans in the form of addition, deletion or modification of gates. The main idea is to translate the circuit netlist to a state transition system based model and verify it against the identified set of functional and behavioral properties that can be affected by any malicious modification in the IC. The model is then intruded with the expected malicious behaviour, and counterexamples are analyzed for deducing potential attack paths. On the basis of the information extracted from the detailed analysis of counterexamples, the designers can merge protection in the original design by embedding runtime hardware monitors. The proposed LTL properties are based on system functional and physical behavior. We propose to use the symbolic model checker nuXmv [8] for analysis by virtue of its ability to handle real numbers and implicit dealing of state counters.

The rest of this paper is organized as follows: Sect. 2 provides an overview of the nuXmv model checker and performance parameters used in our gate models. In Sect. 3, we explained the proposed methodology for hardware intrusion detection followed by our gate modeling in the nuXmv model checker in Sect. 4. In Sect. 5, we have given a case study for our proposed methodology. Section 6 presents the results followed by a comparison with some of the existing schemes in Sect. 7. Finally, the paper concludes in Sect. 8.

2 Preliminaries

In this section, we give a brief introduction to the nuXmv model checker and the performance parameters, i.e., dynamic power and delay, that we have used for gate level modeling in our proposed Hardware Trojan detection scheme. The intent is to facilitate the understanding of the rest of the paper for both hardware security and formal methods communities.

2.1 nuXmv Model Checker

The nuXmv symbolic model checker [8] is a recently developed formal verification tool that extends the capabilities of NuSMV model checker [10], by supporting analysis of infinite state domains. It complements NuSMV's verification techniques by sharing basic functionalities, such as symbol table, boolean encoding of scalar variables, flattening of design, and representation of finite state machines at different levels of abstraction. Moreover, it inherits all the basic model checking algorithms from NuSMV for finite domains using BDDs and SAT. For infinite state transition models, it introduces new data types of unbounded *Integers* and *Reals* and it provides the support of Satisfiability Modulo Theories (SMT), using MathSAT [20], for the analysis of such kinds of designs. The system that is required to be modeled is translated into SMV language, which supports the modular programming approach. The entire system can be distributed into several modules that interact with one another in the MAIN module. The properties to be checked can be expressed in nuXmv using the Linear Temporal Logic (LTL) and Computation Tree Logic (CTL). The specifications are expressed in nuXmv with the help of logical operations like, OR (|), AND (&), Exclusive OR (xor), Exclusive NOR (xnor), equality (<->), implication (->), and temporal operators, like next (X), Globally (G), Finally (F) and until (U). Similarly, the CTL specifications can be written by combining logical operations with quantified temporal operators, like forall finally (AF), exists globally (EG) and exists next state (EX). It is also possible to analyze quantitative characteristics of the state transition system by specifying real-time specifications. Whenever a specified property is determined to be false, a counterexample is constructed and subsequently printed by nuXmv in the form of an error trace of the state space that falsifies the property. We have chosen the nuXmv model checker because it can effectively model continuous values of power consumption and path delays of any given IC.

2.2 Performance Parameters

Gate level characterization has effectively formed the basis of side channel Hardware Trojan detection schemes, which are based on characterizing each gate in terms of its physical and performance parameters. We adopted dynamic power consumption and path delay as the side channel performance parameters for malicious intrusion detection in any given circuit. Equation 1 represents the gate level switching power model [31] that is dependent upon the activity factor α, output capacitance C_L, supply voltage V_{dd}, which has quadratic effect on dynamic power, and operating frequency f. The activity factor is the switching probability that a node of a circuit transitions from 0 to 1, because that is the only time when dynamic power is consumed by the circuit in the CMOS technology. The total output capacitance is the sum of parasitic capacitance of the individual gate and load capacitances at the output node.

$$P_{switching} = \alpha C_{total} V_{dd}{}^2 f \tag{1}$$

We have estimated gate level delays based on individual transitions at the gate inputs using the Elmore delay model [31], which computes the delay by representing each circuit in the form of RC tree. The voltage source is the root of tree, and capacitors are leaves at the ends of the branches. The delay is estimated by the model from a source switching to one of the leaf nodes changing as the sum over each node i of the capacitance C_i on the node, multiplied by the effective resistance R_{is} on the shared path from the source to the node and the leaf. Equations 2 and 3 are used in formulation of the gate level delay model.

$$\tau_{elmore} = \sum_i R_{is} C_i \tag{2}$$

$$t_{delay} = \ln 2 \times \tau_{elmore} \tag{3}$$

3   Proposed Methodology

In this section, we describe our proposed generic framework for the detection of malicious intrusion in any given IC. Our methodology comprises of the following five steps as depicted in Fig. 1.

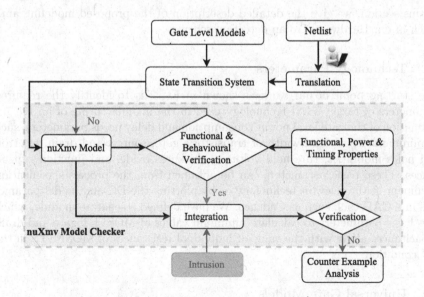

Fig. 1. Proposed framework for Hardware Trojan detection

1. The first step is to develop models for universal gates, including NAND, NOR and NOT. The advantage of these models is that we can build any other complex gate or a complete IC using these three basic gates. These generic models are technology independent and can be customized based on the characteristic parameters of a particular VLSI technology.
2. The next step is to develop a state transition system for any given netlist manually using the individual gate models. Based on the information in the netlist, expressions are specified for computation of both power and individual path delays. The technology parameters, and individual gate models are passed to the main module for required computations.
3. The state-space model is verified in a model checker against LTL properties specified for the IC functionality and performance. The gate fanouts [25] are set to be of variable size, such that model checker can analyze all possible combination of gate sizes in a circuit. The minimum and maximum bounds for circuit power consumption and path delays are determined, which are used to examine the integrity of the circuit.
4. The behaviour of Hardware Trojan is integrated into the model of IC. The intruded model is subsequently verified against the specified power and timing LTL properties.
5. The verification of intruded model generates counterexamples, which are analyzed and translated into the potential attack paths in the IC.

4   nuXmv Modeling

In this section, we give the detailed description of the proposed modeling approach in our Hardware Trojan detection scheme.

4.1   Technology Parameters

The starting point of our work as shown in Fig. 2 is to identify the required parameters of target VLSI technology used in the manufacturing of an IC. An estimation of the gate level power consumption and delay needs parameters, such as minimum length and width of transistor's gate, source, and drain, electron and holes mobilities, threshold voltages, thickness oxide, and junction capacitances. These basic parameters can be obtained from the process specification document of the relevant technology or by plotting the DC and model parameters in a CAD tool, such as Cadence. We have defined a separate module, which uses basic parameters to calculate minimum values of MOSFET gate and drain capacitances along with the value of individual resistances of MOSFETS in the ON condition.

4.2   Universal Gate Models

Based on the technology parameters, we have developed models for the universal gates, i.e., NAND, NOR and NOT as depicted in Fig. 2, in order to estimate

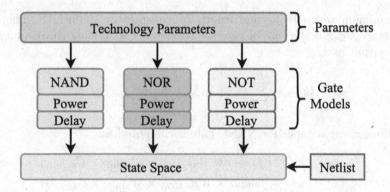

Fig. 2. Gate level modeling

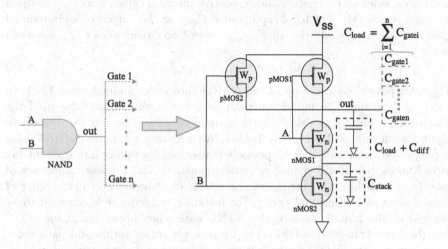

Fig. 3. Composition of two input NAND gate

switching power and delay. These gate models can be in turn used to build more complex gates and circuit elements. The description of the NAND gate model is provided here and all the others have been developed similarly with different parameter values.

A two input NAND gate is composed of two pMOS transistors, connected in parallel, and two nMOS transistors connected in series as shown in Fig. 3. The individual gate capacitances for pMOS and nMOS transistors are given in Eqs. 4 and 5.

$$C_{gatepMOS} = fanout \times WR_{pMOS} \times C_{gminP} \qquad (4)$$

$$C_{gatenMOS} = fanout \times WR_{nMOS} \times C_{gminN} \qquad (5)$$

where WR is the width ratio and C_{gmin} is the minimum gate capacitance for pMOS and nMOS transistor. C_{gmin} is calculated from the oxide capacitance

C_{ox}, minimum width W_{min} and length L of respective MOSFETS. The load capacitance C_{load} is the sum of gate capacitances of individual gates connected at the output node.

$$C_{load} = \sum_{i=1}^{p} C_{gatepMOSi} + \sum_{j=1}^{n} C_{gatenMOSj} \tag{6}$$

The diffusion capacitance for NAND gate is computed as:

$$\begin{aligned} C_{diffusion} = &\left(2 \times fanout \times WR_{pMOS} \times W_{minP} \times C_{dminP}\right) \\ &+ \left(1 \times fanout \times WR_{nMOS} \times W_{minN} \times C_{dminN}\right) \end{aligned} \tag{7}$$

where C_{dmin} is the minimum diffusion capacitance of a MOSFET, calculated using area, sidewall perimeters and respective junction capacitances of the drain diffusion region [31]. The total capacitance C_{total} at the output of an individual gate is computed by addition of $C_{diffusion}$ and load capacitance C_{load} as shown in Eq. 8.

$$C_{total} = C_{load} + C_{diffusion} \tag{8}$$

The total power consumption of the NAND gate is determined using Eq. 1. In order to determine the individual path delays in a circuit, we have used the Elmore delay model to calculate the individual gate delay on the respective input transitions as depicted in Table 1. An accurate estimation of the delay is performed by considering all possible transitions by taking into account the capacitances, which will change or remain constant. Our proposed approach of gate level modeling also considers the effects of charging and discharging of capacitances at the internal nodes. For instance, capacitance is required to be charged at the nMOS stack of the NAND gate when upper transistor is ON and the lower transistor is OFF. The total power consumption and path delay measurements are mainly dependent upon charging and discharging of individual capacitances in an IC. We illustrate this fact by considering a behaviour of a single inverter, which drives the load of two inverters connected at its output node as shown in Fig. 4. At input low, the gate capacitances of NOT2 and NOT3, i.e., C_{g2} and C_{g3} along with the diffusion capacitance C_{d1} of gate NOT1 are charged. The output node of NOT1 transitions to logic high depicted as *state* 1. The compute power (CP) and estimate delay (ED) flags are set to high, indicating the measurement of dynamic power and time required to charge capacitance. At the input high, same capacitance is required to be discharged and output node transitions to *state* 0. The state does not change if the input remains same, indicating no change in dynamic power or path delay. Similarly, behaviour of two input NAND and NOR gates can be represented with the state diagram comprising of four states, and each state having transitions to and from, all other states.

Table 1. Elmore delay calculation NAND gate

Input	Output	Elmore delay
00	1	$(2 \times R_p \times C_{total})/(\text{Fanout} \times WR_{pMOS} \times W_{minP})$
01	1	$(R_n \times C_{total})/(\text{Fanout} \times WR_{nMOS} \times W_{minN})$
10	1	$(R_n \times (C_{total} + C_{stackN}))/(\text{Fanout} \times WR_{nMOS} \times W_{minN})$
11	0	$(R_n \times C_{total})/(\text{Fanout} \times WR_{nMOS} \times W_{minN})$

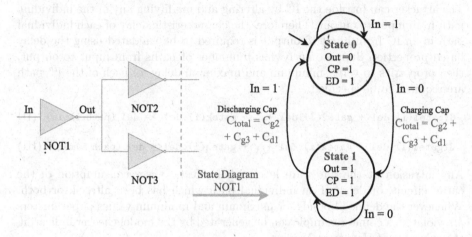

Fig. 4. The state-space model of an inverter

4.3 Netlist Translation

The translation of netlist is accomplished by interconnecting the individual gate modules. A particular gate module is defined by parameters, including variable inputs, transition probabilities, gate capacitances at output, fanout and relevant technology parameters. The transition probabilities along with outputs are passed to all gates connected at the output node of an individual gate. Other gates are constructed using the three basic gates, for instance, the AND gate is constructed using a NAND module followed by a NOT gate. Similarly, netlist of any integrated circuit can be manually translated using basic models of the three gates. The individual fanouts are swept across all the values in order to identify maximum and minimum bounds of switching power and individual path delays.

4.4 Property Specification

The verification of the IC model is carried out by validating the following properties using the bounded model checking (BMC) support for *real* numbers. The performance properties are validated using the nuXmv model checker to ascertain that the given IC remains between the specified boundaries defined for dynamic power and delay parameters. The undesired behaviour of the circuit due to any malicious alteration of circuit can be identified from the generated counterexample. The maximum and minimum bounds for power consumption are identified to validate the power property. The LTL specifications to validate the switching power is defined by adding the power consumed by individual gates in the circuit.

$$G(\text{pwr\_max} >= \text{gate1.pwr} + \text{gate2.pwr} +...+ \text{gaten.pwr} >= \text{pwr\_min}) \quad (I)$$

The attacker can intrude the IC by altering and modifying any of the individual path from input to output. Therefore, the characteristic delay of each individual path in an IC from input to output is required to be validated using the delay based properties. Suppose an IC has p number of paths from input to output, then properties to verify minimum and maximum delay for each of the ith path are required to be specified.

$$G(\text{gate1(i).del} + \text{gate2(i).del} +...+ \text{gatek(i).del} >= \text{del\_(path\_i)min}) \quad (II)$$

$$G(\text{gate1(i).del} + \text{gate2(i).del} +...+ \text{gatek(i).del} <= \text{del\_(path\_i)max}) \quad (III)$$

Any intrusion at the hardware level either affects power consumption of the entire circuit, or delay of an individual path which has been altered, or both. Whenever the defined bounds for maximum and minimum values of parameters are violated, a counterexample can be generated by the model checker indicating the existence of Hardware Trojans.

5 Case Studies

We illustrate usefulness of our proposed framework, by evaluating it on ISCAS85 benchmark circuit C17. We show two types of malicious intrusions on C17 given in [30], and [22] as depicted in Fig. 5a and b respectively. The procedure of modeling and identification of intrusions using nuXmv model checker is explained below.

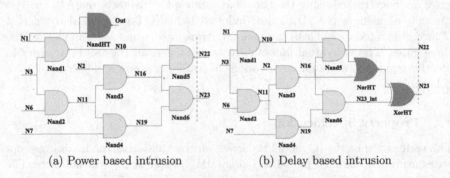

(a) Power based intrusion   (b) Delay based intrusion

Fig. 5. Intruded ISCAS-85 C17 benchmark circuit

5.1 Gate Level Models

The first step in our proposed framework is to acquire the basic gate level models. The ISCAS benchmark circuit C17 comprises of 6 two input NAND gates, and total number of 5 inputs. Only the NAND gate model is required, which constitutes of expressions for diffusion and load capacitances, required to estimate values for both power and path delay. Moreover, the activity factors for switching power computation are also determined for each gate in the circuit. The basic gate models are defined in separate modules in the nuXmv model checker.

5.2 State Space Modeling

The netlist gives the description of connectivity for C17 benchmark circuit, which is translated into the state space. For example, consider the NAND3 gate in Fig. 5a which has inputs N2, and NAND2.out (output of NAND2). The gate along with relevant parameters is described as:

```
NAND3:nand(N2, NAND2.out, 0.5, 0.5, NAND2.P0, NAND2.P1, Fanout3, par.Freq,
    par.Cgmin_p, par.Cgmin_n, par.Vdd, par.Wmin, par.Cdmin_p, par.Cdmin_n,
    par.Csmin_p, par.Csmin_n,par.Rp, par.Rn, NAND5.Cgate, NAND6.Cgate,0, 0);
```

Using the given input signal probabilities of the circuit, we compute the probabilities and activity factor for its each node. For example, input N2 has an input probability of 0.5 for 0 and 1, $P0$ and $P1$ are the probabilities of the second input being 0 or 1, which can be used to calculate the activity factor at the pertinent node of circuit. This follows by the parameters like, operating frequency, input voltage V_{dd}, values of gate and diffusion capacitances, along with the values of ON resistances R_p and R_n for pMOS and nMOS transistors, respectively. The last part of the expression indicates the total load at the output node N16, which is the sum of gate capacitance of NAND5 and NAND6. Typically, gates have the maximum fanout of 4 and minimum fanout of 1 [25]. Similarly, all six NAND gates of C17 circuit are described in the main module of nuXmv to generate the formal model of the given circuit.

5.3 Model Verification

After the state space of the C17 benchmark circuit is defined, the next step is to check the functionality the circuit. There are a total number of $2^5 = 32$ possible input vector for C17 circuit. We verified the functionality of circuit by using certain number of input vectors. The next step is to identify the maximum and minimum bounds for switching power and delay. Our model accuracy requires the values to remain in between these bounds. The power for C17 circuit is maximum when all 6 NAND gates have a maximum fanout equal to 4. Similarly, the minimum bound is determined by computing the power with the minimum fanout of 1. For all sizes of the gates of the C17 benchmark, the power for

C17 is required to remain in between the specified bound. The circuit has four individual paths from inputs to two output, and the bounds for the delay are identified for every single path by computing the combination of individual gate fanouts, which gives the maximum and minimum path delay for every path. The model is termed as verified if all the functional and performance properties are satisfied.

5.4   Hardware Intrusion and Verification

To present the effectiveness of model checking based Hardware Trojan detection technique, we used intruded versions of C17 benchmark given by Wei et al. [30] and Mukhopadhyay et al. [22]. The intrusion of a single two input NAND gate is depicted in Fig. 5a. The addition of the gate only affects the overall power consumption and does not affect its delay since it is not in the path from input to output. The state space for the intruded model is defined with the C17 benchmark circuit along with NANDHT gate. Therefore, when the intruded model of the circuit is validated against the property defined for maximum power, it generates a counterexample. However, intruded model satisfies delay based properties since the NANDHT does not lie in the any of active paths of the circuit. The combinational Trojan in [22] is embedded in the C17 circuit with a NOR and XOR gate. Due to the inserted Hardware Trojan, the power consumption and delay of the circuit increases and LTL properties defined for the maximum power and delay fails.

5.5   Counterexample Analysis

The counterexamples generated by the verification of intruded circuits can be analyzed to identify potential locations of the malicious intrusion. Our proposed approach has an inherent advantage of compositional analysis, as shown in Fig. 6. If the power property defined for the entire IC fails, the analysis may be extended by partitioning the IC into distinct regions or components, and specifying the power properties for the individual parts to isolate Trojan-free and Trojan-inserted regions. For example, for analyzing the power property failure in Fig. 6, we divided the IC into four distinct regions in such a way that each region approximately has an equal number of gates. The power property for each region is verified and the intruded region is subsequently identified, i.e., Region 3. In order to identify the intruded component within the identified region we can further analyze the power property for each component, e.g., component 2 of Region 3.

For instance, whenever input N1 in Fig. 5a switches from 0 to 1 or 1 to 0, the total dynamic power increases and corresponding property for the IC fails. On partitioning the circuit into different regions, each having two NAND gates, we can specify a power property for each individual partition. The first partition comprising of NAND1 and NAND2 will fail the power property on verification, indicating the presence of malicious intrusion along the input N1. Similarly, the delay based properties are specified for each path from input to output, and

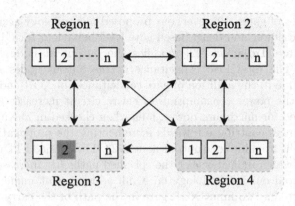

Fig. 6. Counterexample analysis of IC

the failure of the corresponding property will indicate the path along which the circuit has been intruded. The total delay of any path from input N6 to output N23 in Fig. 5b is the sum of the individual delays of NAND gates and intruded gates along the path, resulting in the failure of the specified delay property. The analysis of generated counterexamples for both power and delay can thus be used to identify the potential location of the intrusion in IC.

6   Results and Discussion

We used the version 1.0.1 of the nuXmv model checker along with the Windows 10 Professional OS running on a Core i7 processor, 2.67 GHz, with 6 GB memory for our experiments. We applied our verification methodology on different benchmark circuits as depicted in Table 2. The intruded variant of C17 [30] has 7 NAND gates, and it has one additional gate due to which the dynamic power check fails. The power consumption at a particular node depends upon the sum of gate and diffusion capacitances. Whenever there is an activity at the input of intruded gate, switching power is consumed by delivering energy to charge capacitance at the output node, and then dumping this energy to ground. Our method is effective since we can detect any intrusion even if no load is driven by the intruded gate. The diffusion capacitance $C_{diffusion}$ depends on the size of source and drain region, with wider transistors having proportionally greater diffusion capacitances. We have successfully tested our technique by varying intruded gate sizes, since any transition at input, even with the minimum possible gate size, fails the defined power specifications. The delay property is validated in this case, since we have defined delay bounds on propagation delays of the individual logic paths, and malicious gate in this case does not contribute towards the charging and discharging of capacitances at particular nodes of any path. The technique presented in [30] performs the gate level characterization (GLC) with some error, i.e., GLC error for C17 is 0.0057% [30], which increases with the number of gates. However, our proposed methodology accurately models the dynamic power and delay based gate level behaviour for C17.

The Hardware Trojan in [22] modifies the output at node $N23$ on rare input vectors. The total load capacitance at the output nodes $N23\_int$ and $N16$ increases due to the addition of gate capacitances of XOR and NOR gates. Consequently, the power consumption of entire circuit increases and the LTL property, defined for maximum power, fails when checked in nuXmv. Similarly, added capacitances contribute towards incrementing the propagation delays of the effected paths from input to output node $N23$. The defined LTL delay bounds in nuXmv fail, which indicates that the specified paths has increased delays.

We also tested our methodology on a full adder circuit made by universal gates. We inserted a two input XOR gate in the path of the carry out signal of the full adder with one input as a trigger signal. When the trigger signal stays low, the carry-out remains the same, however, when the trigger is activated, the logic of carry-out changes. The intruded gate, due to its inherent C_{gate}, affects the power usage and delay constraints, and subsequently identified when verified for its integrity in the nuXmv model checker. Similarly we defined the state-space for a 4 bit ripple carry adder (RCA). To overcome complexity, we designed other gates like XOR, using universal gates in separate modules. The instances of these modules are called in the main module while defining the formal model as per the netlist information. After validating the parametric properties of the trusted RCA circuit model, the intrusion is modeled at the third stage of carry-out by inserting a three stage Ring Oscillator (RO), which is enabled using an external trigger signal through a NAND gate. Once enabled, the RO continuously oscillates between the two voltage levels, resulting in more power consumption. It is pertinent to mention that the RO is not inserted along the path of carry. The model verification against the properties indicated that it fails both checks for power and delay bounds. The capacitances of added gates contributes towards the switching power consumption. In case of delay, although an intrusion is not along the path of delay computation, the added gate act as load to the previous gate generating the carry. Thus, a counterexample is also generated in this case by the model checker.

The result indicates that multi-parameter based intrusion detection is more effective than just using a single parameter. If the malicious circuitry is not being detected by the defined bounds for delay then the power property may fail, indicating presence of an intrusion whenever switching activity occurs. The results further elaborate the usefulness of the nuXmv model checker for handing real numbers and bounded model checking (BMC) feature. The extensive simulations for every possible input using traditional methods is a laborious task. In contrast, once a model is defined in a model checker based on the proposed approach, then it takes significantly lesser time and resources to test the integrity of the entire system. The results in Table 2 show that modeling and verification of all the case studies require a 115 MB of memory at maximum, which is around 2% of the available memory of the machine used to acquire these experimental results. Therefore, the proposed approach seems quite scalable to handle larger

Table 2. Timing and memory resources for some of the Intruded circuits detected by our technique.

Circuit	No of gates			Hardware Trojans		Dynamic power			Delay		
	NAND	NOR	NOT	Intrusion	Effect	Check	Memory (MB)	Time (s)	Check	Memory (MB)	Time (s)
C-17	6	—	—	—	—	✓	69	1054	✓	75	1530
C-17 [30]	7	—	—	1 NAND	Power Consumption	✗	47	215	✓	77	550
C-17 [22]	9	1	2	1 XOR 1 NOR	Rare Input Modifications	✗	55	316	✗	54	715
Full Adder	8	1	7	—	—	✓	79	1210	✓	81	1770
HT Full Adder	11	1	9	1 XOR	Externally Triggered Carry Out	✗	61	375	✗	63	886
4 Bit RCA	32	4	28	—	—	✓	103	2715	✓	115	3855
HT 4 Bit RCA	33	4	31	RO	Power Consumption	✗	77	977	✗	79	1224

circuits with the availability of around 16 GB memory. However, the inherent state-space explosion problem of model checking may limit the applicability of the proposed approach for larger circuits and therefore, in these cases, we plan to extend the models to a higher abstraction level.

7   Comparison with Existing Gate Modeling Techniques

The gate level time and power models have been presented previously by different researchers. The timing analysis at the gate level description of a circuit is proposed in [4], where each gate is abstracted as a set of states and individual transitions are characterized by the propagation delay of the falling or rising edge. The propagation delays are determined by using set of differential equations for capacitances or through SPICE simulations. Timing verification for asynchronous circuits, proposed in [7], is based on translating the circuit behavior in terms of transition graphs, which is checked under the assumption that the delays are bounded between two numbers. The formal verification of timed circuits is represented as symbols with unspecified delays in [11]. In this scheme, a set of linear constraints on the symbols are discovered that guarantees the correctness of the circuit. Similarly, a state transition graph based power dissipation model is presented in [16] that considers charging and discharging of the capacitance at the gate output node. The input signal probabilities are used to estimate the expected activity number of each edge in the graph, followed by computing the total consumption by summing each edge. The consumption values of transitions are obtained from SPICE simulation.

The proposed gate modeling technique in this paper takes both power and timing parameters under consideration. Our scheme has an inherent advantage in the perspective of hardware intrusion detection that we take particular VLSI technology and possible variations in fanout and gate sizes in to account as well. Moreover, our model is generic as we estimate power and timing measurements with all possible input transitions without any requirements of simulations with SPICE or other circuit simulators.

8   Conclusions

This paper presents a generic framework based on the formal verification of the integrated circuit (IC) to detect malicious hardware intrusions. Unlike the traditional methods to detect the intrusions in integrated circuits, our solution uses formal models based on multi-parameter side channel information and their validation using a model checker. The ability of nuXmv model checker to handle *real* numbers and the powerful verification methods, based on SAT and SMT solvers, has been successfully utilized to validate dynamic power and path delay parameters, to ascertain integrity of integrated circuits. In the future, we plan to enhance this work by proposing an automated method for netlist translation, and extending the models to higher abstraction level to efficiently handle scalability for larger ICs. Moreover, additional side channel parameters, such as leakage power will also be incorporated in order to strengthen the proposed Hardware Trojan detection scheme.

References

1. Adee, S.: The hunt for the kill switch. IEEE Spectr. **45**(5), 34–39 (2008)
2. Agrawal, D., Baktir, S., Karakoyunlu, D., Rohatgi, P., Sunar, B.: Trojan detection using IC fingerprinting. In: Symposium on Security and Privacy, pp. 296–310. IEEE (2007)
3. Anderson, M.S., North, C., Yiu, K.K.: Towards countering the rise of the silicon Trojan. In: Annual Report. Defence Science and Technology Organisation, DSTO-TR-2220, Australia (2008)
4. Bara, A., Bazargan-Sabet, P., Chevallier, R., Encrenaz, E.: Formal Verification of Timed VHDL Programs. In: Specification & Design Languages, pp. 1–6. IET (2010)
5. Bhasin, S., Regazzoni, F.: A survey on hardware Trojan detection techniques. In: Circuits and Systems, pp. 2021–2024. IEEE (2015)
6. Bhunia, S., Hsiao, M.S., Banga, M., Narasimhan, S.: Hardware Trojan attacks: threat analysis and countermeasures. Proceedings of IEEE **102**(8), 1229–1247 (2014)
7. Bozga, M., Jianmin, H.: Maler: verification of asynchronous circuits using timed automata. Electron. Notes Theoret. Comput. Sci. **65**(6), 47–59 (2002)
8. Cavada, R., Cimatti, A., Dorigatti, M., Griggio, A., Mariotti, A., Micheli, A., Mover, S., Roveri, M., Tonetta, S.: The NUXMV symbolic model checker. In: Biere, A., Bloem, R. (eds.) CAV 2014. LNCS, vol. 8559, pp. 334–342. Springer, Heidelberg (2014). doi:10.1007/978-3-319-08867-9_22
9. Chakraborty, R.S., Wolff, F., Paul, S., Papachristou, C., Bhunia, S.: *MERO*: a statistical approach for hardware Trojan detection. In: Clavier, C., Gaj, K. (eds.) CHES 2009. LNCS, vol. 5747, pp. 396–410. Springer, Heidelberg (2009). doi:10.1007/978-3-642-04138-9_28

10. Cimatti, A., Clarke, E., Giunchiglia, E., Giunchiglia, F., Pistore, M., Roveri, M., Sebastiani, R., Tacchella, A.: NuSMV 2: an opensource tool for symbolic model checking. In: Brinksma, E., Larsen, K.G. (eds.) CAV 2002. LNCS, vol. 2404, pp. 359–364. Springer, Heidelberg (2002). doi:10.1007/3-540-45657-0_29
11. Clarisó, R., Cortadella, J.: Verification of timed circuits with symbolic delays. In: Asia and South Pacific Design Automation Conference, pp. 628–633. IEEE (2004)
12. Di Natale, G., Dupuis, S.: Is side-channel analysis really reliable for detecting hardware Trojans?. In: Design of Circuits and Integrated Systems, pp. 238–242 (2012)
13. Drechsler, R., et al.: Advanced Formal Verification. Springer (2004)
14. Force, T.: High performance microchip supply. In: Annual Report. Defense Technical Information Center (DTIC), USA (2005). http://www.acq.osd.mil/dsb/reports/ADA435563.pdf
15. Jin, Y., Makris, Y.: Hardware Trojan Detection using Path Delay Fingerprint. In: Hardware-Oriented Security and Trust, 2008. pp. 51–57. IEEE (2008)
16. Lin, J.Y., Liu, T.C., Shen, W.Z.: A cell-based power estimation in CMOS combinational circuits. In: Computer-Aided Design, pp. 304–309. IEEE (1994)
17. Lodhi, F.K., Abbasi, I., Khalid, F., Hasan, O., Awwad, F., Hasan, S.R.: A self-learning framework to detect the intruded integrated circuits. In: International Symposium on Circuits and Systems, pp. 1702–1705 (2016)
18. Lodhi, F.K., Hasan, S.R., Hasan, O., Awwad, F.: Hardware Trojan detection in soft error tolerant macro synchronous micro asynchronous (MSMA) pipeline. In: Midwest Symposium on Circuits and Systems. pp. 659–662 (2014)
19. Lodhi, F., Hasan, S., Hasan, O., Awwad, F.: Formal analysis of macro synchronous micro asychronous pipeline for hardware Trojan detection. In: Nordic Circuits and Systems Conference & International Symposium on System-on-Chip, pp. 1–4. IEEE (2015)
20. MathSAT 5: (2016). http://mathsat.fbk.eu/
21. Mitra, S., Wong, H.S.P., Wong, S.: The Trojan-proof chip. IEEE Spectr. **52**(2), 46–51 (2015)
22. Mukhopadhyay, D., Chakraborty, R.S.: Hardware Security: Design, Threats, and Safeguards. CRC (2014)
23. Ngo, X.T., Danger, J.L., Guilley, S., Najm, Z., Emery, O.: Hardware property checker for run-time hardware Trojan detection. In: 2015 European Conference on Circuit Theory and Design (ECCTD), pp. 1–4. IEEE (2015)
24. Qu, G., Yuan, L.: Design THINGS for the internet of things-an EDA perspective. In: International Conference on Computer-Aided Design (ICCAD), pp. 411–416. IEEE (2014)
25. Rabaey, J.M., Chandrakasan, A.P., Nikolic, B.: Digital Integrated Circuits, vol. 2. Prentice Hall (2002)
26. Rai, D., Lach, J.: Performance of delay-based trojan detection under parameter variations. In: Hardware-Oriented Security and Trust, pp. 58–65. IEEE (2009)
27. Rathmair, M., Schupfer, F.: Hardware Trojan detection by specifying malicious circuit properties. In: Electronics Information and Emergency Communication, pp. 317–320. IEEE (2013)
28. Tehranipoor, M., Koushanfar, F.: A survey of hardware trojan taxonomy and detection. IEEE Des. Test Comput. **27**(1), 10–25 (2010)
29. Wang, L., Xie, H., Luo, H.: Malicious circuitry detection using transient power analysis for IC security. In: Quality, Reliability, Risk, Maintenance, and Safety Engineering, pp. 1164–1167. IEEE (2013)

30. Wei, S., Meguerdichian, S., Potkonjak, M.: Malicious circuitry detection using thermal conditioning. IEEE Trans. Inf. Forensics Secur. **6**(3), 1136–1145 (2011)
31. Weste, N., Harris, D.: CMOS VLSI Design: A Circuits and Systems Perspective. Pearson (2011)
32. Xiao, K., Forte, D., Jin, Y., Karri, R., Bhunia, S., Tehranipoor, M.: Hardware Trojans: lessons learned after one decade of research. ACM Transactions on Design Automation of Electronic Systems **22**(1), 1–23 (2016)
33. Zhang, X., Tehranipoor, M.: Detecting hardware Trojans in third-party digital IP cores. In: Hardware-Oriented Security and Trust (HOST), pp. 67–70. IEEE (2011)

Formal Probabilistic Analysis of a WSN-Based Monitoring Framework for IoT Applications

Maissa Elleuch[1,3]($\boxtimes$), Osman Hasan[2], Sofiène Tahar[2], and Mohamed Abid[1]

[1] CES Laboratory, National School of Engineers of Sfax, Sfax University,
Soukra Street, 3052 Sfax, Tunisia
maissa.elleuch@ceslab.org, mohamed.abid@enis.rnu.tn
[2] Department of Electrical and Computer Engineering, Concordia University,
1455 de Maisonneuve W., Montreal, QC H3G 1M8, Canada
{melleuch,o_hasan,tahar}@ece.concordia.ca
[3] Digital Research Center of Sfax, Technopark of Sfax, Sfax, Tunisia

Abstract. Internet of Things (IoT) has been considered as an intuitive evolution of sensing systems using Wireless Sensor Networks (WSN). In this context, energefficiency is considered as one of the most critical requirement. For that purpose, the randomized node scheduling approach is largely applied. The randomness feature in the node scheduling together with the unpredictable deployment make probabilistic techniques much more appropriate to evaluate the coverage properties of WSNs. Classical probabilistic analysis techniques, such as simulation and model checking, do not guarantee accurate results, and thus are not suitable for analyzing mission-critical WSN applications. Based on the most recently developed probability theory, available in the HOL theorem prover, we develop the formalizations of the key coverage performance attributes: the coverage intensity of a specific point and the expected value of the network coverage intensity. The practical interest of our higher-order-logic developments is finally illustrated through formally analyzing the asymptotic coverage behavior of an hybrid monitoring framework for environmental IoT.

Keywords: Theorem proving · Wireless sensor networks · Node scheduling · Performance analysis · Network coverage · Environmental monitoring

1 Introduction

Wireless Sensor Networks (WSN) have emerged as a key enabler technology for the development of the Internet of Things (IoT) paradigm [20,24]. Deployed over a field of interest, smart sensor nodes collaborate together without any human interaction, in order to mainly achieve a monitoring or a tracking task. Such networks are covering limitless applications [28], including home automation, external environmental monitoring and object tracking, and hence integrating WSN technologies into the IoT context [12,20].

© Springer International Publishing AG 2017
C. Artho and P.C. Ölveczky (Eds.): FTSCS 2016, CCIS 694, pp. 93–108, 2017.
DOI: 10.1007/978-3-319-53946-1_6

Due to their restricted size, sensors are basically battery-powered and thus have very critical energy resources. Consider the example of a WSN deployed for forest fire detection, in which the sensor nodes are randomly distributed with a high density. The network should be able to ensure the monitoring of the whole forest area while being functional for a sufficiently long period. Since a wild fire occurs only occasionally, some sensor nodes can be intuitively deactivated to save the network energy. In this context, the k-set randomized scheduling [18] is a kind of scheduling approach, suitable for a wide range of WSN applications, which mainly consists in organizing a given set of nodes by randomly partitioning them into "k" subsets, which work alternatively.

Scheduling sensor nodes for lifetime management purposes is surely a simple and intuitive approach, however it is also crucial to not compromise on the monitoring of the area. For the same forest fire application, the deployed WSN should be also able to cover, i.e., monitor, the outbreak of fires occurring at any point of the area with a high probability. Nevertheless, the coverage performance is completely probabilistic. For instance, some fire outbreaks may not be effectively covered if no nodes are deployed around the fire because of the random node deployment, or the surrounding nodes are inactive, due to random scheduling. Missing fire intrusion, can have devastating consequences.

The performance of the randomized scheduling has been generally analyzed using paper-and-pencil based probabilistic technique [18,25]. The reliability of the obtained analytical models is consolidated through simulation using the Monte Carlo method [19]. However, both paper-and-pencil proof and simulation methods cannot be regarded as completely accurate mainly due to the error proneness of the former and the in-exhaustive nature of the later.

Formal methods overcome the drawbacks of simulation by rigorously using mathematical techniques to validate the analytical model of the given system. Recently, formal methods have gained a growing interest in the context of analyzing wireless sensor networks to analyze their functional or quantitative correctness [3,22,29], but most of the existing work is focused on the validation of their functional aspects only. Nevertheless, rigorous performance evaluation of WSNs constitutes also an extremely challenging aspect.

In this paper, we are interested in providing an accurate performance analysis of WSN randomized scheduling based on the paper-and-pencil models proposed in [18,26]. In earlier work [6,7], we have presented a formalization of the k-set randomized scheduling algorithm and its coverage properties based on a probabilistic framework developed by Hasan [13] in the HOL theorem prover. While sufficient for analyzing the coverage aspects of the original WSN models [18,26], this formalization falls short to reason about other performance aspects of the same algorithm [8], like the detection metrics. In fact, the foremost requirement for reasoning about these WSN aspects in a theorem prover is the availability of the higher-order-logic formalization of probability theory and continuous random variables. In this regard, Hurd's [16] formalization of measure and probability theories is a pioneering work. Building upon this formalization, most of the commonly-used continuous random variables [14] have been formalized using the HOL theorem prover. However, this foundational formalization of probability theory only supports the whole universe as the probability space, which limits its scope in many aspects. In particular the inability to reason about multiple continuous random variables [14] is a major obstacle for modeling and analyzing detection and lifetime properties of WSNs [9]. More recent probability theory formalizations [15,21], however, allow the use of any arbitrary probability space that is a subset of the universe and thus are more flexible than Hurd's and Hasan's formalizations of probability theory. Particularly, Mhamdi's [21] probability theory formalization which is based on extended-real numbers (real numbers including $\pm\infty$), has been included in the HOL theorem prover and thus has been chosen for our work. Therefore, in this paper we propose to use the most recent probability theory developed by Mhamdi [21] in HOL to formally reason about the coverage properties of randomly-scheduled WSN, while emphasizing on the main lessons learned through this experience. The practical interest of the new developments is illustrated through the formal analysis of the asymptotic coverage behavior of a WSN based environmental surveillance framework.

The rest of this paper is organized as follows. We review some related work on the validation of WSNs in Sect. 2. In Sect. 3, we summarize the main requirements of this work. Section 4 provides the foundational probabilistic analysis of the coverage properties. We utilize these developments to formally verify a WSN-based monitoring framework for IoT applications in Sect. 5. Section 6 is devoted to discuss the main results of our work. We finally conclude the paper in Sect. 7.

2   Related Work

Theoretical analysis, also known as paper-and-pencil based probabilistic technique, has been widely used to validate randomized scheduling algorithms for WSN [18,25,26]. Such analysis consists in constructing a theoretical model where the required random variables are determined together with the associated performance metrics. Afterwards, a probabilistic based study is achieved. For validation purposes, simulation, using the Monte Carlo method [19], is finally done.

Traditional model checking technique [2] has been successfully used to validate various aspects in the WSN context. In [22], the formal analysis of the Optimal Geographical Density Control (OGDC) algorithm, which is a kind of randomized scheduling algorithm, is done. Several other prominent works reported on the use of model checking for the analysis of WSN protocols include [10,30]. The main strength of all these methods is their formal models and automatic verification. However, they suffer from the common model checking related problem of state space explosion [2]. Hence, the analysis of the OGDC algorithm [22] has been restricted for WSN with up to 6 nodes in a region of $15\,\text{m} \times 15\,\text{m}$. Furthermore, the work of [30] has pointed out over 1 million generated states for the analysis of a simple property. Furthermore, none of the previous works has provided reliable probabilistic modelling. For example, in [22], a random function, assumed to be 'good', has been used to model the probabilistic behavior.

To cope with these major problems, probabilistic model checking [23] has also been used for the probabilistic functional analysis of wireless systems. Probabilistic model checking allows to capture the probability modelling for both the system and the property of interest. The probabilistic model checker PRISM has been applied quite frequently for the validation of Medium Access Control (MAC) protocols for WSNs [11,29]. Nevertheless, the reasoning support for statistical quantities in most of model checkers suffers from many shortcomings. Indeed, expected performance values are usually obtained through several runs on the built model [29]. The obtained results can hardly be termed as exhaustive and thus formally verified.

On the other hand, very few works based on theorem proving exist in the open literature. The work [4] reports on the use of the PVS system to build a theorem proving based framework for WSN algorithms, with some theories expressing dynamic scenarios like nodes mobility and link quality changes [4]. While the PVS framework is supposed to be extended with some "dynamic" scenarios in [4], the randomness aspect has been characterized by a pseudo-random generator. The nodes mobility, specified by the random walk pattern, has been also specified through a recursive function.

Unlike the PVS framework which is limited by the probability support of the PVS system, the work, described in this paper, provides very accurate formalizations of the randomized scheduling algorithm based on the sound probability support of the HOL theorem prover. In addition, the presented formalizations are generic and completely valid for all the parameter values.

3   Preliminaries

3.1   Probabilistic Analysis in HOL

A probability measure P is basically a measure function on the sample space Ω and an event is a measurable set within the set F of events which are subsets of Ω. By definition, a random variable is a measurable function, satisfying the condition that the inverse image of a measurable set is also measurable [21].

Definition 1. ⊢ ∀X p. real_random_variable X p =
          prob_space p ∧
          (∀x ∈ p_space p ⇒ X x ≠ NegInf ∧ X x ≠ PosInf) ∧
          X ∈ measurable (p_space p,events p) Borel.

where X designates the random variable, p is a given probability space, $NegInf$ and $PosInf$ are the higher-order-logic formalizations of negative infinity or positive infinity, and $Borel$ is the HOL definition of the Borel sigma algebra.

The probability distribution of a random variable is specified as the function that accepts a random variable X and a set s and returns the probability of the event $\{X \in s\}$.

Definition 2. ⊢ ∀X p.
 distribution p X = (λs. prob p (PREIMAGE X s ∩ p_space p)).

In the discrete case, the expectation of the random variable X has been formalized in HOL as follows.

Theorem 1. ⊢ ∀X p. (real_random_variable X p) ∧ FINITE (IMAGE X (p_space p))
 ⇒ (expectation p X =
$\sum_{\text{IMAGE X (p\_space p)}}$ (λr. r × Normal (distribution p X {r}))).

where (IMAGE X (p_space p)) designates the list of values taken by the random variable X over the sample space (p_space p).

3.2 The k-set Randomized Scheduling Algorithm

During the initialization stage, the k-set randomized scheduling is run in parallel on every node as follows [18]. Each node starts by randomly picking a number, denoted by i, ranging from 0 to $(k-1)$, where k is the number of subsets or partitions. A node s_j is thus assigned to the ith sub-network, designated by S_i, and will activate itself only during the scheduling round of that subset. At the end of the algorithm, k disjoint sub-networks are created. These subsets will be working independently and alternatively. Figure 1 shows a small WSN of eight sensor nodes, which is randomly portioned into two sub-networks; S_0 and S_1. Each node randomly chooses a number 0 or 1 in order to be assigned to one of these two sub-networks. Suppose that nodes 0; 2; 5, randomly choose the number 0 and thus join the subset S_0, whereas nodes 1; 3; 4; 6; 7, select the number 1 and will be in the subset S_1. These two sub-networks will work by rounds, i.e., once the nodes 1; 3; 4; 6; 7, illustrated by the dashed circles, will be active, the remaining nodes 0; 2; 5, will be at the sleep state, and vice-versa.

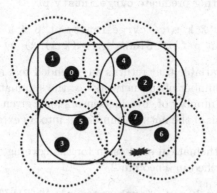

Fig. 1. The k-set randomized scheduling for $(n = 8)$ nodes and $(k = 2)$ subsets.

4 Formalization of the Network Coverage Intensity

Within a wireless sensor network, a given point is said to be covered, if any occurring event at this point, is detected by at least one active node with a given probability. According to [18], the coverage intensity of a specific point; C_p, inside the monitored area is defined as the average time during which the point is covered in a whole scheduling cycle of length $k \times T$. A given point is covered if the current active subset contains at least one node, i.e., is not empty.

Let X be the random variable describing the total number of non-empty subsets, the coverage intensity of a given point in the monitored area, C_p, as originally specified in [18], is

$$C_p = \frac{E[X] \times T}{k \times T}. \tag{1}$$

where $E[X]$ denotes the expectation of X, which is described as:

$$X = \sum_{j=0}^{k-1} X_j. \tag{2}$$

where X_j is the Bernoulli random variable whose value is 1 in case of non-empty subset. A non-empty sub-network is described by a Bernoulli random variable with the complement probability of $\left(1 - \frac{1}{k}\right)^c$ [6], where c is the number of covering sensors for a given point.

Definition 3. $\vdash \forall X$ p k c.
   sbst_non_empty_rv X p k c = bernoulli_distr_rv X p $\left(1 - \left(1 - \frac{1}{\&k}\right)^c\right)$.

In higher-order logic, we model the coverage behavior of a specific point (Eq. (1)) by the following predicate cvrge_intsty_pt.

Definition 4. $\vdash \forall$p X k s c. cvrge_intsty_pt p X k s c =
       expectation p (λx. SIGMA (λi. (X i) x) s) / (&k).

where X: a random variable that returns an extended real number, p: the probability space, k: the number of sub-networks, s: the summation set whose cardinality is k, and c: the number of covering sensors for a given point. The operator & allows the conversion of the natural number m into its extended number counterpart.

The following mathematical expression for the coverage intensity of a point has been formally verified in Theorem 2.

Theorem 2. $\vdash \forall X$ p k s c. (prob_space p) $\wedge$ (FINITE s) $\wedge$ (1 < k)
   $\wedge$ (CARD s = k) $\wedge$ ($\forall$i. i $\in$ s $\Rightarrow$ sbst_non_empty_rv (X i) p k c)
   $\Rightarrow$ (cvrge_intsty_pt p X k s c = Normal $\left(1 - \left(1 - \frac{1}{k}\right)^c\right)$).

- The assumption ($\forall$i. i $\in$ s $\Rightarrow$ sbst_non_empty_rv (X i) p k c) indicates that every element of the set s is a random variable sbst_non_empty_rv (Definition 3).

– The HOL function Normal is used to convert a real value to its corresponding value in an extended real.

The proof of the above theorem is mainly based on lemmas about the linearity of the expectation property, which in turn required some reasoning on the integrability of some functions as well as operations from the Lebesgue theory. For most of these lemmas, it was a prerequisite to verify the measurability of the used events, along with some analysis on extended reals.

The whole network can be now statistically described by a single performance metric; C_n, which is the average or the expectation value of the coverage intensity over all points of the monitored area.

$$C_n = E[C_p]. \tag{3}$$

According to the expression of C_p, shown in Theorem 2, we can write

$$C_n = E[1 - \left(1 - \frac{1}{k}\right)^c]. \tag{4}$$

Based on the above equation, we notice how the value of C_n depends mainly on c which is the number of nodes covering a given point of the field. Intuitively, we can assimilate the fact of covering a point or not to a Bernoulli trial with the probability $q = \frac{r}{a}$ [18]. Considering the variable c among the n nodes of the network, it becomes a Binomial random variable (C) with the probability given in Eq. (5). Thereby, the network coverage intensity C_n, shown in Eq. (4), is not a simple expectation, but rather an expectation of a function of a random variable.

$$Pr(C = j) = C_n^j \times \left(\frac{r}{a}\right)^j \times \left(1 - \left(\frac{r}{a}\right)\right)^{n-j}. \tag{5}$$

where C_n^j is the binomial coefficient, r is the size of the sensing area of each sensor, a is the size of the monitored area, and $\left(\frac{r}{a}\right)$ is the probability that each sensor covers a given point. The Binomial random variable with n trials and success probability $q = \left(\frac{r}{a}\right)$ has been formalized in HOL as follows.

Definition 5. ⊢ ∀X p q n. binomial_distr_rv X p q n =
    (real_random_variable X p) ∧
    (IMAGE X (p_space p) = IMAGE (λx.&x) (count (SUC n))) ∧
    (∀m. &m ∈ (IMAGE X (p_space p)) ⇒
    (distribution p X {&m} = &(binomial n m) × q^m × (1 − q)^{(n−m)}).

where X is a real random variable on the probability space p, and IMAGE (λx.& x) (count (SUC n)) gives the support of the Binomial. The function binomial, used in the above definition, is the higher-order-logic formalization of the binomial coefficient for reals.

The coverage intensity of the whole WSN with n nodes has been formally specified by the function cvrge_intsty_network, shown in Definition 6. The latter takes as parameters: X: a random variable that returns an extended real number, p: the probability space, s: the summation set used in Definition 4, k: the number of sub-networks, C: the random variable describing the number of covering nodes, n: the total number of nodes, and q: the probability that each sensor covers a given point.

Definition 6. $\vdash \forall X$ p k s C n q.
  cvrge_intsty_network p X k s C n q =
  expectation p (λx. cvrge_intsty_pt p X k s (num (C x))).

where the function **expectation** designates the higher-order-logic formalization of the expectation of a random variable that returns an extended real, and the values (num(C x)), in the above definition, are the output values of the random variable C. The function **num**, used here, converts an extended real; (&m), to its corresponding natural value m, using the real function **floor**.

    Based on the higher-order-logic formalizations developed so far, we have been able to formally verify the final network coverage intensity as in Theorem 3.

Theorem 3. $\vdash \forall$p X k s C n q. (prob_space p) $\wedge$ (0 < q < 1) $\wedge$
  (events p = POW (p_space p)) $\wedge$ (1 $\leq$ n) $\wedge$ (1 < k) $\wedge$ FINITE s $\wedge$
  (CARD s = k) $\wedge$ (sn_covers_p C p q n) $\wedge$
  (expectation p C $\neq$ PosInf) $\wedge$ (expectation p C $\neq$ NegInf) $\wedge$
  ($\forall$i x. (i $\in$ s) $\wedge$ (x $\in$ p_space p) $\Rightarrow$
        sbst_non_empty_rv (X i) p k (num(C x)))
  $\Rightarrow$ (cvrge_intsty_network p X k s C n q = Normal $(1 - (1 - \frac{q}{(\&k)})^n)$).

- The assumption (events p = POW (p_space p)) describes the set of events to be the power set of the sample space Ω.
- The assumptions (1 $\leq$ n) ensures that the WSN include at least one node, while (0 < q < 1) checks that the probability q lies in $[0..1]$.
- sn_covers_p is the Binomial random variable (Definition 5) with a finite expectation, i.e., (expectation p C $\neq$ PosInf) $\wedge$ (expectation p C $\neq$ NegInf). The variables (PosInf) and (NegInf) are the higher-order-logic formalizations of positive infinity and negative infinity, respectively.
- The function (sbst_non_empty_rv (X i) p k (num(C x))) is the function specified in Definition 3.

The proof of Theorem 3 is primarily based on Theorem 4 which verifies the expectation of a function of a random variable. Additionally, the current proof also required the application of the linearity of the expectation property. Finally, a considerable amount of real analysis associated to the Binomial theorem for reals, and to the summation function has been needed.

Theorem 4. $\vdash \forall$C p q n k.
  (prob_space p) $\wedge$ (1 < k) $\wedge$ (0 < q < 1) $\wedge$
  (events p = POW (p_space p)) $\wedge$ (1 $\leq$ n) $\wedge$ (sn_covers_p C p q n)
  $\Rightarrow$ (expectation p (λx. f_fct (num (C x)) k) = Normal $(1 - \frac{q}{(\&k)})^n)$.

where the function f_fct is defined as follows

$$\texttt{f\_fct x k} = \texttt{Normal} \left(1 - \frac{1}{k} \right)^x. \qquad (6)$$

The proof of Theorem 4 has been possible using intermediate results on the injectivity of some functions, as well as, some properties related to the random variables functions. A lot of reasoning associated with the use of extended real and the floor function, has also been required.

In this section, we presented our new higher-order-logic formalizations of the k-set randomized scheduling for wireless sensor networks, using the recently developed probability theory available in the HOL theorem prover [21]. These formalizations have been then utilized to formally reason about the coverage performance properties. The corresponding HOL code of the current formalizations is available at [5]. Due to fundamental differences in the foundations of the two probability theories in [13,21], the current resulting formalizations is completely different from the previous one [6]. Indeed, the new probability theory allows to cater for arbitrary probability spaces and is thus more generic and complete compared to the previous formalization in which the probability space has to be the universe of a set. Moreover, the specification of the randomized algorithm has been found to be much more intuitive with [21]. Unlike the work in [6], the developed proofs required much less reasoning about sets and lists producing thus less lengthy proofs. However, these proofs have been more laboured involving usually results from the three HOL theories: Lebesgue, measure and extended reals. A deep learning of all theoretical foundations of [21] was thus required to successfully achieve the target formalizations in the HOL theorem prover. In the next section, we will illustrate how the developed generic theorems extremely facilitate the formal analysis of real-world WSN applications.

5   Application: Formal Analysis of a WSN-based Monitoring Framework for IoT Applications

Numerous frameworks for environmental monitoring based on WSN have been hence proposed in the literature [1,27]. These systems can be seamlessly integrated to build an extended IoT framework for low-cost, persistent and efficient services [12,17]. Due to the new constraints of the IoT environment, deployed WSN should have a smart behavior regarding the power availability while performing a good coverage of any intrusion. The randomized node scheduling has been proposed for use to save energy in the context of an heterogeneous surveillance framework for environmental monitoring [27]. Such framework considers collaboration between sensor nodes, mobile robots and RFID tags, to ensure efficient surveillance. Using specific sensors designed for IoT [17], this framework can realize a whole IoT structure.

In this section, we focus on formally analyzing the coverage performances of the hybrid surveillance framework proposed in [27] adopted for IoT applications. The nodes can hence have any sensing area r, and are deployed into a circular region of a radius R with a total size of a, whereas the success probability q of a sensor covering a point is $q = \frac{r}{a}$. Such framework has been primarily analyzed using a paper-and-pencil model, which has been then validated through some simulation scenarios evaluating the expected coverage and the maximum number of subsets [27]. It would be interesting to provide a more rigorous technique to validate the proposed paper-and-pencil model. Based on the formal development achieved so far, we show in this section how we are able to carry out an accurate asymptotic analysis of the probabilistic coverage according to the key design parameters: n; the total number of sensor and k; the number of subsets.

We designate the generic network coverage intensity (`cvrge_intsty_network p X s k C n q`), shown in Definition 6, by (`Cn_wsn p X s k C n q`), that has been checked in HOL as

$$\texttt{Normal} \left(1 - \left(1 - \frac{q}{k}\right)^{n}\right). \tag{7}$$

5.1   Formal Analysis Based on the Number of Nodes

Setting the number of subsets to k and targeting a network coverage intensity Cn_wsn of at least t, we verify, in Lemma 1, the minimum number of sensors; n_{min}, that are necessary to deploy in the context of our monitoring framework.

Lemma 1. $\vdash \forall p\ X\ s\ k\ C\ n\ q\ t.\ (1 \leq n) \wedge (1 < k) \wedge (0 < q < 1) \wedge$
$(0 < t < 1) \wedge (\texttt{Normal}\ t \leq \texttt{Cn\_wsn}\ p\ X\ s\ k\ C\ n\ q)$
$\Rightarrow \left\lceil \frac{\ln(1-t)}{\ln\left(1-\frac{q}{k}\right)} \right\rceil \leq \&n.$

The higher-order-logic proof of the above lemma is based on some properties of transcendental functions and arithmetic reasoning.

We have been able to formally verify, in Lemma 2, that the network coverage intensity Cn_wsn is a growing function of n, i.e., a larger node number n is responding to a better coverage. For the monitoring framework, much more points of the area are expected to be covered, since it is likely that many more covering nodes are deployed in its surrounding area.

Lemma 2. $\vdash \forall p\ X\ s\ k\ C\ q.\ (1 < k) \wedge (0 < q < 1)$
$\Rightarrow (\texttt{mono\_incr}\ (\lambda n.\ \texttt{real}(\texttt{Cn\_wsn}\ p\ X\ k\ s\ C\ n\ q))).$

where the function `real` is used to convert the network coverage intensity of type extended real to its corresponding real value, and `mono_incr` is the HOL definition of an increasing sequence.

While Cn_wsn increases with the increase of the number of nodes n, as verified in Lemma 2, the next lemma shows how the network coverage intensity Cn_wsn approaches 100% when n becomes infinite, independently of the monitoring application.

Lemma 3. $\vdash \forall p\ X\ s\ k\ C\ q.\ (1 < k) \wedge (0 < q < 1)$
$\Rightarrow (\lim_{n \to +\infty} (\lambda n.\ \texttt{real}(\texttt{Cn\_wsn}\ p\ X\ s\ k\ C\ n\ q)) = 1).$

5.2   Formal Analysis Based on the Number of Subsets

Targeting a network coverage intensity of at least t, we successfully verify, in Lemma 4, the upper bound on the number of disjoint subsets k for a given n.

Lemma 4. $\vdash \forall p$ X s k C n q. $(1 \leq n) \wedge (0 < t < 1) \wedge$
$(0 < q < 1) \wedge (1 < k) \wedge$ (Normal $t \leq$ (Cn_wsn p X s k C n q))
$\Rightarrow k \leq \dfrac{q}{1 - e^{\frac{\ln(1-t)}{(\&n)}}}$.

The above result is interesting for practical WSN applications which necessitate adjustable performance measurement quality for energy preserving purposes.

We have been able to formally check, in Lemma 5, that the network coverage intensity Cn_wsn definitely decreases when the WSN is partitioned into a quite large number of sub-networks k.

Lemma 5. $\vdash \forall p$ X s C n q. $(1 \leq n) \wedge (0 < q < 1)$
$\Rightarrow$ (mono_decr ($\lambda k.$ real (Cn_wsn p X s k C n q))).

where the HOL function mono_decr defines a decreasing sequence.

We also formally confirm, in Lemma 6, that increasing the number of deployed nodes n gives smaller network coverage and hence a poor performance of the deployed application.

Lemma 6. $\vdash \forall p$ X s C n q. $(1 \leq n) \wedge (0 < q < 1)$
$\Rightarrow$ ($\lim\limits_{k \to +\infty}$ ($\lambda k.$ real (Cn_wsn p X p s k C n q)) = 0).

The above lemma has been successfully verified in HOL using intermediate results associated to real and sequential limits.

5.3   Formal Analysis Based on Uniform Partitions

We closely investigate the asymptotic coverage behavior of our monitoring framework in the case of a *uniform* split of the nodes. Here, n can be written as $k \times m$, where m is the number of nodes per subset.

In particular, as the number of sub-networks k goes infinite, the upper limit of the network coverage Cn_wsn has been formally verified in Lemma 7.

Lemma 7. $\vdash \forall p$ X s C m q. $(0 < q < 1)$
$\Rightarrow \lim\limits_{k \to +\infty}$ ($\lambda k.$ real(Cn_wsn p X s k C (m $\times$ k) q)) = 1 - $e^{-q \times (\&m)}$.

The proof of the above lemma has been quite tricky requiring the important result $\lim\limits_{k \to +\infty} (1 + \frac{x}{k})^k = e^x$, which had to be proved in HOL beforehand.

Based on Lemma 7, we can hence verify that when m becomes very large, the uniform network coverage will surely approach 100%. Such result is considered as a second verification of Lemma 3 in the case where n and k are proportional.

Lemma 8. $\vdash \forall X$ p s C q. $(0 < q < 1)$
$\Rightarrow \lim\limits_{m \to +\infty} (\lambda m. \lim\limits_{k \to +\infty} (\lambda k.\ \text{real}(\text{Cn\_wsn p X s k C (m} \times \text{k) q})) = 1.$

The current analysis, presented in this section, distinctly shows how our theoretical developments, described in Sect. 4, match pretty well the original paper-and-pencil models of the randomized scheduling, available in the open literature [18,26].

6   Discussion

The main motivation of the current work is to provide a rigorous approach for the probabilistic performance evaluation of the k-set randomized scheduling algorithm for wireless sensor networks. The randomness in the scheduling approach and the node deployment makes the accuracy of the performance evaluation of such algorithm very critical, especially given the major limitations of classical techniques and the safety-critical of most WSN applications. In this regard, this paper describes the main formalizations of the k-set randomized scheduling and its coverage properties using the new probability theory available within the HOL4 theorem prover [21]. These higher-order-logic formalizations resulted from the porting process of our previous formalizations [6,7], developed within a precedent probabilistic framework of the HOL theorem prover [13]. The practical usefulness of our approach is shown in Sect. 5, where we formally analyzed the coverage performance of a general purpose surveillance framework based on WSN for IoT applications.

The higher-order-logic formalizations, presented in this paper, consumed approximatively 730 lines of code in the HOL4 theorem prover. On the other hand, the formal analysis of our application took only 200 lines of HOL code for the verification of most of the lemmas. Nevertheless, the proofs of Lemmas 7 and 8 have been quite tedious consuming in total 500 lines of HOL code, since the mathematical theorem $\lim\limits_{k \to +\infty} (1 + \frac{x}{k})^k = e^x$, was missing in HOL. The latter result required a lot of real analysis related to the exponential function as a power series and many other properties for the sequence convergence.

The generic nature of the theorem proving technique and the high expressibility of higher-order logic allows us a considerable amount of flexibility in several aspects. Indeed, the formalizations, presented in this paper, primarily constitutes a successful automation of the paper-and-pencil models [18,26] of the k-set randomized scheduling and its coverage performance within a higher-order-logic proof assistant. Through this work, we therefore clearly assert the complete accordance of the resulting formal developments with the mathematical models, increasing thus the confidence on the developed theory. Given the discussion, presented in Sect. 2, it is certain that other analysis techniques can never have this efficiency. Actually, the existing probabilistic models of the randomized scheduling are not so reliable either regarding the complete set of assumptions or the correctness of the manual mathematical analysis, which may include human errors. In addition, while previous simulation methods usually rely on pseudo-random modelling, we have been able to provide an appropriate modelling of the inherent randomness of the algorithm of interest. Besides, unlike probabilistic model checkers where statistical properties are not so accurately specified, we have been able to achieve formal and precise analysis of the network coverage as a statistical measure of the coverage intensity for a specific point. On the other hand, the formal performance analysis of the coverage behavior of the environmental framework clearly shows the usefulness of our theoretical developments. Such verification enables reliable asymptotic reasoning of the deployed WSN. Compared to the asymptotic analysis already done in [7], we have been able to enrich our analysis with new valuable results. At the end, it is important to note that the presented application is a simple case study illustrating the practical interest of our work, but the claimed generic results can be obviously applied to any other WSN application as well.

To successfully achieve the current work, we have experienced many difficulties. Firstly, although the initial paper-and-pencil models [18,26] are depending on simple discrete random variables, the major challenge was to correctly translate these models of a real WSN algorithm into higher-order logic. These analytical modelling of real-world systems is effectively very intuitive, and the original mathematical models [18,26] are usually missing detailed explanations either when describing the probabilistic analysis or when applying the probability rules. In addition, the assumptions of the original model are never presented exhaustively. A deep investigation step was thus required in order to correctly understand all missing steps and achieve then efficiently the target higher-order-logic formalizations. For that purposes, a good background on probability coupled with a sound knowledge of the WSN context, are usually required for an effective understanding of the probabilistic reasoning.

Secondly, the choice of porting our previous higher-order-logic formalizations [6,7] into a new probability theory [21], was, at once, tough and time consuming. As previously mentioned, such choice has been primarily motivated by the fact that we were targeting more evolutive probabilistic analysis of the k-set randomized scheduling with the formalization of further performance aspects in the near future [8]. These aspects should require some probabilistic features which are not available in [13]. Moreover, while the new HOL specification seems to be more straightforward in the new probability theory, we had to get extensive understanding of all the corresponding mathematical foundations including extended reals, measure and Lebesgue theories in order to correctly conduct the probabilistic analysis. Nevertheless, the existing results from the formalized probability theory helped us to keep the amount of proof efforts reasonable.

7 Conclusions

In this paper, we presented a reliable approach for the formal analysis of the coverage performances of wireless sensor networks using the k-set randomized scheduling to save energy. This formalization enables us to formally verify the coverage related characteristics of most WSNs using the k-set randomized scheduling. To show the practical interest of our foundational results, we apply them to perform the formal probabilistic analysis of an hybrid monitoring framework for environmental Internet of Things (IoT) applications. Such framework can be adapted for any kind of monitoring application using WSN as well.

On the other hand, the produced results are thoroughly generic, i.e., valid for all parameter values. It is clear that such results cannot be achieved in simulation or probabilistic model checking based approach. Moreover, it has been possible to provide precise formal reasoning on the statistical coverage using expectation. Finally, unlike most of the existing work that focuses on the validation of the functional aspects of WSN algorithms, our work is distinguishable by addressing the performance aspects. Finally, the proposed solution allowed us to build upon our coverage formalizations to develop our whole methodology [8] in a single coherent formalism. In particular, the current results have been very helpful for our work on the higher-order-logic formalizations of the detection properties of WSNs [9], based on the paper-and-pencil analysis of [26]. It has been useful to formally check the relationship between coverage and detection showing that coverage reflects detection [18].

References

1. Aslan, Y., Korpeoglu, I., Ulusoy, O.: A framework for use of wireless sensor networks in forest fire detection and monitoring. Comput. Environ. Urban Syst. **36**(6), 614–625 (2012)
2. Baier, C., Katoen, J.P.: Principles of Model Checking. The MIT Press, Cambridge (2008)
3. Ballarini, P., Miller, A.: Model checking medium access control for sensor networks. In: Proceedings of the 2nd Symposium on Leveraging Applications of Formal Methods, Verification and Validation, pp. 255–262. IEEE Computer Society (2006)
4. Bernardeschi, C., Masci, P., Pfeifer, H.: Analysis of wireless sensor network protocols in dynamic scenarios. In: Guerraoui, R., Petit, F. (eds.) SSS 2009. LNCS, vol. 5873, pp. 105–119. Springer, Heidelberg (2009). doi:10.1007/978-3-642-05118-0_8
5. Elleuch, M.: Formalization of the coverage properties of WSNs in HOL (2015). http://hvg.ece.concordia.ca/projects/prob-it/wsn.php
6. Elleuch, M., Hasan, O., Tahar, S., Abid, M.: Formal analysis of a scheduling algorithm for wireless sensor networks. In: Qin, S., Qiu, Z. (eds.) ICFEM 2011. LNCS, vol. 6991, pp. 388–403. Springer, Heidelberg (2011). doi:10.1007/978-3-642-24559-6_27
7. Elleuch, M., Hasan, O., Tahar, S., Abid, M.: Formal probabilistic analysis of a wireless sensor network for forest fire detection. In: Symbolic Computation in Software Science, Electronic Proceedings in Theoretical Computer Science, vol. 122, pp. 1–9. Open Publishing Association (2013)
8. Elleuch, M., Hasan, O., Tahar, S., Abid, M.: Towards the formal performance analysis of wireless sensor networks. In: Proceedings of the 22nd Workshop on Enabling Technologies: Infrastructure for Collaborative Enterprises, pp. 365–370. IEEE Computer Society (2013)

9. Elleuch, M., Hasan, O., Tahar, S., Abid, M.: Formal probabilistic analysis of detection properties in wireless sensor networks. Formal Aspects Comput. **27**(1), 79–102 (2015)

10. Fehnker, A., Fruth, M., McIver, A.K.: Graphical modelling for simulation and formal analysis of wireless network protocols. In: Butler, M., Jones, C., Romanovsky, A., Troubitsyna, E. (eds.) Methods, Models and Tools for Fault Tolerance. LNCS, vol. 5454, pp. 1–24. Springer, Heidelberg (2009). doi:10.1007/978-3-642-00867-2_1

11. Fruth, M.: Probabilistic model checking of contention resolution in the IEEE 802.15.4 low-rate wireless personal area network protocol. In: Proceedings of the 2nd Symposium on Leveraging Applications of Formal Methods, Verification and Validation, pp. 290–297. IEEE Computer Society (2006)

12. Hart, J., Martinez, K.: Towards an environmental Internet of Things [IoT]. Earth Space Sci. **2**, 1–7 (2015)

13. Hasan, O.: Formal probabilistic analysis using theorem proving. Ph.D. thesis, Concordia University, Montreal, QC, Canada (2008)

14. Hasan, O., Tahar, S.: Formalization of continuous probability distributions. In: Pfenning, F. (ed.) CADE 2007. LNCS (LNAI), vol. 4603, pp. 3–18. Springer, Heidelberg (2007). doi:10.1007/978-3-540-73595-3_2

15. Hölzl, J., Heller, A.: Three chapters of measure theory in Isabelle/HOL. In: Eekelen, M., Geuvers, H., Schmaltz, J., Wiedijk, F. (eds.) ITP 2011. LNCS, vol. 6898, pp. 135–151. Springer, Heidelberg (2011). doi:10.1007/978-3-642-22863-6_12

16. Hurd, J.: Formal verification of probabilistic algorithms. Ph.D. thesis, University of Cambridge, Cambridge, UK (2002)

17. Lazarescu, M.: Design of a WSN platform for long-term environmental monitoring for IoT applications. IEEE J. Emerg. Sel. Topics Circ. Syst. **3**(1), 1–6 (2013)

18. Liu, C., Wu, K., Xiao, Y., Sun, B.: Random coverage with guaranteed connectivity: joint scheduling for wireless sensor networks. IEEE Trans. Parallel Distrib. Syst. **17**(6), 562–575 (2006)

19. MacKay, D.: Introduction to Monte Carlo methods. In: Proceedings of NATO Advanced Study Institute on Learning in Graphical Models, pp. 175–204. Kluwer Academic Publishers (1998)

20. Mainetti, L., Patrono, L., Vilei, A.: Evolution of wireless sensor networks towards the internet of things: a survey. In: Proceedings of the 19th International Conference on Software, Telecommunications and Computer Networks, pp. 1–6. IEEE (2011)

21. Mhamdi, T.: Information-theoretic analysis using theorem proving. Ph.D. thesis, Concordia University, Montreal, QC, Canada, December 2012

22. Ölveczky, P.C., Thorvaldsen, S.: Formal modeling and analysis of the OGDC wireless sensor network algorithm in real-time Maude. In: Bonsangue, M.M., Johnsen, E.B. (eds.) FMOODS 2007. LNCS, vol. 4468, pp. 122–140. Springer, Heidelberg (2007). doi:10.1007/978-3-540-72952-5_8

23. Rutten, J., Kwaiatkowska, M., Normal, G., Parker, D.: Mathematical Techniques for Analyzing Concurrent and Probabilisitc Systems. CRM Monograph Series. American Mathematical Society, Providence (2004)

24. Whitmore, A., Agarwal, A., Xu, L.: The internet of things-a survey of topics and trends. Inf. Syst. Front. **17**(2), 261–274 (2015)

25. Wu, K., Gao, Y., Li, F., Xiao, Y.: Lightweight deployment-aware scheduling for wireless sensor networks. Mob. Netw. Appl. **10**(6), 837–852 (2005)

26. Xiao, Y., Chen, H., Wu, K., Sun, B., Zhang, Y., Sun, X., Liu, C.: Coverage and detection of a randomized scheduling algorithm in wireless sensor networks. IEEE Trans. Comput. **59**(4), 507–521 (2010)

27. Xiao, Y., Zhang, Y.: Divide-and conquer-based surveillance framework using robots, sensor nodes, and RFID tags. Wirel. Commun. Mob. Comput. **11**(7), 964–979 (2011)
28. Yick, J., Mukherjee, B., Ghosal, D.: Wireless sensor network survey. Comput. Netw. **52**(12), 2292–2330 (2008)
29. Zayani, H., Barkaoui, K., Ayed, R.B.: Probabilistic verification and evaluation of backoff procedure of the WSN ECo-MAC protocol. Int. J. Wirel. Mob. Netw. **12**(1), 156–170 (2010)
30. Zheng, M., Sun, J., Liu, Y., Dong, J.S., Gu, Y.: Towards a model checker for NesC and wireless sensor networks. In: Qin, S., Qiu, Z. (eds.) ICFEM 2011. LNCS, vol. 6991, pp. 372–387. Springer, Heidelberg (2011). doi:10.1007/978-3-642-24559-6_26

Shared-Variable Concurrency, Continuous Behaviour and Healthiness for Critical Cyberphysical Systems

Richard Banach[1(✉)] and Huibiao Zhu[2]

[1] School of Computer Science, University of Manchester,
Oxford Road, Manchester M13 9PL, UK
banach@cs.man.ac.uk
[2] Shanghai Key Laboratory of Trustworthy Computing,
MOE International Joint Laboratory of Trustworthy Software,
International Research Center of Trustworthy Software,
East China Normal University, Shanghai 200062, China
hbzhu@sei.ecnu.edu.cn

Abstract. In the effort to develop critical cyberphysical systems, existing computing formalisms are extended to include continuous behaviour. This may happen in a way that neglects elements necessary for correct continuous properties and correct physical properties. A simple language is taken to illustrate this. Issues and risks latent in this kind of approach are identified and discussed under the umbrella of 'healthiness conditions'. Modifications to the language in the light of the conditions discussed are described. An example air conditioning system is used to illustrate the concepts presented, and is developed both in the original language and in the modified version.

1 Introduction

With the massive proliferation in computing systems that interact with the real world, spurred by the tumbling costs of processors, memory and sensor/actuator equipment, the need for reliable methods to construct such systems has never been greater, especially since so many of these systems have high consequence aspects if they fail to behave as intended. In the light of this drive, systematic methodologies from the discrete formalisms world are being adapted to incorporate the needs of the physical behaviours that are now intrinsic to these systems. While this is entirely appropriate as a broad objective, in reality, many such initiatives may turn out skewed in the execution, in that a great emphasis is placed on the discrete aspects of such an extended formalism, to the neglect of needs

The work reported here was done while Richard Banach was a visiting researcher at E.C.N.U. The support of E.C.N.U. is gratefully acknowledged.

Huibiao Zhu is supported by National Natural Science Foundation of China (Grant No. 61361136002) and Shanghai Collaborative Innovation Center of Trustworthy Software for Internet of Things (ZF1213).

C. Artho and P.C. Ölveczky (Eds.): FTSCS 2016, CCIS 694, pp. 109–125, 2017.
DOI: 10.1007/978-3-319-53946-1_7

coming from the continuous aspects, especially regarding the more subtle of these pertaining to continuous behaviour, and to credible physical properties. The interplay between these worlds can also fail to get the attention it requires. The balance of emphasis perceptible in typical texts in this area such as [1,2] gives a good indication of this situation.

In this paper we intend to address this perceived imbalance by examining an example language for concurrent discrete update and critically analysing the consequences that follow when continuous update facilities are added in a relatively naïve way. We describe this critical analysis as bringing some 'healthiness considerations' into play, by analogy with the terminology used in UTP [3]. Having brought these out, we show how to modify our original language to better take them into account within the syntax (where possible). We discuss how remaining points need to be addressed semantically. It is worth saying that our language is one that we would not necessarily use seriously for such applications, but actually, its very lack of obvious suitability serves to better highlight the points we make.

We illustrate the above by developing a simple case study concerning the steady state operation of an air conditioning system, this being a system where there is enough *a priori* physical behaviour to exemplify some of what we discuss abstractly. We give a development in the original language, and a revised version in the revised language.

The rest of the paper is as follows. In Sect. 2 we present our initial language, and our initial attempt at adding continuous behaviour, specified using differential equations (DEs). Discussing the semantics of this, even relatively informally, leads to a substantial detour regarding the possibilities available when DEs are involved. In Sect. 3 we give our initial AC system development. In Sect. 4 we turn to the healthiness considerations, enlarging the earlier semantic discussion to include further issues. Section 5 then modifies the initial language syntactically, where possible. Section 6 redevelops the AC system. Section 7 considers some related approaches. Section 8 concludes.

2   An Initial Concurrent Language

Here is the syntax of our initial language. It is a fairly conventional concurrent shared variable language, allowing delays of a specified number of time units.

Declarations:
$$Decl ::= [x : T [= x_0] ;]^*$$
Discrete behaviours:
$$Db ::= x := e \mid \{xs := es\} \mid @b \mid \#r$$
Constructs:
$$P0 ::= Db$$
Programs:
$$Pr0 ::= P0 \mid Name \mid [Name =] Decl ; Pr0 \mid Pr0 ; Pr0$$
$$\mid \textbf{if } b \textbf{ then } Pr0 \textbf{ else } Pr0 \textbf{ fi} \mid \textbf{while } b \textbf{ do } Pr0 \textbf{ od} \mid Pr0 \parallel Pr0$$

As well as this syntax, we use parentheses in the usual way. In connection with this definition we note the following:

(1) All variables used have to be declared with their types in a declaration block *Decl* in whose scope (defined as usual) their uses occur.

(2) The discrete variable assignment, $x := e$, is *atomic*, so that no action can interleave the reading the variables of e and writing the result to x. The vacuous assignment is written **skip**. Each variable has to be assigned an initial value (in terms of constants and already assigned variables) before it can be used. Initialisation is optionally taken care of during declaration.

(3) The simultaneous assignment $\{xs := es\}$ merely defines a *package* of several atomic updates, which are effected at the same instant.

(4) The discrete event-guard, @b, is enabled when the guard b holds; otherwise it is disabled and waits; b is a Boolean condition. #r represents a delay of r time units.

(5) Program constructs are familiar. **if** b **then** P **else** Q **fi** is the conditional, and **while** b **do** P is iteration. P ; Q is sequential composition. Shared-variable concurrency is expressed via $P \parallel Q$, where P and Q can contain the behaviours outlined.

Semantically, if we momentarily disregard the delay #r, everything is quite conventional and we do not need to repeat the details. A language like $Pr0$ expresses updates to variables, which are related to each other via the usual syntactically derived causality relation, but there is no indication about how these updates might relate to the real world. In practice, (real world counterparts of) the atomic updates are usually understood to occur at isolated moments of real time, but there is no absolute necessity for this, e.g. if we interpret according to the conventions of the duration calculus [4].[1]

When we now reconsider the delay #r, things change. We are obliged to take note of real world time. Consequently we take the view that all (packages of) update execution instances have their own specific isolated points in time at which they execute.

The preceding sets the scene for introducing continuous variable update.

Continuous behaviours:
$$Cb ::= @g \mid [iv]\, \mathcal{D}\, \boldsymbol{x} = F(\boldsymbol{x}, \boldsymbol{y}, \tau) \text{ until } g$$
Constructs:
$$P1 ::= Db \mid Cb$$
Programs:
$$Pr1 ::= P1 \mid Name \mid [Name =]\, Decl\, ;\, Pr1 \mid Pr1\, ;\, Pr1 \mid \ldots \text{ etc.}$$

Regarding the above we make the following further comments:

(6) Declarations may now include continuous variables as well as discrete variables.

(7) The command @g waits for its guard g to be satisfied. It is like @b except that g may now contain continuous variables.

---

[1] In this paper we wish to sidestep the race conditions that arise when two (packages of) updates which read each others' left hand side variables execute at exactly the same moment.

(8) The differential equation (DE) command $[iv] \mathcal{D} \boldsymbol{x} = F(\boldsymbol{x}, \boldsymbol{y}, \tau)$ **until** g first guards the entry point of executing the DE until the initial conditions on the variables of the DE system (expressed in $[iv]$) are satisfied (execution is delayed if they are not). Once $[iv]$ is satisfied, the current values of the variables being updated define the DE's initial values, and the behaviour specified by the DE continues ($\mathcal{D}$ denotes the time derivative), until the preempting guard g is satisfied or the DE itself becomes infeasible. The preempting guard g is a Boolean condition, like @g.

Semantically, the leeway we had in interpreting pure discrete events, evaporates when we add differential equations. At least it does so if we want a credible correspondence with the real world. While pure discrete event formalisms may, quite sensibly, be studied axiomatically, this is never the case for DEs.

In conventional pure and applied mathematics, the ingredients of differential equations are always first interpreted with respect to a semantic domain that is stipulated in advance (albeit often implicitly in the case of applied mathematics). Different choices of such semantic domains are justified on grounds of the differing generality that they permit in the properties of the functions that are deemed to solve those differential equations, see e.g. [5]. Accordingly, to embed behaviours defined by differential equations into our language in a sound way, we must first pay some attention to matters of operational semantics for the whole language. We base our treatment here on fairly standard interpretations of state based discrete constructs and of DE systems.

Working bottom-up, the fundamental concept is the state σ, a mapping from each variable v to a value in its type: $v \mapsto \sigma(v)$. We also need clocks, written generically as τ. A clock is a continuous real variable whose time derivative is fixed at 1. The phrase 'a clock is started' means that a fresh clock, initialised to 0, starts to run from the beginning of the semantic interpretation of some non-atomic construct of interest.

The Db part of the language is unsurprising. The discrete atomic variable assignment, $x := e$, sends the state σ to $\sigma[\sigma(e)/x]$, which is identical to σ, except at x, which becomes $\sigma(e)$. Similarly for packaged atomic updates.

For @b, if b is true in the current state, then the program completes successfully. Otherwise a clock is started, and runs as long as it takes for the environment to make b true, at which point the program completes.

For #r, if $r \leq 0$, then the program completes successfully. Otherwise a clock is started, and runs for $r > 0$ time units, at which point the program completes.

For the continuous behaviours, for @g, since g may contain continuous variables, the true-set of g must be **closed**. With this proviso, if g is true in the current state, then the program completes successfully. Otherwise a clock is started, and runs as long as it takes for the environment to make g true, at which point the program completes.

For the DE forms, we first mention some generalities.

If we write a general first order differential equation as $\Phi(\boldsymbol{v}, \mathcal{D}\boldsymbol{v}, t) = 0$, where $\boldsymbol{v}$ is some tuple of real variables, $\mathcal{D}\boldsymbol{v}$ is a corresponding tuple of real variables intended to denote the derivatives of $\boldsymbol{v}$, and Φ is an arbitrary real-valued function, then nothing can be said about whether any sensible interpretation of such an equation exists. See e.g. [5], or any other rigorous text on DEs, for a wealth of counterexamples that bear this out. Accordingly, rigorous results on differential equations that cover a reasonably wide spectrum of cases, are confined to DE forms that fit a restricted syntactic shape and satisfy specific semantic properties. The best known such class covers first order families that can be written in the form:

$$\mathcal{D}\,\boldsymbol{x} = \boldsymbol{F}(\boldsymbol{x}, \tau) \quad \text{or} \quad \mathcal{D}\,\boldsymbol{x} = \boldsymbol{F}(\boldsymbol{x}, \boldsymbol{y}, \tau)$$

Here, the left hand form refers to a closed system of variables $\boldsymbol{x}$, whereas the right hand form also permits the presence of additional external controls $\boldsymbol{y}$. As well this syntactic shape, conditions have to be demanded on the vector of functions $\boldsymbol{F}$ and on the entry conditions of the behaviour to be defined by these definitions.

For simplicity, we assume that the vector of functions $\boldsymbol{F}$ is defined on a closed rectangular region, where for each $\boldsymbol{x}$ component index i we have a Cartesian component $x_i \in [x_{iL} \ldots x_{iU}]$, and for each $\boldsymbol{y}$ component index j we have a Cartesian component $y_j \in [y_{jL} \ldots y_{jU}]$, and where the time dependence of $\boldsymbol{F}$ has been normalised to a clock $\tau \in [0 \ldots \tau_f]$, with τ_f maximal, which starts when the DE system starts.

For each x_i component, x_{iL} is either $-\infty$ or a finite real number, and x_{iU} is either $+\infty$ or a finite real number, and if both are finite, then $x_{iL} < x_{iU}$. Similarly for the y_j components. We denote this region by $XY \times T$, where XY refers to all the $\boldsymbol{x}, \boldsymbol{y}$ components, and T refers to clock time. We write X for just the $\boldsymbol{x}$ components and Y for just the $\boldsymbol{y}$ components, so that $XY = X \times Y$.

To guarantee existence of a solution the vector $\boldsymbol{F}$ must satisfy a Lipschitz condition:

$$\exists K \bullet K \in \mathbb{R} \land \forall \boldsymbol{x}_1, \boldsymbol{y}_1, \boldsymbol{x}_2, \boldsymbol{y}_2, \tau \bullet (\boldsymbol{x}_1, \boldsymbol{y}_1) \in XY \land (\boldsymbol{x}_2, \boldsymbol{y}_2) \in XY \land \tau \in T \Rightarrow$$
$$\|\boldsymbol{F}(\boldsymbol{x}_1, \boldsymbol{y}_1, \tau) - \boldsymbol{F}(\boldsymbol{x}_2, \boldsymbol{y}_2, \tau)\|_\infty \leq K \|(\boldsymbol{x}_1, \boldsymbol{y}_1) - (\boldsymbol{x}_2, \boldsymbol{y}_2)\|_\infty$$

Here, we have used the supremum norm $\|\cdot\|_\infty$ since it composes best under logical operations. For finite dimensional systems, any norm is just as good; see [6,7]. Additionally, we require that $\boldsymbol{F}$ is continuous in time for all $\boldsymbol{y}(\tau) \in Y$.

With the above in place, if $\boldsymbol{x}_0$ is an initial value for $\boldsymbol{x}$ such that $\boldsymbol{x}_0 \in X$, then the standard theory for existence and uniqueness of solutions to DE systems guarantees us a solution $\boldsymbol{x}(\tau)$ for $\tau \in [0 \ldots \tau_{\boldsymbol{x}_0}]$, where $\tau_{\boldsymbol{x}_0} \leq \tau_f$, with $\boldsymbol{x}(\tau)$ differentiable in the interval $[0 \ldots \tau_{\boldsymbol{x}_0}]$ and satisfying the DE system, and such that we have $\forall \tau \bullet \tau \in [0 \ldots \tau_{\boldsymbol{x}_0}] \Rightarrow \boldsymbol{x}(\tau) \in X$. See [5] for details.

Let us abbreviate $[iv]\,\mathcal{D}\,\boldsymbol{x} = F(\boldsymbol{x}, \boldsymbol{y}, \tau)$ **until** g, to $[iv]\,\mathcal{DE}$ **until** g below. For soundness, we assume all the properties above regarding F hold, but it is impractical to include in the syntax all the data needed to establish them. Even including such data would still leave the problem of proving the properties needed — not trivial in general. So our view is that the presence of F in the language construct is accompanied, behind the scenes, by the needed data, together with proofs that the requisite properties hold.

Along with the properties of F, we need to know that on entry to $\mathcal{DE}$, the iv properties hold. This means that $[x_0 \in X \wedge P(x_0)]$, where $P(x_0)$ denotes any properties needed beyond the domain requirement $x_0 \in X$. The semantics of iv is as for any other guard. If iv holds, then the guard succeeds immediately, and execution of $\mathcal{DE}$ commences. If iv fails, then the process pauses, a clock is started, and it runs until the environment makes iv true, at which point the guard succeeds.

Assuming the guard has succeeded, a fresh clock is started to monitor the progress of the solution to $\mathcal{DE}$ — this clock is the one that is referred to as τ in the expression $F(x, y, \tau)$. We are guaranteed that the solution exists for some period of time.[2]

There remains the preemption guard g. As for @g, for the preemption moment to be well defined, we demand that the true-set of g is **closed**. If during the period $[0 \ldots \tau_{x_0}]$ for which we have a solution, g becomes true, execution of the solution is stopped and the execution of the whole construct $[iv]\,\mathcal{DE}$ **until** g succeeds. If during the period $[0 \ldots \tau_{x_0}]$, g never becomes true, then as in other cases, the execution of $[iv]\,\mathcal{DE}$ **until** g stops once τ_{x_0} is reached. This completes the operational semantics of the DE construct.

Thus far we have covered the semantics of individual constructs in terms of their individual durations. DEs, positive delays, and unsatisfied guards have all acquired non-zero durations. Non-positive delays and immediately satisfied guards are instantaneous, but since they do not change the state, we can allow them to complete immediately.

Atomic updates *do* change the state though. And to ensure that (packages of) atomic changes of state take place at isolated points in time, to execute an update, we start a clock which runs for a finite, unspecified, (but typically short) time, during which a non-clashing time point is chosen and the update is done. Non-clashing means that the update is separated from time points specifying other semantic events.

The remaining outer level constructors offer few surprises. Sequential composition, P_1 ; P_2, starts by executing P_1, and if it terminates after a finite time, then P_2 is started. The conditional **if** b **then** P_1 **else** P_2 **fi** is familiar. Depending on the (instantaneous) truth value of b, the execution of either P_1 or P_2 is started, and the other is forgotten. For iteration, **while** b **do** P, if b is false, the construct terminates. If b is true, the execution of P is started. If it completes in finite time, the whole process is repeated. The parallel construct $P_1 \parallel P_2$ denotes programs P_1 and P_2 running concurrently.

With the above, we can describe the runs of a program, having characteristics that are consistent with the physical picture we would want in a formalism that includes DEs, by giving, for each variable, a function of time that gives its value at each moment. For discrete variables, such a function is piecewise constant,

---

[2] The period of time during which the solution exists may be very short indeed. If x_0 is right at the boundary of X and F is directed towards the exterior of XY, then τ_{x_0} may equal 0, and the initial value may be all that there is. This makes the $\mathcal{DE}$ execution equivalent to **skip**.

being constant on left-closed right-open intervals, with an atomic update at t_α say, taking the left-limit value at t_α to the actual value at t_α. For continuous updates running till τ_g, we remove the final value of an interval $[0 \dots \tau_g]$, getting a left-closed right-open interval again, and interpreting the guard g as the left-limit value at τ_g.

3 Example: An Air Conditioning System

We illustrate how the language $Pr1$ works via a simplified air conditioning example. Although failures in AC systems are typically not critical, the kind of modelling needed, and the issues to be taken into account regarding the modelling, are common to systems of much higher consequence, making the simple example useful.

The AC system is controlled by a *User*. The user can switch it on or off, using the boolean $runAC$. The user can also increase or decrease the target temperature by setting booleans $tempUp$ and $tempDown$. Since $Pr1$ does not have pure events as primitives, the AC system reacts on the rising edges of $tempUp$ and $tempDown$, resetting these values itself (whereas it reacts to both the rising and falling edges of $runAC$).

Here then is the *User* program. In the following, we assume available a function rnd, that returns a random non-negative integer value. Note that $runAC$, $tempUp$ and $tempDown$ are not declared here since they need to be declared in an outer scope.

$User =$
    while true
    do #(rnd) ; $runAC :=$ **true** ; $cnt : \mathbb{N} =$ rnd ;
        while $cnt > 0$
        do #(rnd) ; **if** rnd % 2 **then** $tempUp :=$ **true else** $tempDown :=$ **true fi**
        od ;
        $runAC :=$ **false**
    od

The above models the nondeterministic behaviour of the user by using random waits between user events, and random counts of temperature modification commands. This is evidently a bit clumsy, but is adequate for purposes of illustration.

The AC apparatus consists of a room unit and an external unit. It operates on a Carnot cycle, in which a compressible fluid (passed between the two units via insulated piping) is alternately compressed and expanded. The fluid is compressed in the external unit to raise its temperature higher than the surroundings, where it is cooled by forced ventilation to (close to) the temperature of the surroundings. The fluid is then expanded, cooling it, so that, in the room unit, it is cooler than the room, and forced ventilation with the room's air warms it again, thus cooling the room. The cycle runs continuously. The inefficient thermodynamics of the Carnot cycle means this process cannot work without a constant input of energy, making AC systems expensive to run.

Our simplified model of AC operation depends on a number of temperature variables, reflecting the structure of the Carnot cycle: θ_S is the room temperature set by the user; θ_R is the current room temperature; θ_X is the temperature of the external unit's surroundings; θ_{FH} is the temperature of the fluid when compressed; θ_{FL} is the temperature of the fluid when expanded. All of these are real valued.

When an AC system is started, each part will be at the temperature of its own surroundings, and there will be a transient phase during which the AC system reaches its operating conditions. For simplicity we ignore this, and our model starts in a state in which all components are initialised to their operating conditions. Consequently θ_{FH}, θ_{FL} and θ_X are assumed constant, so do not require their own dynamical equations.

For simplicity we further assume that θ_{FH} is independent of other quantities, and that θ_{FL} is lower than θ_{FH} by an amount proportional to $\theta_{FH0} - \theta_{X0}$. We also assume that when operating, the AC system cools the room air according to a linear law.

$ACapparatus =$
$\quad \theta_S : \mathbb{N} \cap [S_L \ldots S_H] = \theta_{S0} \;; \theta_R : \mathbb{R} \cap [R_L \ldots R_H] = \theta_{R0} \;;$
$\quad [\; \theta_X : \mathbb{R} \cap [X_L \ldots X_H] = \theta_{X0} \;;$
$\quad\quad \theta_{FH} : \mathbb{R} = \theta_{FH0} \;; \theta_{FL} : \mathbb{R} = \theta_{FL0} = \theta_{FH0} - K_X(\theta_{FH0} - \theta_{X0}) \;; \;]$
$\quad$ **while true**
$\quad$ **do** $@(runAC = \textbf{true}) \;;$
$\quad\quad$ **while** $runAC = \textbf{true} \wedge \theta_R > \theta_S$
$\quad\quad$ **do** $[\; \theta_R \in [R_L \ldots R_H] \;]$
$\quad\quad\quad \mathcal{D}\,\theta_R = -K_R(\theta_R - \theta_{FL})$ **until**
$\quad\quad\quad (\theta_R = \theta_S \vee tempUp = \textbf{true} \vee tempDown = \textbf{true} \vee runAC = \textbf{false}) \;;$
$\quad\quad\quad$ **if** $tempUp = \textbf{true}$
$\quad\quad\quad$ **then** $\{tempUp, \theta_S := \textbf{false}, \min(\theta_S + 1, S_H)\}$
$\quad\quad\quad$ **elsif** $tempDown = \textbf{true}$
$\quad\quad\quad$ **then** $\{tempDown, \theta_S := \textbf{false}, \max(\theta_S - 1, S_L)\}$
$\quad\quad\quad$ **elsif** $\theta_R = \theta_S$
$\quad\quad\quad$ **then** $@(\theta_R = \theta_S + 1)$
$\quad\quad\quad$ **else skip**
$\quad\quad\quad$ **fi** ;
$\quad\quad$ **od** ;
$\quad\quad @(\theta_R \geq \theta_S + 1)$
$\quad$ **od**

Putting *User* and *ACapparatus* together gives us the complete system.

$ACsystem =$
$\quad runAC : \mathbb{B} = \textbf{false} \;; tempUp : \mathbb{B} = \textbf{false} \;; tempDown : \mathbb{B} = \textbf{false} \;;$
$\quad (User \;\|\; ACapparatus)$

Note that in the above, while *runAC* works as a toggle, *tempUp* and *tempDown* are reset by the apparatus. Finally, we recognise that for a sensibly behaved system, we would need a considerable number of relations to hold between all the constants that implicitly define the static structure of the system.

4   Healthiness Considerations

At this point we step back from the detailed discussion of the example to cover a number of general considerations that arise when physical systems interact with computing formalisms.

[1] Allowing all variables of interest to be considered as functions of time yields a convenient uniformity between isolated discrete updates and continuous updates. Treating the two kinds in different ways can lead to a certain amount of technical awkwardness, at the very least.

[2] When variables are functions of time, values at individual points in time have no physical significance. Only values aggregated over an interval of time make sense physically, and for these to be well defined, the functions of time in question have to be well behaved enough (e.g. 'continuous', although 'integrable' would actually suffice).

[3] In dealing with CPS systems we must take into account the consequences of using differential equations. In a sense we have already fallen into covering this quite extensively in discussing the semantics of our prototypical language in Sect. 2. The existence of solutions to arbitrary DEs cannot be taken for granted without the imposition of appropriate sufficient conditions. An easy way to ensure this is to impose strict syntactic restrictions on the permitted DEs, e.g. by insisting that they are linear.

[4] Physics is relentlessly *eager*. In conventional discrete system formalisms, assuming that the discrete events in question are intended to correspond with real world events, the precise details of the correspondence with moments of time is seldom critical (other than for explicitly timed systems), and more than one interpretation is permissible, provided the causal order of events remains the same. As soon as physical behaviour enters the scene though, this choice disappears. If one physical behaviour stops, another must take over immediately, as the universe does not 'go on hold' until some new favourable state of affairs arises.

[5] Point [4] places quite strong restrictions on the semantics of languages intended for the integrated descriptions of computing and physical behaviour, since many of the options available for discrete systems simply disappear. Although it is perfectly possible to design languages that ignore this consideration and integrate continuous behaviour and discrete behaviour in an arbitrary fashion, even though they may be perfectly consistent mathematically, unless they take due consideration of the requirements of the physical world, they are irrelevant for the description of real world systems.

[6] Points [4] and [5] boil down to a requirement that descriptions of physical behaviour must be guaranteed to be *total* over time. Languages intended for

CPS and critical systems should not permit gaps in time during which the behaviour of some physical component is undefined.

[7] The requirements of the last few points can be addressed by having separate formalisms for the discrete and continuous behaviours of the whole system and having a well thought out framework for their interworking. However, in cases of multiple cooperating formalisms, it is always the cracks between the formalisms that make the most hospitable hiding places for bugs, so particular vigilance is needed to prevent that.

[8] The impact of the preceding points may be partly addressed by careful syntactic design — we demonstrate this to a degree in Sect. 5. However, most aspects are firmly rooted in the semantics. In this regard, a language framework that puts such semantic criteria to the fore is highly beneficial. The semantic character of most of the issues discussed implies that an approach restricted to syntactic aspects can only achieve a very limited amount.

[9] The implications of the heavily semantic nature of most of the issues discussed above further implies the necessity of having runtime abortion as an ingredient of the operational semantics of any language suitable for the purposes we contemplate. Although this is seldom an issue *per se* for practical languages, which must include facilities for division, hence for division by zero at runtime, it is nevertheless perfectly possible to contemplate languages in which all primitive expression building operations are total, and hence to dispense with runtime abortion, even if such languages are of largely theoretical interest.

The overwhelmingly semantic nature of the preceding discussion motivates our referring to the matters raised as 'healthiness conditions'. (The nomenclature is borrowed from UTP [3], where appropriate structural conditions that play a similar role are baptised thus.) Checking that the necessary conditions hold for a given system, compels checking that the relevant criteria, formulated as suits the language in question, hold for the system at runtime (for the entire duration of the execution). Depending on the language and how it is structured, this may turn out to be more convenient or less convenient.

5   An Improved Concurrent Language

Taking on board the discussion in Sect. 4, we redesign our language as follows.

$$Decl ::= [x : T [= x_0] ;]^*$$
$$Db ::= x := e \mid \{xs := es\} \mid @b \mid \#r$$
$$Pr0 ::= Db \mid Decl ; Pr0 \mid Pr0 ; Pr0$$
$$\mid \textbf{if } b \textbf{ then } Pr0 \textbf{ else } Pr0 \textbf{ fi} \mid \textbf{while } b \textbf{ do } Pr0 \textbf{ od} \mid Pr0 \parallel Pr0$$
$$CbE ::= [iv] \, \mathcal{D} \, x = F(x, y, \tau) \textbf{ until } g \mid \textbf{obey } Rstr \textbf{ until } g$$
$$Pr2 ::= CbE \mid Pr2 ; Pr2$$
$$\mid \textbf{if } b \textbf{ then } Pr2 \textbf{ else } Pr2 \textbf{ fi} \mid \textbf{while } b \textbf{ do } Pr2 \textbf{ od} \mid Pr2 \parallel Pr2$$
$$PrSys ::= Name \mid [Name =] Decl ; PrSys \mid Pr0 \mid Pr2 \mid PrSys \parallel PrSys$$

In the above grammar, the healthiness considerations that can be addressed via the syntax have been incorporated. Thus, there is a visible separation between the previous discrete program design $Pr0$ (which remains unchanged), and the provisions made for describing physical behaviour $Pr2$, which have been restructured.

Specifically, there are now no facilities for $Pr2$ processes to wait. Furthermore, they can only be combined with discrete processes at top level, precluding their sudden appearance part way through a system run. This also means that they must be declared at top level, reflected in the design of the $PrSys$ syntax.

Note the additional **obey** clause for physical behaviour. This permits relatively loosely defined behaviour to be specified in cases where more prescriptive behaviour via a DE is not desired or is impossible due to lack of knowledge, etc. This replaces use of waiting clauses in the earlier grammar. Note that DE behaviour and **obey** behaviour are the *only* permitted ways of describing continuous behaviour at the bottom level.

Although we have ensured that $Pr2$ processes cannot wait for syntactic reasons, we have to ensure that they can't wait for semantic reasons either. Thus we must stipulate what happens in the DE and **obey** cases when one or other of their syntactic components fails. Taking the DE case first, if iv does not evaluate to **true**,[3] then the whole top level $PrSys$ process must abort, that is to say, execution terminates abruptly in a failing state. If F fails to satisfy the conditions for existence of a DE solution, then the top level $PrSys$ process aborts. If g does not evaluate to **true** at some moment in the DE solution, in case that the duration of the DE solution τ_f is finite, then when τ_f is reached, the top level $PrSys$ process aborts. Turning to the **obey** case, if $Rstr$ does not evaluate to **true** in a left closed right open time interval starting from the moment the **obey** construct is encountered (or amounts to **skip** at that moment), then top level $PrSys$ process aborts. If g does not evaluate to **true** at some moment during the **true** interval of $Rstr$, in case that the duration of the **true** interval of $Rstr$, say τ_f, is finite, then when τ_f is reached, the top level $PrSys$ process aborts.

Having defined the improved language, we can check over how it addresses the healthiness conditions described earlier. Re. [1], we have already stipulated that all variables depend on time in our description of the semantics, so [1] is covered. Re. [2], this is again implicit in our semantics. Likewise, [3] is also covered by our relatively detailed discussion of DEs. Re. [4], we have designed the syntax to prohibit explicit lazy behaviour in the continuous domain, and this is backed up by the semantics which disallows lazy behaviour arising from runtime conditions — this justification extends to point [5], and this, combined with the fact that DE behaviour and **obey** behaviour are the only permitted ways of describing continuous behaviour at the bottom level guarantee totality over time *provided* the behaviour described by the syntax is well defined semantically, covering point [6]. Points [7] and [8] are things that can be achieved syntactically, and our design does so. Point [9] indicates the necessity of having runtime aborts in the semantics, this being forced by the eagerness of physical behaviour. The need for this also arose in our remarks regarding point [6].

---

[3] That is to say, it evaluates to **false**, or fails to evaluate at all.

The heavy dependence on semantics of this discussion raises the question of how we can be sure that any system that is written down defines a sensible behaviour. In purely discrete languages, there is a well trodden route from the syntactic structure of a system description to verification conditions that confirm the absence of runtime errors.

The same approach extends to languages containing continuous update, such as ours. The syntactic structure of such a language can be analysed to elicit all the dependencies between different syntactic elements that can arise at runtime, and these dependencies can be used to create template verification conditions. Given a specific model, the generic template verification conditions can be instantiated to the elements of the model to provide sufficient (although not necessarily necessary) conditions for runtime well definedness. Still, it has to be conceded that such conditions can be more challenging than in the discrete case because of the more subtle nature of aspects of continuous mathematics.

Although we do not give a comprehensive account of the verification templates for our (improved) language (it has, after all, been constructed just for illustrative purposes), we can give an indication of a couple of them.

Thus, if the flow of control reaches an DE construct $[iv]\mathcal{D}x = F(x, y, \tau)$ **until** g we need to know the initial value guard will succeed. We can ensure statically that this will be the case if the DE construct occurs in a case analysis whose collection of guards covers all values that could be generated.

Similarly, once a DE construct has been preempted by its preemption guard becoming true, we need to ensure that there is a viable continuous successor behaviour for the physical process to engage in. This is helped in our case by the syntax, and can be supported by a proof that the truth of the preemption guard enables some syntactically available successor option.

In the discrete part of the language, the success of an **if** statement can be assured provided there is a default **else** clause to capture any exceptional cases. And so on.

Still, achieving full static assurance of freedom from runtime errors may require fully simulating the system, which will usually be impractical. Much depends on the language design. To help the process, languages may be designed in which all expression forming constructs are guaranteed to denote (e.g. *in extremis* by not having division in the language). Such languages may help in the verified design of critical systems.

6   The Running Example, Improved

In the light of the preceding discussions, we return to our running example and restructure it for the improved language. For simplicity we will omit the bracketed constant declarations that appeared in the earlier *ACapparatus*. We also keep the definition of the *User* the same, as that conforms to the syntax of the improved language. Regarding the *ACapparatus*, it requires some significant restructuring.

Firstly, the previous design mixed discrete and continuous update in a fairly uncritical manner. Thus the DE $\mathcal{D}\theta_R = -K_R(\theta_R - \theta_{FL})$, describing the fluid behaviour, is mixed with discrete updates to θ_S, done at the behest of the *User*. Worse, when the DE is preempted, no physical behaviour is defined for the fluid — the *ACapparatus* just hangs around waiting for the next opportunity to do some cooling. This is not really acceptable: the fluid does not stop being a physical system, subject to the laws of nature, just because, with our focus on the *ACapparatus* design, we have no great interest in its behaviour during a particular period.

Our restructured design separates the physical from the discrete aspects. The earlier *ACapparatus* is split into an *ACcontroller* process, looking after the discrete updates, and a *ACfluid* process, which describes the physical behaviour of the fluid.

Normally, the *User* would communicate with the *ACcontroller*, which would then control the *ACfluid*, but we are a bit sloppy, and allow the *User*'s *runAC* variable to also directly control the *ACfluid*, thus sharing the fluid control between the *User* and the *ACcontroller*. The latter therefore just controls the θ_S value while *runAC* is **true**.

The *ACfluid* process, now constrained by the restricted syntax for physical processes, describes the fluid's properties at all times. At times when the DE behaviour is not relevant, an **obey** clause defines default behaviour, amounting to θ_R remaining within the expected range. The separation of control and fluid allows us to make the fluid responsible for detecting temperature and to only initiate the DE behaviour when the temperature is at least a degree above the set point θ_S. Of course this is rather unrealistic, and a more credible (and detailed) design would involve sensors under the control of the *ACcontroller* to manage this aspect.

```
ACcontroller =
    while true
    do @(runAC = true) ;
        while runAC = true ∧ θR > θS
        do @(tempUp = true ∨ tempDown = true ∨ runAC = false) ;
            if tempUp = true
            then {tempUp, θS := false, min(θS + 1, SH)}
            elsif tempDown = true
            then {tempDown, θS := false, max(θS − 1, SL)}
            fi
        od
    od
ACfluid =
    while true
    do obey θR ∈ [RL ... RH] until runAC = true ;
        if θR ≥ θS + 1
        then [ θR ∈ [RL ... RH] ] D θR = −KR(θR − θFL)
                until (θR = θS ∨ runAC = false)
        else obey θR ∈ [RL ... RH] until θR ≥ θS + 1 ∨ runAC = false
        fi
    od
```

Putting all three components together gives us the complete system.

$ACsystem =$
$\quad runAC : \mathbb{B} = \textbf{false} \; ; tempUp : \mathbb{B} = \textbf{false} \; ; tempDown : \mathbb{B} = \textbf{false} \; ;$
$\quad (User \; \| \; (\; \theta_S : \mathbb{N} \cap [S_L \ldots S_H] = \theta_{S0} \; ; \theta_R : \mathbb{R} \cap [R_L \ldots R_H] = \theta_{R0} \; ;$
$\quad\quad ACcontroller \; \| \; ACfluid \;) \;)$

7 Related Approaches

It is fair to say that the critical systems industry is rather conservative — advocating radical new ways of doing things that do not enjoy the highest levels of trust risks major disasters in the field. Even the newer standards in key fields, such as DO-178C (for avionics [8]), ISO 26262 (for automotive systems [9]), IEC 62304 (for medical devices [10]), or CENELEC EN 50128 (for railway systems [11]), are still heavily weighted in favour of mandating specific testing strategies, and other practices heavily rooted in traditional development techniques. Thus the entry of formal techniques into the standardised critical systems development portfolio is rather cautious, despite the strong evidence in niche quarters about the dependability that can be gained by appropriate use of formal development, suitably integrated into the wider system engineering process. This is as much because entrenched industrial practice cannot move as nimbly as one might hope, even when the evidence for attempting to do so is relatively strong.

Here, we briefly comment on some approaches that compare with our exercise to realign a candidate language for utility in the cyberphysical and critical systems arena.

In the cyberphysical systems area [12–14], we can point to the extensive survey [15], which covers a wide spectrum of research into cyberphysical systems, and the tools and techniques used in that sphere. As we might expect, despite the relative newness of the cyberphysical systems area, formal approaches are somewhat overshadowed by more traditional and simulation based techniques. Again, this is due to the fact that cyberphysical systems still have to be built, and this falls back on traditional approaches.

The older survey [16] is more linguistically based and covers a large spectrum of languages and tools for hybrid systems. One is struck by the typically low expressivity in the continuous sphere of many of the systems discussed there, motivated, of course, by the desire for decidability of the resulting languages and systems. For decidability reasons, most of these are based on variations of the hybrid automaton concept [17–19]. In fact, for simple linear behaviours, e.g. $\mathcal{D}x = K$, with K constant, there is very little difference between using a DE as just quoted, and using an expression $x' = x + K\Delta T$ where ΔT is the duration of the behaviour.

Neverthless, many of the formalisms in these sources are focused on the single goal of hybrid or continuous behaviour, to the exclusion of more general computing concerns. This leads to the 'bugs in between formalisms' risk noted earlier, when multiple formalisms need to be combined.

Closer to our perspective is the work of Platzer [20], supported by the Key-Maera tool [21]. This supports the kind of modelling exemplified in this paper, with a strong focus on verification. Alternatively there is the Hybrid Event-B formalism [22,23]. This is an extension of the pure discrete event formalism Event-B [24], building on the earlier classical B-Method [25], (which is still actively used in critical applications in the urban rail sector [26]). The extension is expressly designed to avoid the kind of traps regarding continuous behaviour and verification that we illustrated earlier in this paper.

Thus far our discussion has avoided mentioning noise or randomness. This is legitimate when the physical considerations imply that it is negligible. But if sources of uncertainty are significant, then probabilistic techniques need to be taken on board. These add nontrivial complication to the semantics of any language. An indication of the issues that can arise can be found in [27,28].

8   Conclusion

Motivated by the current dramatic proliferation in critical and cyberphysical systems, especially in urbanised areas all over the world, in the preceding sections, we examined the problem of extending typical existing, more conventional formalisms for programming, to allow them to incorporate the needed physical behaviour that is a vital ingredient of these systems. Such integrated formalisms can come into their own if we contemplate the *integrated* verification of critical cyberphysical systems, in which we seek to avoid the possibilities of there being bugs that hide in the semantic cracks between separate formalisms that are used to check separate parts of the behaviour.

Rather than being comprehensive, our approach in this paper has been to illustrate the range of issues to be considered, by taking a somewhat prototypical shared variable language for concurrent sequential programming, and extending it in a relatively naïve way to incorporate continuous behaviour. We then critically examined the consequences of this, and identified a number of issues that are not always taken sufficient account of when embarking on such an extension exercise. For want of a pithy name, we termed these 'healthiness considerations', by analogy with the nomenclature used in UTP. This done, we showed how the earlier naïve syntax could be improved to partially address some of these issues, the remainder being the responsibility of the semantics.

We illustrated our particular solution with a simplified air conditioning system, giving the core steady state behaviour in both the original and improved formulations.

It is important to emphasise that we do not claim that the details of our solution (even in the case of our specific language) are unique. One could resolve the same issues in a number of ways that differed in the low level detail. Nevertheless, the broad sweep of the things needing to be considered would remain similar.

We also do not claim that our language (and its improved version) are to be particularly recommended for critical cyberphysical system development. In many ways, the issues we have striven to highlight are brought our more clearly in a language which one would rather *not* choose to use.

We can liken the urge to match the surface syntactic features of the language as closely as possible to what is needed by the semantics of the physical considerations, with the longstanding process whereby machine code was superseded by assembly language, which was superseded by higher level languages, etc., in each case the desire being to raise the level of abstraction in such a way as to preclude as many user level errors as possible by making them syntactically illegal (or simply impossible to express), and backing this up semantically.

It is to be hoped that the insights from an exercise like the one we have undertaken can help to improve the broader awareness of the issues lurking under the bonnet when formalisms for critical and cyberphysical systems are designed in future.

References

1. Alur, R.: Principles of Cyberphysical Systems. MIT Press, Cambridge (2015)
2. Lee, E., Shesha, S.: Introduction to Embedded Systems: A Cyberphysical Systems Approach, 2nd edn. (2015). LeeShesha.org
3. Hoare, T., He, J.: Unifying Theories of Programming. Prentice-Hall, Englewood Cliffs (1998)
4. Zhou, C., Hoare, T., Ravn, A.: A calculus of durations. Inf. Process. Lett. **40**, 269–276 (1991)
5. Walter, W.: Ordinary Differential Equations. Graduate Texts in Mathematics, vol. 182. Springer, New York (1998)
6. Horn, R., Johnson, C.: Matrix Analysis. Cambridge University Press, Cambridge (1985)
7. Horn, R., Johnson, C.: Topics in Matrix Analysis. Cambridge University Press, Cambridge (1991)
8. DO-178C. http://www.rtca.org
9. ISO 26262. http://www.iso.org/iso/home/store/catalogue_tc/catalogue_detail. htm?csnumber=54591
10. IEC 62304. https://webstore.iec.ch/preview/info_iec62304ed1.0en_d.pdf
11. CENELEC EN 50128. https://www.cenelec.eu/dyn/www/f?p=104:105
12. Sztipanovits, J.: Model integration and cyber physical systems: a semantics perspective. In: Butler, M., Schulte, W. (eds.) FM 2011. LNCS, vol. 6664, p. 1. Springer, Heidelberg (2011). doi:10.1007/978-3-642-21437-0_1. http://sites.lero.ie/download.aspx?f=Sztipanovits-Keynote.pdf
13. Willems, J.: Open dynamical systems: their aims and their origins. Ruberti Lecture, Rome (2007). http://homes.esat.kuleuven.be/~jwillems/Lectures/2007/ Rubertilecture.pdf
14. National Science and Technology Council. Trustworthy cyberspace: strategic plan for the federal cybersecurity research and development program (2011). http://www.whitehouse.gov/sites/default/files/microsites/ostp/fed_ cybersecurity_rd_strategic_plan_2011.pdf
15. Geisberger, E., Broy M. (eds.): Living in a networked world. Integrated research agenda cyber-physical systems (agendaCPS) (2015). http://www. acatech.de/fileadmin/user_upload/Baumstruktur_nach_Website/Acatech/root/ de/Publikationen/Projektberichte/acaetch_STUDIE_agendaCPS_eng_WEB.pdf

16. Carloni, L., Passerone, R., Pinto, A., Sangiovanni-Vincentelli, A.: Languages and tools for hybrid systems design. Found. Trends Electron. Des. Autom. **1**, 1–193 (2006)

17. Henzinger, T.: The theory of hybrid automata. In: Proceedings of IEEE LICS-96, pp. 278–292. IEEE (1996). http://mtc.epfl.ch/~tah/Publications/the_theory_of_hybrid_automata.pdf

18. Alur, R., Courcoubetis, C., Henzinger, T.A., Ho, P.-H.: Hybrid automata: an algorithmic approach to the specification and verification of hybrid systems. In: Grossman, R.L., Nerode, A., Ravn, A.P., Rischel, H. (eds.) HS 1991-1992. LNCS, vol. 736, pp. 209–229. Springer, Heidelberg (1993). doi:10.1007/3-540-57318-6_30

19. Alur, R., Dill, D.: A theory of timed automata. Theor. Comput. Sci. **126**, 183–235 (1994)

20. Platzer, A.: Logical Analysis of Hybrid Systems: Proving Theorems for Complex Dynamics. Springer, Heidelberg (2010)

21. Symbolaris. http://www.symbolaris.org

22. Banach, R., Butler, M., Qin, S., Verma, N., Zhu, H.: Core hybrid event-B I: single hybrid event-B machines. Sci. Comput. Prog. **105**, 92–123 (2015)

23. Banach, R., Butler, M., Qin, S., Zhu, H.: Core hybrid event-B II: multiple cooperating hybrid event-B machines. Sci. Comp. Prog. (2017, to appear)

24. Abrial, J.R.: Modeling in Event-B: System and Software Engineering. Cambridge University Press, Cambridge (2010)

25. Abrial, J.R.: The B-Book: Assigning Programs to Meanings. Cambridge University Press, Cambridge (1996)

26. Clearsy. http://www.clearsy.com/en/

27. Zhu, H., Qin, S., He, J., Bowen, J.: PTSC: probability, time and shared-variable concurrency. Innov. Syst. Softw. Eng. **5**, 271–284 (2009)

28. Zhu, H., Yang, F., He, J., Bowen, J., Sanders, J., Qin, S.: Linking operational semantics and algebraic semantics for a probabilistic timed shared-variable language. J. Log. Alg. Prog. **81**, 2–25 (2012)

Parametrized Verification

Applying Parametric Model-Checking Techniques for Reusing Real-Time Critical Systems

Baptiste Parquier[1,2(✉)], Laurent Rioux[1], Rafik Henia[1], Romain Soulat[1], Olivier H. Roux[2], Didier Lime[2], and Étienne André[2,3]

[1] THALES Research and Technology, 1 Avenue Augustin Fresnel,
91120 Palaiseau, France
[2] IRCCyN, 1 Rue de la Noë, 44300 Nantes, France
baptiste.parquier@eleves.ec-nantes.fr
[3] Université Paris 13, Sorbonne Paris Cité, LIPN, CNRS, UMR 7030,
93430 Villetaneuse, France

Abstract. Due to the increase of complexity in real-time safety-critical systems, verification and validation costs have significantly increased. A straightforward way to reduce costs is to reuse existing systems, adapting them to new requirements, so as to avoid new costly developments. Our aim is to verify during the development strategy definition phase whether the existing products can be reused and adapted for a new customer, by identifying key parameters to be tuned in order to reuse existing products. Performing efficient verification is therefore crucial.

In this paper, we focus on the performance requirement aspects. Nowadays, model-checking techniques have improved significantly to verify the performances of real-time systems. However, model-checking cannot address real-time systems where some timing constants are unknown or uncertain. Parametric model-checking leverage this shortcoming by identifying parameter ranges for which the system is correct. We report here on an experiment of the evaluation of the use of these formal techniques applied to automatize the synthesis of good parameter ranges for system reuse in the setting of the environment requirements for an aerial video tracking system.

Keywords: Real-time systems · Safety-critical systems · Formal methods · Parametric verification · Performance verification · Case study · Avionics

1 Introduction

Performance verification is a common discipline in system and software engineering. In practice, it is very common to spend a lot of effort in performance

This work is partially supported by the ANR national research program ANR-14-CE28-0002 PACS ("Parametric Analyses of Concurrent Systems").

© Springer International Publishing AG 2017
C. Artho and P.C. Ölveczky (Eds.): FTSCS 2016, CCIS 694, pp. 129–144, 2017.
DOI: 10.1007/978-3-319-53946-1_8

engineering especially for certified products. Standards specify a complete and precise safety process to follow in order to be certified (e. g., DO-178C in the avionics domain). There is a need to reduce the time and efforts related to design such real-time systems considering performance requirements. We would like to experiment and verify if the current state of the art on performance verification tools are able to cope with industrial needs. We will not address the whole performance engineering process. We will focus on the performance verification in a particular context: an industrial company plans to reuse an existing real-time safety-critical system for the needs of a new client to cut costs and delays. However, this client is coming with its own performance requirements that differs from what the system was originally designed for. Our use case is an aerial video tracking device. Its mission is safety-critical for the whole system and, therefore, has to be certified according to the DO-178C standard.

To this end, we have to demonstrate the software architecture meets the performance requirements, which implies that the system has to satisfy all the deadline requirements in all (and in particular the worst) situations.

A conventional way at THALES—but also in other industrial companies—to tackle this problem is to evaluate the performance of the current system. The system is taken as is and if it satisfies the client performance requirements, the system can be reused as it stands. If not, experts check how to modify environment parameters—typically sources of activation of the system—and try to identify a new configuration where the system can meet its new requirements. This is time consuming and costly. Therefore, generally only few configurations are tested and evaluated, and quite often, none of them meets the requirements. As a consequence when the activity is seen as too costly, the "reuse" strategy is dropped.

We report here on an experimentation to apply formal techniques on an aerial video tracking system by THALES, in a way to tool-up the identification of the good environment parameters to reuse the system. Our methodology is as follows:

1. We first identified the most appropriate formalisms and formal techniques to validate the performance and identify the good environment parameters: we chose to use parametric stopwatch automata (PSwAs) and parametric stopwatch Petri nets (PSwPNs), two formalisms for modeling and verifying preemptive real-time systems with parameters. These two formalisms benefit from state-of-the-art model-checkers (IMITATOR for PSwAs and ROMÉO for PSwPNs).

2. We then devised a way to model the system needed for performance validation, using the identified formalisms.

3. We then studied how to measure the trust in the results produced by IMITATOR and ROMÉO: In this regard, we exploit diversity: the use of several techniques giving the very same results is a great source of confidence. Nevertheless, diversity can only be reached if the alternatives used are truly different and cannot both fail due to some common weaknesses.

Organization of the Paper. Sect. 2 presents the aerial video tracking system developed by THALES, and its new requirements. Section 3 presents the state of the art of available verification techniques, in particular formal methods using parameterization. Section 4 introduces the tools ROMÉO and IMITATOR respectively for parametric stopwatch Petri nets and parametric stopwatch automata. Section 5 provides the modeling of the case-study into both formalisms. Finally we present experimental results in Sect. 6 and we conclude with Sect. 7.

2   Industrial Case-Study

2.1   Specifications

This case-study is an aerial video tracking system designed by THALES, used in intelligence, surveillance, reconnaissance, tactical and security applications. Figure 1 presents the two major functions of this system:

1. The video frame processing function, which receives frames from the camera and sends them to the cockpit to be displayed for the pilot.
2. The tracking and camera control function, which gives the control commands to the camera from the aircraft sensor data. The study focuses on this part of the system.

The objective of the tracking and camera control function is to control the camera position according to the plane trajectory. The camera has to always focus on the same target, whatever the plane trajectory is.

The system is characterized by strict constraints on timing. One major timing problem consists in calculating the timing latencies for the functions in the "Tracking and Camera control" part.

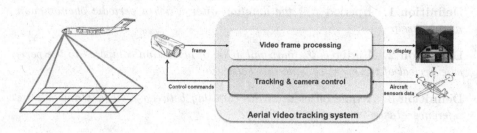

Fig. 1. Organization of the aerial video tracking system

"Tracking and Camera control" is decomposed in 4 subfunctions: Processing (T2), Target position prediction (T5), Tracking control (T6) and Camera control (T7). All sub-functions share the same computing resource, i. e., work on the same CPU. Figure 2 illustrates how all those sub-functions communicate with each other and how much time they require on the computing resource. (The red arrow in Fig. 2 is not considered for now, and will be used later on.)

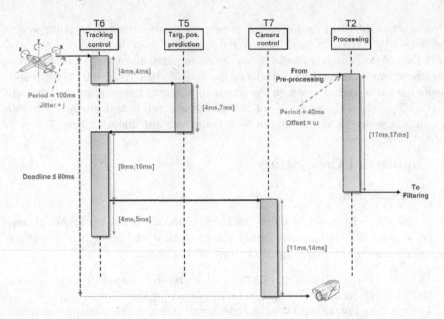

Fig. 2. Tracking and camera control: time description (Color figure online)

The system has the following characteristics:

- All tasks are triggered by the arrival of data at their inputs;
- There is a preemptive scheduling for the computing resource;
- Tasks are prioritized in this order: T2 > T6 > T5 > T7.

Let us now introduce various definitions.

Definition 1. *A period τ is the duration after which a periodic phenomenon repeats itself.*

Definition 2. *A jitter is the maximal delay of activation compared to the periodic arrival of the event causing this activation.*

Definition 3. *A time offset ω is the time lag between an event and a time reference—taken arbitrarily.*

Definition 4. *In a system, a stimulus is an external activation that periodically sends a signal to one or multiple tasks. It is fully characterized by: 1. A period, 2. A jitter, 3. A time offset.*

Example 1. In our case-study, there are two stimuli as shown in Fig. 2:

- The first one activating T6—tracking control: period 100 ms, jitter j, no offset—this stimulus is chosen as reference,
- The second one activating T2—processing: period 40 ms, no jitter, offset $ω$.

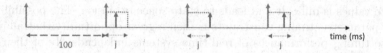

Fig. 3. A 30 ms jitter on a 100 ms period stimulus (Color figure online)

Example 2. Figure 3 illustrates a periodic stimulus with a period of 100 ms and a jitter j, that activates a task. The periodic stimulus sends data to the task in order to activate it (blue arrows in Fig. 3). Because of the jitter, the activation of the task happens between 0 and j time units after the stimulus (red arrows).

The jitter j represents a potential delay due to the communication network in the aircraft. It is not something that can be determined at design time: the best a designer can do is to take into account that there will be a possible delay in the final system and ensure the system will behave according to the requirements whatever the jitter is. Until now, system environment ensured that:

$$j = 30\,\text{ms}$$

The offset ω might be used to change the reference between T6's and T2's activations. An offset is something the designer can tune to ensure the system good behavior.

2.2 Main Objective

Our main objective is to reuse an existing system for new customers, which means the system has to meet all new performance requirements. More precisely, in this experiment, we consider the situation where a new customer wants to modify the following requirement to the aerial video tracking system: "The end-to-end latency between the activation of task T6 and the termination of task T7 shall be lower than 80 ms." The new end-to-end latency requirement is depicted in red in Fig. 2.

Our aim is to compute new timing specifications of the system so that this additional requirement can be met. However, the heart of the system must not change. As the system is expected to be reused as is, we can only modify the timing specifications of external activations: tune the offset between stimuli, or change the jitter requirements.

2.3 Our Constraints: A Parametric Approach

In our case study, jitter and offset can be seen as parameters. Moreover, even timing properties can be expressed parametrically, as timing constraints make sense only in the context of a given concrete environment. For example, a maximal delay of the system response has to be at most two times the minimal delay, or the transmission time in the communication protocol could be left as a parameter. Performing non-parametric model-checking of the systems for different concrete values is difficult and leads to state-space explosion. The possibility to specify parametric timing constraints is then a great opportunity that allows to evaluate timing performances of real-time systems independently of their particular implementation.

We summarize the main needs for a parametric approach:

- Parameters allow to cope with the early uncertainties in developing an industrial system;
- Parameters allow to investigate robustness of some of the design choices;
- If the system is proven wrong, the whole verification process has to be carried out again;
- Considering a wide range of values for constants allows for a more flexible and robust design.

3 Related Works

3.1 Response Time and Latency Analysis

As mentioned in [21], many research papers have already addressed the problem of parametric schedulability analysis, especially on single processor systems. Bini and Buttazzo [10] proposed an analysis of fixed priority single processor systems, which is used as a basis for this paper.

Parameter sensitivity can be also be carried out by repeatedly applying classical schedulability tests, like the holistic analysis [19]. One example of this approach is used in the MAST tool [13], in which it is possible to compute the *slack* (i. e., the percentage of variation) with respect to one parameter for single processor and for distributed systems by applying binary search in that parameter space [19].

A similar approach is followed by the SymTA/S tool [14], which is based on the *event-stream* model [20]. Another interesting approach is the Modular Performance Analysis (MPA) [23], which is based on Real-Time Calculus. In both cases, the analysis is compositional, therefore less complex than the holistic analysis. In [16], a real time system is modeled using a high level variant of timed automata including design timed parameters and is analyzed using the UPPAAL tool. Nevertheless, these approaches are not fully parametric, in the sense that it is necessary to repeat the analysis for every combination of parameter values in order to obtain the schedulability region.

3.2 Parametric Formalisms for Real-Time Systems

The literature proposes mainly two formalisms to model and verify systems with timing parameters: parametric timed automata [3] and parametric time Petri nets [22]. Both formalisms are subject to strong undecidability results, even with low numbers of parameters [18], syntactic restrictions such as strict constraints [12], or with restricted parameter domains, such as bounded rationals [18], or (unbounded) integers [3] (see [5] for a survey). Undecidability is not necessarily a problem: semi-algorithms were defined (e. g., [3,6,15]) and safe under-approximations were also proposed (e. g., [8,15]).

For many real-time systems, in particular when subject to preemptive scheduling, these formalisms are not expressive enough. As a consequence, we therefore use extensions of parametric timed automata and parametric time Petri nets augmented with stopwatches, yielding parametric stopwatch automata [21], and parametric stopwatch Petri nets [22].

To the best of our knowledge, the only tools using as basis formalism these two formalisms are IMITATOR [7] for parametric stopwatch automata, and ROMÉO [17] for parametric stopwatch Petri nets. In this work, we evaluate the capabilities of both tools using the industrial case study.

4   Tools

We briefly present both tools in the following. Using tools is an opportunity to increase the confidence in our results. We believe this offers us the diversity we seek for in our approach, because the tools are developed by different teams, and based on different theories: parametric stopwatch Petri nets vs. parametric stopwatch automata, that implies different models.

By doing that, the confidence one can have in both tools increases considerably: if both tools give the same results, the odds that they are both wrong is clearly very low, and therefore the confidence is high.

4.1   ROMÉO

ROMÉO[1] [17] is a software studio for parametric analysis of time Petri nets and some of their hybrid extensions (such as parametric stopwatch Petri nets). It is available for Linux, MacOSX and Windows platforms and consists of a graphical user interface (GUI) to edit and design PSwPNs, and a computation engine.

ROMÉO supports the use of parametric linear expressions in the time intervals of the transitions, and allows to add linear constraints on the parameters to restrict their domain. Finally, ROMÉO provides a simulator and an integrated TCTL model-checker [11].

4.2   IMITATOR

IMITATOR[2] [7] is a software for parametric verification and robustness analysis of real-time systems. It relies on the formalism of networks of parametric timed automata, augmented with integer variables and stopwatches. Parameters can be used both in the model and in the properties.

IMITATOR is fully written in OCaml, and makes use of the Parma Polyhedra Library [9]. It is available under the GNU General Public License.

---

[1] http://romeo.rts-software.org.
[2] http://www.imitator.fr.

5 Modeling the Case-Study

Modeling the system in both tools was one of the challenges of this work. Each theory has its particularities, and translating the case-study specifications according to the associated theory was sometimes problematic. This part presents the modeling choice we made to obtain an equivalent model of the aerial video tracking system, both with ROMÉO and IMITATOR.

Modeling reentrancy. In our models, we decompose the task T6—tracking control—in three different tasks:

– T6_1, duration [4, 4] ms
– T6_2, duration [9, 10] ms
– T6_3, duration [4, 5] ms

This decomposition simplifies the analysis of the transmission of data between T6, T5 and T7—shown Fig. 2. Indeed, with this modification there is no more transmission inside a task. However, the system's behavior needs to stay unmodified: there can not be two cycles T6_1 to T6_3 overlapping. After an activation of T6—i. e., T6_1—it is impossible to have a new one before its termination—i. e., T6_3 termination.

Definition 5. *We define a cycle between two tasks T and T'—T causing the activation of T'—as the time elapsed between the activation of task T and the termination of T' caused by this activation.*

The phenomenon of overlapped cycles is called *reentrancy*, e. g., when there are at least two T6's activation before any T7's termination.

5.1 ROMÉO

We give in Fig. 4 the rules that we use to translate the aerial video tracking system into PSwPNs. Each element needed in the system—task, stimulus, synchronization (blue arc) and priority (red arc)[3]—is translated (in that order). The whole formal model is constructed by linking by an arc the elements (pattern) constituting the system. As an example, for the periodic task $T2$, the *Periodic Stimulus* pattern is linked to the *Task* pattern by an arc between *Jitter_transition* to *Task_place*. According to these few rules, we obtained a PSwPN net modelling the case-study.

Remark 1. In ROMÉO, there is no explicit time unit: it is inherent to the model. Every duration in the case-study is in ms, so the time value given by ROMÉO will be in ms.

---

[3] The use of timed (resp. discrete) inhibitor arc (red arc) leads to the modeling of preemptive (resp. non-preemptive) scheduling.

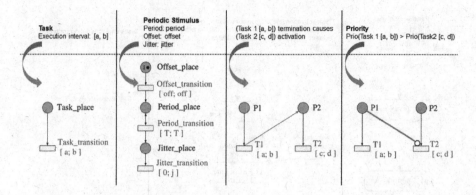

Fig. 4. Translating the system (top) into ROMÉO (bottom) (Color figure online)

In this model, there are two parameters: *jitter*—corresponding to the maximal delay j of the first stimulus defined in Sect. 2.1—and *offset*—corresponding to the offset ω of the second stimulus.

To be consistent with the case-study, the following constraints are defined:

$$jitter \leq 30 \quad \& \quad offset \in [0, 40) \tag{1}$$

Remark 2. There is no need for a larger range for the offset: T2 is activated every 40 ms (periodic stimulus), so we review all possible cases with these bounds.

To be able to compute a latency, an observer is needed.[4] An observer is another time Petri net linked to the initial net that needs to be observed. It does not change the behavior of the observed part, and—by asking the right property to the model-checker and thanks to a parameter—it allows to compute the worst latency between two tasks.

5.2 IMITATOR

We give in Fig. 5 the translation rules to build the IMITATOR model. Constraints on the model are defined in the same way as with ROMÉO in Eq. (1). The whole formal model is constructed by synchronizing the elements (pattern) constituting the system. The IMITATOR synchronization model is such that all PSwAs declaring an action must synchronize together on this action. As an example, for the periodic task $T2$, the *Periodic Stimulus* pattern is synchronized with the *Task* pattern by the *activate_task* action.

Remark 3. As in ROMÉO, there is no explicit time unit in IMITATOR.

---

[4] Observers (also called testing automata) were studied in [1,2], and a library of common observers was proposed in [4].

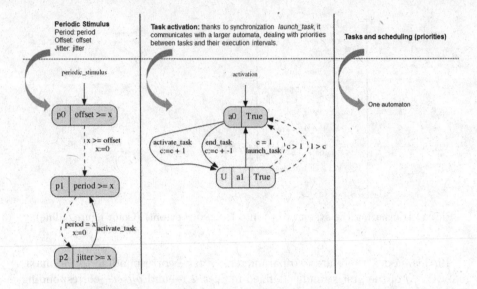

Fig. 5. Translating the system (top) into IMITATOR (bottom)

6   Experiment Results

6.1   Hardware

The computation was conducted on a regular personal computer running Linux 64 bits 3.10 GHz and 4 GiB memory. Models and experiment results are available at www.imitator.fr/FTSCS16.

For our analysis, as explained in Sect. 2.2, we are interested in checking that the worst-case end-to-end latency—from activation of the Tracking control task to termination of the Camera control task as defined in Sect. 2.1—does not exceed 80 ms.

6.2   Worst-Case Scenario

We have computed the worst latency for the basic configuration: i.e., with a 30 ms jitter – the activation of T6 in Fig. 2 may happen between 0 and 30 ms after the arrival of the stimulus. If this worst latency between the T6's activation and T7's termination is less than 80 ms, this configuration of the system meets the requirements.

Table 1 presents the results obtained with both ROMÉO and IMITATOR. In this table and the following, the *Performance ratio* denotes a comparison between the computing times of the two tools. The fastest is taken as reference.

Both tools give the same result: the worst time is 117 ms. It is really reassuring. As explained in Sect. 4, this allows the designer to have a strong confidence in this result.

Table 1. Case-study: 30 ms jitter, no offset

Worst-case end-to-end latency		
Software	ROMÉO	IMITATOR
Response	**117 ms =**	**117 ms**
Memory	16.2 MB	342.3 MB
Computing time	0.6 s	34.3 s
Performance ratio (time)	1	57

The used tools are able to produce traces for the worst cases. This is of prime interest for someone designing a system as it allows him to understand the existing bottlenecks and to be able to easily address them.

Figure 6 shows this worst-case scenario. The worst time is reached because of reentrancy when all tasks have their longest duration. Indeed, the task T7—the one with the lowest priority—does not have the time to end before the launching of a new cycle. It is then preempted by all the other tasks. The reentrancy is possible because of the jitter. There are only 70 ms between both activations of task T6 (tracking control).

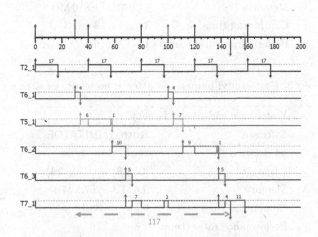

Fig. 6. Gantt chart of the worst-case scenario

Moreover, the end-to-end delay requirement given by the client is not met.

$$117 \text{ ms} > 80 \text{ ms}$$

In the next part, we investigate if the modification of environment parameters could fix it.

6.3   Exploitation of Parameters

In this part, we are interested in addressing the capabilities of the tools to explore different parameter valuations in order to meet requirements. As presented in Sect. 2, to modify the external sources of activations—i. e., stimuli—we have two parameters we can operate on: the offset ω between the stimuli, and the jitter j before the activation of T6—tracking control. As a consequence, the designer is allowed to change the value of the offset in order to meet the end-to-end requirements. Otherwise, (s)he has to fix the maximal jitter the system can tolerate according to the same requirements.

The results (condition on both parameters ω and j) of Table 4 are more general and covers the results of the previous two. However, Tables 2 and 3 allow to compare the tools and to understand the compromise between the relevance of the result and the memory and the computing time required to obtain this result.

Table 2. Case-study: 30 ms jitter, parametric offset

Worst-case end-to-end latency		
Software	Roméo	IMITATOR
$wt \leq 80$ ms	$\bot$ $=$ $\bot$	
Memory	64.0 MB	1,816 MB
Computing time	3.3 s	3 min 35 s
Performance ratio (time)	1	65

Table 3. Case-study: parametric jitter j, no offset, $wt \leq 80$ ms

Worst-case end-to-end latency		
Software	Roméo	IMITATOR
$wt \leq 80$ ms	**true** $=$ **true**	
j (ms)	**[0, 26)** $\Leftrightarrow$ **[0, 26)**	
Memory	9.6 MB	267.8 MB
Computing time	0.5 s	38.1 s
Performance ratio (time)	1	76

Offset Only. We are now interested in finding a constraint on the offset such that the 80 ms requirement is met. The observer is set to check that the end-to-end delay is below 80 ms. The offset between the two tasks is set as a parameter. The model checkers will produce a constraint on the offset such that the requirement is always met.

Both model-checkers output $\bot$, which denotes that no parameter valuations are such that the system meets the performance requirement. This means that no offset valuation can satisfy this requirement.

Remark 4. We have run a full analysis, performed by parameterizing both the offset and the end-to-end delay in the observer: this analysis, in fact, showed that no matter the offset, the worst case will always be 117 ms.

This ability to produce a negative result is also of prime interest for a system architect. It allows to reduce the design exploration time. In this case, the architect knows that tweaking the offset will never be successful.

Since acting on the offset was not enough, reducing the jitter's specification becomes essential.

Reducing the Jitter. In this part, we explore another part of the design space: reducing the jitter. We are interested in finding jitter valuations that allows the system to meet its end-to-end maximal delay requirement. If we find a working configuration, we will take the highest authorised jitter's value to put in the new requirements: it gives more flexibility to the system, allowing more flexibility for the external sources of events.

Jitter Only. In this part, we only use one parameter for the jitter's value:

$$j \in [0, 30] \text{ ms, } \textit{the offset is set at } \omega = 0$$

Once again, the results are still the same for both tools. According to Table 3: *to meet its requirement, the system shall have a jitter $j \in [0, 26)$ ms if the offset is left at $\omega = 0$.*

However, reducing the jitter can be expensive. We will investigate the possibility to have a higher jitter value by allowing a different offset ω.

Offset and Jitter. In this part, we parametrize both the offset ω, and the jitter j—there are now two parameters in our models. To reduce the state-space, we add the following constraints:

$$\omega \in [0, 40) \text{ ms } \& \quad j \in [0, 30] \text{ ms} \tag{2}$$

In Table 4 are the results we obtained using this configuration: once again, both tools agreed.

Table 4. Case-study: 2 parameters (jitter j & offset ω), $wt \le 80$ ms

Worst-case end-to-end latency			
$wt \le 80$ ms	**true**	**true**	**true**
ω (ms)	[0, 6)	[0, 26)	[0, 40)
j (ms)	[0, 29)	[0, 29)	[0, 26)
Condition	$-j + \omega > -23$	$-j + \omega > -3$	none
ROMÉO	Memory: 117.3 MB—Computing time: 7.5 s		
IMITATOR	Memory: 2,017 MB—Computing time: 6 min 36 s		

For a system architect point of view, having the full constraints allows to make smart industrial choices. With these results, one of the smartest thing to do in order to have *worst time* $\leq$ 80 ms is, for example, to use 6 ms offset with 28 ms jitter. These two values are allowed by the results model-checkers gave us, and it is one of the highest jitter we can have.

6.4   Tool Comparison

In our experimentations, ROMÉO has always performed better than IMITATOR in terms of time and memory consumption. Therefore, ROMÉO seems to be a promising tool for future industrial use. It would be interesting to know why there is such a gap between these model-checkers, although they use a very similar notion of symbolic state, and a common internal representation using the Parma Polyhedra Library [9]. Here are some hypotheses:

- Both PSwAs and PSwPNs use *clocks*, i. e., real-valued variables. The number of clocks significantly impacts the model checking performance. A main difference is that clocks are created statically in PSwAs (hence in IMITATOR), whereas they are dynamic in PSwPNs (hence in ROMÉO) and are therefore fewer in this latter case.
- The reentrancy phenomenon is well managed in ROMÉO, thanks to the Petri net theory—it is just multiple tokens in one place—whereas in IMITATOR, the reentrancy is made possible by adding variables and automata, which necessarily impacts the efficiency.

In addition, note that the distributed capabilities of IMITATOR were not used in our comparison.

Nevertheless, IMITATOR and ROMÉO gave us the same results: this is crucial for confidence in our results. Tool redundancy is used in some certification processes to lower the certification level needed for each tool. Having several tools with distinct underlying techniques, formalisms, and libraries that output the same results, can help in cheaper certifications.

7   Conclusion

In this paper, we faced a concrete industrial need concerning an aerial video tracking system made by THALES: can this system meet an additional end-to-end delay?

With our study, we used parametric model checking to investigate possible designs and answer this question. We used two different tools using formal methods—IMITATOR and ROMÉO. By doing that, and checking certain properties on our models, we have now a precise idea of what we have to do to respect this requirement. Moreover, both tools drew the same conclusions: that is reassuring, both for these two tools and for our models. More important, it also validates the estimated performances presented in this paper.

This kind of approach was able to give us solutions to our questions. Even if there is no certification yet, this study allows to glimpse the potential of model-checking techniques using parameters for industrial use.

In the future, THALES R&D engineers want to promote the use of model-checking software for industrial practices, and implement it in design and analysis tools already available. Therefore, the next step is to test the limitation of the selected tool: by creating models with a large pallet of specifications, and see if the model-checker can manage every feature. If the tool passes the exam, there is an upscaling process: from any system modeled with THALES' tool, automatically generate a model fit for our model-checker.

Acknowledgment. The authors would like to thank Violette Lecointre for her participation at modeling the case-study with ROMÉO.

References

1. Aceto, L., Bouyer, P., Burgueño, A., Larsen, K.G.: The power of reachability testing for timed automata. In: Arvind, V., Ramanujam, S. (eds.) FSTTCS 1998. LNCS, vol. 1530, pp. 245–256. Springer, Heidelberg (1998). doi:10.1007/978-3-540-49382-2_22
2. Aceto, L., Burgueño, A., Larsen, K.G.: Model checking via reachability testing for timed automata. In: Steffen, B. (ed.) TACAS 1998. LNCS, vol. 1384, pp. 263–280. Springer, Heidelberg (1998). doi:10.1007/BFb0054177
3. Alur, R., Henzinger, T.A., Vardi, M.Y.: Parametric real-time reasoning. In: STOC, pp. 592–601. ACM (1993)
4. André, É.: Observer patterns for real-time systems. In: ICECCS, pp. 125–134. IEEE Computer Society (2013)
5. André, É.: What's decidable about parametric timed automata? In: Artho, C., Ölveczky, P.C. (eds.) FTSCS 2015. CCIS, vol. 596, pp. 52–68. Springer, Heidelberg (2016). doi:10.1007/978-3-319-29510-7_3
6. André, É., Chatain, T., Encrenaz, E., Fribourg, L.: An inverse method for parametric timed automata. Int. J. Found. Comput. Sci. **20**(5), 819–836 (2009)
7. André, É., Fribourg, L., Kühne, U., Soulat, R.: IMITATOR 2.5: a tool for analyzing robustness in scheduling problems. In: Giannakopoulou, D., Méry, D. (eds.) FM 2012. LNCS, vol. 7436, pp. 33–36. Springer, Heidelberg (2012). doi:10.1007/978-3-642-32759-9_6
8. André, É., Lime, D., Roux, O.H.: Integer-complete synthesis for bounded parametric timed automata. In: Bojańczyk, M., Lasota, S., Potapov, I. (eds.) RP 2015. LNCS, vol. 9328, pp. 7–19. Springer, Heidelberg (2015). doi:10.1007/978-3-319-24537-9_2
9. Bagnara, R., Hill, P.M., Zaffanella, E.: The Parma Polyhedra Library: toward a complete set of numerical abstractions for the analysis and verification of hardware and software systems. Sci. Comput. Program. **72**(1–2), 3–21 (2008)
10. Bini, E.: The design domain of real-time systems. PhD thesis, Scuola Superiore Sant'Anna (2004)
11. Boucheneb, H., Gardey, G., Roux, O.H.: TCTL model checking of time Petri nets. J. Logic Comput. **19**(6), 1509–1540 (2009)
12. Doyen, L.: Robust parametric reachability for timed automata. Inf. Process. Lett. **102**(5), 208–213 (2007)

13. González Harbour, M., Gutiérrez García, J.J., Palencia Gutiérrez, J.C., Drake Moyano, J.M.: MAST: modeling and analysis suite for real time applications. In: ECRTS, pp. 125–134. IEEE Computer Society (2001)

14. Henia, R., Hamann, A., Jersak, M., Racu, R., Richter, K., Ernst, R.: System level performance analysis - the SymTA/S approach. IEE Proc. Comput. Digital Tech. **152**(2), 148–166 (2005)

15. Jovanović, A., Lime, D., Roux, O.H.: Integer parameter synthesis for real-time systems. IEEE Trans. Softw. Eng. **41**(5), 445–461 (2015)

16. Le, T.T.H., Palopoli, L., Passerone, R., Ramadian, Y.: Timed-automata based schedulability analysis for distributed firm real-time systems: a case study. Int. J. Softw. Tools Technol. Transf. **15**(3), 211–228 (2013)

17. Lime, D., Roux, O.H., Seidner, C., Traonouez, L.-M.: Romeo: a parametric model-checker for petri nets with stopwatches. In: Kowalewski, S., Philippou, A. (eds.) TACAS 2009. LNCS, vol. 5505, pp. 54–57. Springer, Heidelberg (2009). doi:10.1007/978-3-642-00768-2_6

18. Miller, J.S.: Decidability and complexity results for timed automata and semi-linear hybrid automata. In: Lynch, N., Krogh, B.H. (eds.) HSCC 2000. LNCS, vol. 1790, pp. 296–310. Springer, Heidelberg (2000). doi:10.1007/3-540-46430-1_26

19. Palencia Gutiérrez, J.C., González Harbour, M.: Schedulability analysis for tasks with static and dynamic offsets. In: IEEE Real-Time Systems Symposium, pp. 26–37. IEEE Computer Society (1998)

20. Richter, K., Ernst, R.: Event model interfaces for heterogeneous system analysis. In: DATE, pp. 506–513. IEEE Computer Society (2002)

21. Sun, Y., Soulat, R., Lipari, G., André, É., Fribourg, L.: Parametric schedulability analysis of fixed priority real-time distributed systems. In: Artho, C., Ölveczky, P.C. (eds.) FTSCS 2013. CCIS, vol. 419, pp. 212–228. Springer, Heidelberg (2014). doi:10.1007/978-3-319-05416-2_14

22. Traonouez, L.-M., Lime, D., Roux, O.H.: Parametric model-checking of stopwatch Petri nets. J. Univ. Comput. Sci. **15**(17), 3273–3304 (2009)

23. Wandeler, E., Thiele, L., Verhoef, M., Lieverse, P.: System architecture evaluation using modular performance analysis: a case study. Int. J. Softw. Tools Technol. Transf. **8**(6), 649–667 (2006)

Parameterised Verification of Stabilisation Properties via Conditional Spotlight Abstraction

Nils Timm[(⊠)] and Stefan Gruner

Department of Computer Science, University of Pretoria, Pretoria, South Africa
{ntimm,sgruner}@cs.up.ac.za

Abstract. Parameterised verification means to check properties of an arbitrary number of uniform processes composed in parallel. We introduce an approach to parameterised verification of stabilisation properties. Our approach exploits the fact that stabilisation happens *incrementally*, and thus, also can be verified incrementally. We systematically search for a provable *partial* stabilisation property and then verify *full* stabilisation under the assumption of partial stabilisation. In order to prove partial stabilisation we use a novel *stabilisation cutoff* technique. A proven partial stabilisation property allows us to apply our new technique *conditional spotlight abstraction* (CSA). CSA summarises an arbitrary number of processes into a finite model such that verification can be performed via model checking. Based on a prototype tool we were able to verify several protocols implemented as parameterised systems.

1 Introduction

Parameterised systems consist of an unbounded number of uniform processes running in parallel in an asynchronous interleaving fashion. Practical examples can be found in all sorts of distributed algorithms, like mutual exclusion or leader election. Such systems are often charged with safety-critical computations. Thus, techniques for establishing the correctness of parameterised systems are of great importance. Correctness is typically defined in terms of temporal logic properties. Parameterised verification involves to check whether certain properties hold regardless of the number of processes in the system, which is undecidable in general. Existing approaches are typically incomplete or restricted to certain properties and classes of systems. Even if a method principally allows to solve a verification task, efficiency is still a matter, since the practical applicability of verification techniques is limited by the state explosion problem.

Here we introduce an automatic technique for parameterised verification of stabilisation properties under fairness. Stabilisation is a liveness property and thus particularly hard to verify. It claims that all computations of a system will eventually reach a desired configuration and remain there forever. Hence, stabilisation can capture properties like the absence of deadlocks and livelocks, or the achievement of self-stabilisation in fault-tolerant systems. Our technique exploits the fact that stabilisation happens *incrementally*, and thus, also can be verified incrementally. We first determine a provable *partial* stabilisation

© Springer International Publishing AG 2017
C. Artho and P.C. Ölveczky (Eds.): FTSCS 2016, CCIS 694, pp. 145–160, 2017.
DOI: 10.1007/978-3-319-53946-1_9

property and then verify *full* stabilisation under the assumption of partial stabilisation. Our approach allows us to reduce parameterised verification to a fixed number of model checking runs on small models. As an illustrating example we consider a leader election system composed of a parameterised number of processes $P_1 \parallel \ldots \parallel P_n$ where the property of interest is of the form:

$$stabilisation \; \equiv \; \mathbf{F}\underbrace{\Big((\mathbf{G}\,leader)[1] \wedge (\mathbf{G}\,terminated)[n-1]\Big)}_{stability}$$

which expresses that *eventually* one process will be the leader forever and $n-1$ processes will be terminated forever. Stabilisation happens incrementally in the sense that some form of partial stability will always arise before (full) stability will arise. A partial stabilisation property corresponding to our example may look as follows: $partial\,stabilisation \; \equiv \; \mathbf{F}\underbrace{\Big((\mathbf{G}\,terminated)[n-d]\Big)}_{partial\,stability}$

Thus, we expect that eventually $n-d$ processes will be terminated forever before full stability arises. Verifying partial stabilisation is also undecidable, but we will see that it is typically more likely and less computationally expensive to achieve a definite outcome in checking partial stabilisation than in directly checking full stabilisation. In our approach we systematically search for a provable property $\mathbf{F}(partial\,stability)$ corresponding to the full stabilisation property of interest. In order to prove $\mathbf{F}(partial\,stability)$ we use a novel *stabilisation cutoff detection* technique. Cutoffs [8] refer to the size of an instance of a parameterised system that is sufficiently large to check a certain property and to transfer the result to all larger instances. Once some $\mathbf{F}(partial\,stability)$ is proven, we check for full stabilisation under the assumption that *partial stability* holds. For verification under assumptions we have developed *conditional spotlight abstraction* (CSA). CSA is a technique based on 3-valued abstraction [12] that allows to construct a finite abstraction of a parameterised system by summarising certain processes into an approximative component. Summarising processes involves a loss of information. However, a key feature of CSA is that an already proven property can be used as a condition over the summarised processes, which allows to preserve significantly more information compared to an unconditional abstraction. Since CSA yields a sound 3-valued approximation, definite verification results obtained for the abstraction can be transferred to the original parameterised system.

With our approach we provide an automatic and efficient solution to parameterised verification of stabilisation properties. The efficiency of our approach results from the fact that we split the overall verification task into the verification of partial stabilisation and the verification of full stabilisation assuming partial stabilisation. For solving the sub tasks we developed the specially tailored techniques *stabilisation cutoff detection* and *conditional spotlight abstraction*. This allows us to reduce parameterised verification to a fixed number of model checking runs on small system instances resp. abstractions. Since we deal with an undecidable problem, our method is not complete and thus might not always terminate with a result. However, based on a prototype tool we were able to successfully verify several network protocols implemented as parameterised systems. Preliminary experiments show promising performance results.

2   Basic Definitions

We start with the systems we consider. A *parameterised system* $Sys(n)$ consists of $n > 1$ uniform processes composed in parallel: $Sys(n) = \|_{i=1}^{n} P_i$. It is defined over a set of variables $V = V_g \cup V_l \times \{1, \ldots, n\}$ where V_g is a set of global variables and V_l is a set of local variables with an indexed copy (V_l, i) for each processes P_i. The state space over V corresponds to the set S_V of all type-correct valuations of the variables. Given a state $s_V \in S_V$ and an expression e over V, then $s_V(e)$ denotes the valuation of e in s_V. An example system implementing a simple leader election protocol is shown in Fig. 1.

y : **semaphore where** $y = true$;
$turn$: **bool where** $turn = true$;
$done$: **bool where** $done = true$;

$$\|_{i=1}^{n} P_i ::$$

```
loop forever do
  0: acquire y;
  1: if(turn)
    2: turn := false;
    3: done := false;
    4: release y;
    5: await done;
    6: release y;
  else
    7: turn := true;
    8: done := true;
    9: loop forever do
        [Terminated]
```

Fig. 1. Example system.   **Fig. 2.** Control flow representation.

We have n replicated processes operating on the global variables y, $turn$ and $done$. There are no explicit local variables in this example, but we regard the processes' location counters as special local variables. Each P_i can be formally represented as a *control flow graph* (CFG) $G_i = (Loc_i, \delta_i, \tau_i)$ where Loc_i is a set of control locations, $\delta_i \subseteq Loc_i \times Loc_i$ is a transition relation, and $\tau_i : Loc_i \times Loc_i \to Op_i$ is a function labelling transitions with operations from a set Op_i:

Definition 1 (Operations). *Let $V_g \cup (V_l, i) = \{v_1, \ldots, v_m\}$ be the variables associated with a process P_i. The set of operations Op_i of P_i on these variables consists of statements of the form $assume(e) : v_1 := e_1, \ldots, v_m := e_m$ where $e, e_1, \ldots, e_m$ are expressions over $V_g \cup (V_l, i)$.*

Hence, an operation consists of a guard and an assignment part. We sometimes just write e instead of $assume(e)$. We omit the guard if it is *true*. Moreover, we just write *skip* if there is neither a guard nor an assignment part. A CFG G_i corresponding to the processes of the example system is depicted in Fig. 2. G_i also illustrates the semantics of the operations *acquire*, *release* and *await*.

We assume that a deterministic initialisation is given by an assertion $\varphi = \varphi_g \wedge \bigwedge_{i=1}^{n} \varphi_i$ over V such that φ_g initialises the global variables and each φ_i uniformly initialises the counters and local variables of the processes. For our example we assume $\varphi = (y \wedge turn \wedge done \wedge \bigwedge_{i=1}^{n}(loc_i = 0))$ where loc_i is the location counter of P_i. A computation of a system corresponds to a sequence where in each step one process is non-deterministically selected and the operation at its current location is attempted to be executed. If the execution is not blocked by a guard, the variables are updated according to the assignment part and the process advances to the consequent location. The overall state space S corresponds to the state set over V combined with the possible locations, i.e., $S = \times_{i=1}^{n} Loc_i \times S_V$. Hence, each $s \in S$ is a tuple $s = \langle l_1, \ldots, l_n, s_V \rangle$ where each $l_i \in Loc_i$ and $s_V \in S_V$. As state space models we use Kripke structures (KS).

Definition 2 (Kripke Structure). *A Kripke structure over a set of atomic predicates AP is a tuple $M = (S, S_0, R, L)$ where*

- *S is a set of states with a subset $S_0 \subseteq S$ of initial states,*
- *$R \subseteq S \times S$ is a total transition relation,*
- *$L : S \times AP \to \{true, false\}$ is a function labelling states with predicates.*

A path π of a Kripke structure is an infinite sequence of states $s_0 s_1 s_2 \ldots$ with $s_0 \in S_0$ and $R(s_i, s_{i+1})$. π_i denotes the i-th state of π whereas π^i denotes the i-th suffix $\pi_i \pi_{i+1} \pi_{i+2} \ldots$ of π. Moreover, $\Pi_M^{S_0}$ denotes the set of *all* paths starting in S_0 of M. A system can be represented as a Kripke structure as follows:

Definition 3 (Systems as Kripke Structures). *Let $Sys(n) = \|_{i=1}^{n} P_i$ be a system over V where each P_i is given by a CFG $G_i = (Loc_i, \delta_i, \tau_i)$. Let $Pred$ be a predicate set over V and let φ be an initialisation predicate. The corresponding KS is $M = (S, S_0, R, L)$ over $AP = Pred \cup \{(loc_i = j) | i \in [1..n], j \in Loc_i\}$ with*

- *$S := \times_{i=1}^{n} Loc_i \times S_V$,*
- *$S_0 := \{s \in S | s(\varphi) = true\}$,*
- *$R(\langle l_1 \ldots, l_n, s_V \rangle, \langle l_1' \ldots, l_n', s_V' \rangle) := \bigvee_{i=1}^{n}(R_i(\langle l_i, s_V \rangle, \langle l_i', s_V' \rangle) \wedge \bigwedge_{j \neq i}(l_j = l_j' \wedge \bigwedge_{v \in (V_l, j)} s_V(v) = s_V'(v)))$*
  where
  $R_i(\langle l_i, s_V \rangle, \langle l_i', s_V' \rangle) = \delta_i(l_i, l_i') \wedge s_V(e) \wedge \bigwedge_{k=1}^{m} s_V'(v_k) = s_V(e_k)$
  assuming that $\tau_i(l_i, l_i') = assume(e) : v_1 := e_1, \ldots, v_m := e_m,$

– $L(\langle l_1 \ldots, l_n, s_V \rangle, p) := s_V(p)$ *for any $p \in Pred$,*

– $L(\langle l_1 \ldots, l_n, s_V \rangle, (loc_i = j)) := \begin{cases} true & if \ l_i = j \\ false & else \end{cases}$.

Representing a system as a KS typically involves the application of *predicate abstraction* [3]. Since our example system is solely defined over variables with a *Boolean* domain, we can directly take the variables as predicates, i.e., $Pred := V$. Paths of KS are considered for the evaluation of temporal logic properties. Here we consider the temporal logic LTL.

Definition 4 (LTL Model Checking). *Let $M = (S, S_0, R, L)$ over AP be a KS. Then the evaluation of an LTL formula Ψ over AP on a path $\pi \in \Pi_M$, written $[\pi \models \Psi]$, is defined as follows*

$$
\begin{aligned}
[\pi \models p] &:= L(\pi_0, p) \\
[\pi \models \neg\Psi] &:= \neg[\pi \models \Psi] \\
[\pi \models \Psi \wedge \Psi'] &:= [\pi \models \Psi] \wedge [\pi \models \Psi'] \\
[\pi \models \mathbf{G}\,\Psi] &:= \bigwedge_{i\in\mathbb{N}} [\pi^i \models \Psi] \\
[\pi \models \mathbf{F}\,\Psi] &:= \bigvee_{i\in\mathbb{N}} [\pi^i \models \Psi] \\
[\pi \models \Psi\,\mathbf{U}\,\Psi'] &:= \bigvee_{i\in\mathbb{N}} \left([\pi^i \models \Psi'] \wedge \bigwedge_{0 \leq j < i} [\pi^j \models \Psi] \right)
\end{aligned}
$$

Evaluating Ψ on entire KS is model checking*: $[M, S_0 \models \Psi] := \bigwedge_{\pi \in \Pi_M^{S_0}} [\pi \models \Psi]$.*

Thus, given a system $Sys(n)$, an initialisation predicate φ, a set AP, and $\Psi \in$ LTL, we can construct the corresponding KS M and check whether $[M, S_0 \models \Psi]$ holds. This tells us whether the system satisfies the property specified by Ψ or not. For convenience, we typically just write $[Sys(n), \varphi \models \Psi]$ when we refer to the associated model checking problem. In *parameterised verification* one wants to show that a property holds for *all* possible instances of a system:

$$
\forall n > 1 : [Sys(n), \varphi_g \wedge \bigwedge_{i=1}^{n} \varphi_i \models \Psi]
$$

We implicitly assume *strong fairness* for all verification tasks, i.e., each operation that is infinitely often enabled will be infinitely often executed:

$$
fair \equiv \bigwedge_{i=1}^{n} \bigwedge_{(l_i, l_i') \in \delta_i} (\mathbf{GF}\,(enabled(l_i, l_i')) \rightarrow \mathbf{GF}\,(executed(l_i, l_i')))
$$

Strong fairness guarantees that all processes always eventually proceed in a computation of a concurrent system. Fairness assumptions are essential in order to verify stabilisation properties under realistic conditions. In our approach we focus on the stabilisation properties of the following form:

$$
\Psi \equiv \mathbf{F}\left((\mathbf{G}\,\phi_1)[m_1] \wedge \ldots \wedge (\mathbf{G}\,\phi_k)[m_k] \right)
$$

where $\phi_1, \ldots, \phi_k$ are predicate expressions over V_l and $m_1, \ldots, m_k \in \mathbb{N}$. Here we make use of the following abbreviations:

Definition 5 (Abbreviations). *Let $Sys(n)$ be a system over $V = V_g \cup V_l \times \{1, \ldots, n\}$. Let ϕ be a predicate expression over V_l and $m \leq n$. Then*

$$\phi[m] \equiv \bigvee_{i_1=1}^{n} \cdots \bigvee_{i_m=1}^{n} (\bigwedge_{j=1}^{m} \phi_{i_j})$$
$$(\mathbf{G}\,\phi)[m] \equiv \bigvee_{i_1=1}^{n} \cdots \bigvee_{i_m=1}^{n} (\bigwedge_{j=1}^{m} \mathbf{G}\,\phi_{i_j})$$

assuming that $i_1, \ldots, i_m$ pairwise disjoint.

Stabilisation is a crucial property for several kinds of parameterised systems. It claims that eventually a number of m_i processes will be forever in a state characterised by ϕ_i. For instance, the verification task

$$\forall n > 1 : [Sys(n), \varphi_g \wedge \varphi[n] \models \mathbf{F}\left((\mathbf{G}\,leader)[1] \wedge (\mathbf{G}\,terminated)[n-1]\right)]$$

(where $\varphi[n]$ abbreviates $\bigwedge_{i=1}^{n} \varphi_i$) expresses that for all instances of the system, eventually there one process will be forever the leader and $n-1$ processes will be forever terminated. For our leader election system and its processes P_i we define $terminated = (loc_i = 9) \wedge \bigwedge_{j \neq 9} \neg(loc_i = j)$ and $leader_i = (loc_i = 5) \wedge \bigwedge_{j \neq 5} \neg(loc_i = j)$, i.e., the leader will be the process that is eventually at location 5 forever. In the remainder we introduce an incremental approach to parameterised verification of stabilisation via *conditional spotlight abstraction*.

3   Conditional Spotlight Abstraction

Spotlight abstraction [12] allows to automatically abstract away entire processes of a parameterised system by summarising them in a single approximative process $P^\perp$. It is based on *predicate abstraction* [3] and *3-valued logic* $\mathcal{K}_3$ [5]. Thus, predicates in resulting state space models can take the values *true*, *false* and *unknown*, and the exploration of such models is known as *3-valued model checking* [2]. *Unknown* is used to represent the loss of information due to abstraction. The general idea of spotlight abstraction is to neglect the control flow of a selection of processes and to combine their behaviour in a single abstract operation $op^\perp$ that is continuously executed by $P^\perp$. The operation $op^\perp$ on 3-valued predicates approximates each concrete operation op on global variables that is potentially executed by a process summarised in $P^\perp$. The approximation relation '$\preceq$' on operations is defined based on $\mathcal{K}_3$. A detailed description of the spotlight principle and of 3-valued approximation can be found in [12,14]. Here we briefly illustrate classical spotlight abstraction and its limitations. Thereafter, we introduce our enhancement *conditional spotlight abstraction* (CSA) and show how it overcomes the drawbacks of the classical approach.

Parameterised verification requires to check some property of interest for each possible instance of a parameterised system $Sys(n) = P_1 \parallel \ldots \parallel P_n$. Spotlight abstraction allows to construct *one* abstract system that approximates *all* instances of the concrete system. In a first step a *spotlight size* is chosen which is a fixed $c \in \mathbb{N}$. Now c processes are explicitly considered in the abstract system whereas the parameterised number of $n - c$ processes is summarised in $P^{\perp}$:

$$Sys(n) = \underbrace{P_1 \parallel \ldots \parallel P_c}_{= Sys(c)} \parallel \underbrace{P_{c+1} \parallel \ldots \parallel P_n}_{\succeq P^{\perp}}$$

In the finite abstraction $Sys(c) \parallel P^{\perp}$ the approximative process is defined as

$$P^{\perp} :: \bigcirc \hspace{-0.6em} \curvearrowright op^{\perp}$$

such that $\forall op \in Op : op^{\perp} \preceq op$, where Op is the set of concrete operations occurring in the program code of the processes to be summarised in $P^{\perp}$. Thus, $op^{\perp}$ approximates each operation that is potentially executed by $P_{c+1}, \ldots, P_n$. Since we have uniform processes in parameterised systems, the number of potentially executed operations is finite. In our example system, the global predicates (resp. variables) y, $turn$ and $done$ are modified by the summarised processes. Since there exist both, operations that set these predicates to *true* and operations that set them to *false*, the application of spotlight abstraction yields an approximative process $P^{\perp}$ that continuously executes

$$op^{\perp} \equiv y := unknown, \; turn := unknown, \; done := unknown.$$

Hence, in computations of $Sys(c) \parallel P^{\perp}$ we may lose all definite information with regard to the values of y, $turn$ and $done$.

The approximation relation on operations can be generalised to processes and entire systems. From [14] we get that $\forall n > c : Sys(c) \parallel P^{\perp} \preceq Sys(n)$, i.e., a spotlight abstraction $Sys(c) \parallel P^{\perp}$ approximates all instances of $Sys(n)$ with n greater than c. Moreover, we get the following lemma with regard to the preservation of temporal logic properties under spotlight abstraction:

Lemma 1. *Let $Sys(c) \parallel P^{\perp}$ be a spotlight abstraction of a parameterised system $Sys(n)$ with initialisation predicate $\varphi_g \wedge \varphi[n]$ and let Ψ be an LTL formula. Then*

$$(\forall n > c : [Sys(n), \varphi_g \wedge \varphi[n] \models \Psi]) = \begin{cases} true & if \; [Sys(c) \parallel P^{\perp}, \varphi_g \wedge \varphi[c] \models \Psi] = true \\ false & if \; [Sys(c) \parallel P^{\perp}, \varphi_g \wedge \varphi[c] \models \Psi] = false \end{cases}$$

Hence, each *definite* result obtained under spotlight abstraction can be transferred to the original parameterised verification task. Note that verification under spotlight abstraction may also yield an *unknown* result, which does not allow to draw any conclusion about the original task. This also concerns our example task $\forall n > c : Sys(n), \varphi_g \wedge \varphi[n] \models \mathbf{F}\left((\mathbf{G}\, leader)[1] \wedge (\mathbf{G}\, terminated)[n-1]\right)$. Solving $Sys(c) \parallel P^{\perp}, \varphi_g \wedge \varphi[c] \models \mathbf{F}\left((\mathbf{G}\, leader)[1] \wedge (\mathbf{G}\, terminated)[c-1]\right)$ yields *unknown*. Thus, verification via spotlight abstraction fails in this case. Although it has been demonstrated that the spotlight principle allows to solve certain simple verification tasks [14], the major drawback of this approach is its rigorous concept of abstraction: The behaviour of entire processes is abstracted away, which frequently causes a loss of crucial information and thus makes the verification of systems operating on many global variables virtually impossible. Another drawback is that verification via classical spotlight abstraction is limited to properties that solely refer to the c concrete processes.

We now introduce *conditional spotlight abstraction* (CSA). Our enhanced approach allows to overcome the drawbacks of classical spotlight abstraction by exploiting already proven properties of the system under consideration. For a parameterised system typically *many* temporal logic properties are of interest where some properties are easier to verify than others. Certain properties might have been already successfully verified while others are still unproven. In particular, we will see in a later section that checking stabilisation properties can be done *incrementally* by first proving some form of partial stabilisation and second checking (full) stabilisation under the assumption of partial stabilisation. Thus, it is a realistic scenario that an LTL formula Ψ has to be verified assuming that another formula Ψ' holds. In fact, the initialisation predicate of a parameterised system is a trivial form of such an assumption. While the initialisation predicate is inherently temporal operator-free, we now show that assumptions containing temporal operators can be utilised to significantly increase the precision of the spotlight principle. Our CSA incorporates assumptions in the form of temporal logic formulas in the construction of the approximative process $P^{\perp}$.

We start with an illustrating example for conditional spotlight abstraction. For our leader election system $Sys(n)$ the LTL formula

$$\Psi' \equiv \mathbf{F}\left(\underbrace{(\mathbf{G}\,terminated)[n-c] \wedge \varphi_g \wedge \varphi[c]}_{=:\,\psi'}\right)$$

may have been already proven for some fixed $c \in \mathbb{N}$. Thus, we can assume that for all possible instances eventually $n - c$ processes will be forever terminated and c processes will be (still or again) in their initial configuration. The actual property of interest

$$\Psi \equiv \mathbf{F}\left(\underbrace{(\mathbf{G}\,leader)[1] \wedge (\mathbf{G}\,terminated)[n-1]}_{=:\,\psi}\right),$$

i.e., eventually exactly one leader forever, may be still unproven. For proving Ψ via CSA we make use of the following temporal logic inference rule:

$$\begin{array}{rl} (1): & \psi_1 \to \mathbf{F}\,\psi_2 \\ (2): & \psi_2 \to \mathbf{F}\,\psi_3 \\ \hline (3): & \psi_1 \to \mathbf{F}\,\psi_3 \end{array}$$

Thus, if, assuming ψ_1, eventually ψ_2 holds and, assuming ψ_2, eventually ψ_3 holds, then we can obviously conclude that, assuming ψ_1, eventually ψ_3 holds. In our example we have that (1): $\forall n > c : [Sys(n), \varphi_g \wedge \varphi[n] \models \mathbf{F}\,\psi']$ is already proven, i.e., assuming $\varphi_g \wedge \varphi[n]$, eventually ψ' holds. Now we take ψ' as the new initialisation assumption and check whether $\mathbf{F}\,\psi$ holds (2):

$$\forall n > c : \underbrace{P_1 \parallel \dots \parallel P_c}_{Sys(c),\varphi_g,\varphi[c]} \parallel \underbrace{P_{c+1} \parallel \dots \parallel P_n}_{P^{\perp}_{\mathbf{G}\,terminated}}, \underbrace{(\mathbf{G}\,terminated)[n-c] \wedge \varphi_g \wedge \varphi[c]}_{\psi'} \models \mathbf{F}\,\psi$$

We see that the new initial condition ψ' points at a spotlight abstraction with c concrete processes in their initial configuration and $n - c$ processes to be summarised in $P^\perp$. We additionally get from ψ' that the summarised processes are terminated forever, which allows us to augment the summary process with the condition $\mathbf{G}\,terminated$ where $terminated = (loc = 9) \wedge \bigwedge_{j \neq 9} \neg(loc = j)$. Hence, $\mathbf{G}\,terminated$ is a constraint on the control flow of each P_{c+1} to P_n and thus also on the potentially executed operations. The abstract operation $op^\perp$ executed by $P^\perp_{\mathbf{G}\,terminated}$ only has to approximate operations that are consistent with the constraint, i.e., operations from $Op_{\mathbf{G}\,terminated} = \{\tau(l, l') \in Op \,|\, l = 9 \wedge l' = 9\} = \{skip\}$. For our example the approximative process looks as follows:

$$P^\perp_{\mathbf{G}\,terminated} \;::\; \overset{\downarrow}{\bigcirc}\!\!\rightleftharpoons skip$$

i.e., by exploiting the proven fact that eventually $(\mathbf{G}\,terminated)[n - c]$ holds we get that the summarised processes will never again affect any global predicates. The general definition of the approximative process under CSA is as follows:

Definition 6 (Approximative Process under CSA). *Let* $P, \ldots, P'$ *be processes to be summarised under CSA and let* $\mathbf{G}\,\phi$ *be a constraint over the processes where* ϕ *temporal operator-free. Let* Op *be the set of operations occurring in* $P, \ldots, P'$. *Then the approximative process* $P^\perp_{\mathbf{G}\,\phi}$ *summarising* $P, \ldots, P'$ *continuously executes an operation* $op^\perp$ *with* $\forall op \in Op_{\mathbf{G}\phi} : op^\perp \preceq op$ *where*

$$Op_{\mathbf{G}\,\phi} = \{\tau(l, l') \in Op \,|\, Con\{\phi, (loc = l) \wedge (loc = l') \wedge e \wedge \bigwedge_{j=1}^{m}(v_j = e_j)\}\}$$

assuming that $\tau(l, l')$ *is of the form* $assume(e) \;:\; v_1 := e_1, \ldots, v_m := e_m$.

Here Con denotes logical consistency, i.e., $Con\{\phi_1, \phi_2\}$ holds if $\phi_1 \wedge \phi_2$ is not contradictory. We now get the following theorem with regard to the preservation of temporal logic properties under conditional spotlight abstraction:

Theorem 1 (Conditional Spotlight Abstraction). *Let* $Sys(n)$ *be a parameterised system with initialisation predicate* $\varphi_g \wedge \varphi[n]$. *Moreover, let* $\Psi' = \mathbf{F}\,\psi' = \mathbf{F}\left((\mathbf{G}\,\phi)[n - c] \wedge \phi'\right)$ *be an LTL formula with temporal operator-free sub formulae* ϕ *and* ϕ', *and* Ψ' *holds for all instances of the system. Then for all LTL formulae of the form* $\mathbf{F}\,\psi$ *the following holds:*

$$(\forall n > c : [Sys(n), \varphi_g \wedge \varphi[n] \models \mathbf{F}\,\psi]) = \begin{cases} true & if \;\; [Sys(c) \,\|\, P^\perp_{\mathbf{G}\,\phi}, \phi' \models \mathbf{F}\,\psi] = true \\ false & if \left(\begin{matrix} [Sys(c) \,\|\, P^\perp_{\mathbf{G}\,\phi}, \phi' \models \mathbf{F}\,\psi] = false \\ and \;\; \psi \rightarrow \mathbf{G}\neg\psi' \end{matrix} \right) \end{cases}$$

Proof. *See* http://www.cs.up.ac.za/cs/ntimm/proofs.pdf

Thus, having that $\mathbf{F}\left((\mathbf{G}\,\phi)[n - c] \wedge \phi'\right)$ holds for all instances of $Sys(n)$ we can take $(\mathbf{G}\,\phi)[n - c] \wedge \phi'$ as a new initialisation assumption and construct the corresponding CSA $Sys(c) \,\|\, P^\perp_{\mathbf{G}\,\phi}$. Next we check whether the property of interest holds for the CSA. Since CSA approximates all instances of the system, a *true* result can be immediately transferred to the original verification task. In order to transfer a *false* result, we additionally have to ensure that the assumption ψ' can only hold *before* ψ holds, which is done by the constraint $\psi \rightarrow \mathbf{G}\neg\psi'$. Checking the validity of the constraint typically does not require an extra verification run but already follows from the semantics of LTL.

Coming back to our example for conditional spotlight abstraction, checking $Sys(c) \parallel P_{\mathbf{G}\,terminated}^{\perp}, \varphi_g \wedge \varphi[c] \models \mathbf{F}\left((\mathbf{G}\,leader)[1] \wedge (\mathbf{G}\,terminated)[c-1]\right)$ yields *true* and Theorem 1 allows us to transfer this result to all system instances. Since we applied CSA under the condition $(\mathbf{G}\,terminated)[n-c]$ for the summarised processes and we showed that $(\mathbf{G}\,terminated)[c-1]$ holds for the concrete processes P_1 to P_c, we can even conclude that eventually $n-1$ processes will be forever terminated, i.e., we get that

$$\forall n > c : [Sys(n), \varphi_g \wedge \varphi[n] \models \mathbf{F}\left((\mathbf{G}\,leader)[1] \wedge (\mathbf{G}\,terminated)[n-1]\right)]$$

holds, which completes our conditional verification task[1]. By exploiting an already proven property that restricts the behaviour of the processes to be summarised we were able to construct a finite and small abstraction of a parameterised system that comprised all relevant details for a definite verification result. Thus, CSA can help to overcome the lack of precision of classical (spotlight) abstraction. Moreover, we are able to combine properties that follow from the assumption $((\mathbf{G}\,terminated)[n-c])$ and properties that result from verification under CSA $((\mathbf{G}\,terminated)[c-1])$ to an overall property $((\mathbf{G}\,terminated)[n-1])$. Note that we defined and illustrated CSA based on the case where the already proven Ψ' and the actual property of interest Ψ are of the form $\mathbf{F}(\mathbf{G}\,\phi)$ resp. $\mathbf{F}\,\psi$, i.e., properties that *eventually* hold. This is particularly useful for our incremental approach to stabilisation checking that we introduce in the next section. CSA also works if the condition is of the form $\mathbf{G}\,\phi$, i.e., it holds *instantly*. Then we can even check for arbitrary properties Ψ and are not restricted to $\mathbf{F}\,\psi$ properties.

4   Incremental Parameterised Verification via CSA

We now introduce a technique for parameterised verification of stabilisation properties via CSA. Our technique is based on a search for a provable assumption for CSA in the form of a partial stabilisation property. As discussed in the basics section, formulae characterising (full) stabilisation are of the form

$$\Psi \equiv \mathbf{F}\underbrace{\left((\mathbf{G}\,\phi_1)[m_1] \wedge \ldots \wedge (\mathbf{G}\,\phi_k)[m_k]\right)}_{=:\,\psi}$$

where $\phi_1, \ldots, \phi_k$ are predicate expressions over V_l. Stabilisation means that eventually a number k of stability properties holds, whereas stability means that

---

[1] The cases $1 < n \le c$ are decidable and can be easily proven via model checking.

forever some property ϕ holds. A formula Ψ' characterises *partial* stabilisation with regard to a (full) stabilisation formula Ψ if it is of the form

$$\Psi' \equiv \mathbf{F}\left(\underbrace{(\mathbf{G}\,\phi_1)[m_1'] \wedge \ldots \wedge (\mathbf{G}\,\phi_k)[m_k']}_{=:\,(\mathbf{G}\,\phi)[d]} \wedge \underbrace{\phi_1'[m_1 - m_1'] \wedge \ldots \wedge \phi_k'[m_k - m_k']}_{=:\,\phi'[n-d]}\right)$$

$$\underbrace{\phantom{\mathbf{F}\left((\mathbf{G}\,\phi_1)[m_1'] \wedge \ldots \wedge (\mathbf{G}\,\phi_k)[m_k'] \wedge \phi_1'[m_1 - m_1'] \wedge \ldots\right)}}_{=:\,\psi'}$$

where $m_1' \leq m_1, \ldots, m_k' \leq m_k$. Thus, partial stabilisation Ψ' with regard to some full stabilisation Ψ denotes that eventually $m_i' \leq m_i$ processes will stabilise in ϕ_i whereas $m_i - m_i'$ processes will reach ϕ_i' (and may or may not stabilise in ϕ_i later). For convenience, we from now on assume a simple partial stabilisation property of the form $\Psi' = \mathbf{F}((\mathbf{G}\,\phi)[d] \wedge \phi'[n-d])$. If $\Psi = \mathbf{F}\,\psi$ is a full stabilisation property and $\Psi' = \mathbf{F}\,\psi'$ is a corresponding partial stabilisation property then ψ characterises full stability whereas ψ' characterises partial stability.

In case a parameterised system stabilises then this naturally happens *incrementally*. Hence, some form of partial stability will always be reached before full stability will be reached. In our method we exploit this fact as follows: Given a stabilisation property of interest $\mathbf{F}\,\psi$, we systematically look for a corresponding provable partial stabilisation property $\mathbf{F}\,\psi'$. Then we assume partial stability and check for full stabilisation via conditional spotlight abstraction. Verifying partial stabilisation of a parameterised system is of course also undecidable in general. However, we will see that it is typically more likely and less computationally expensive to achieve a definite outcome in checking partial stabilisation than in directly checking full stabilisation. Our approach is based on *cutoff* arguments that allow us to reduce parameterised verification to a finite number of model checking runs. For illustrating our approach we again consider our leader election example where the stabilisation property of interest is

$$\Psi \equiv \mathbf{F}\left(\underbrace{(\mathbf{G}\,leader)[1] \wedge (\mathbf{G}\,terminated)[n-1]}_{=:\,\psi}\right)$$

and a corresponding partial stabilisation property is of the form

$$\Psi' \equiv \mathbf{F}\left(\underbrace{(\mathbf{G}\,terminated)[d] \wedge \varphi_g \wedge \varphi[n-d]}_{=:\,\psi'}\right),$$

i.e., we expect that for some fixed $d \in \mathbb{N}$ eventually d processes will be stabilised in *terminated* and $n - d$ processes P_i will be (still or again) in their initial configuration φ_i before full stabilisation will be reached. Note that it is a general assumption in verification that some basic form of abstraction, e.g., predicate abstraction, has been applied to the system. Under predicate abstraction local process computations that are not relevant to the interprocess communication are typically summarised into abstract regions. Thus, the configuration φ_i commonly characterises such a region and not only a single state, which makes our partial stabilisation property less restrictive. In order to prove that Ψ' holds for all instances of $Sys(n)$, we make use of the following cutoff theorem.

Theorem 2 (Cutoff-Based Stabilisation Checking). *Let $Sys(n)$ be a system with initialisation predicate $\varphi_g \wedge \varphi[n]$. Let $c, d \in \mathbb{N}$ be fixed with $d \leq c$ and ϕ be temporal operator-free LTL formula. Then the following implication holds:*

$$[Sys(c+1), \varphi_g \wedge \varphi[c+1] \models (\varphi[1]) \, \mathbf{U} \, ((\mathbf{G}\,\phi)[d] \wedge \varphi_g \wedge \varphi[c+1-d])]$$
$$\Rightarrow \forall n > c : [Sys(n), \varphi_g \wedge \varphi[n] \models \mathbf{F} \, ((\mathbf{G}\,\phi)[d] \wedge \varphi_g \wedge \varphi[n-d])]$$

Proof. *See* http://www.cs.up.ac.za/cs/ntimm/proofs.pdf

A cutoff refers to the size of an instance that is sufficiently large to check a certain property of interest and to transfer the result to all larger instances as well. We adapt this concept as follows: If a parameterised system satisfies some partial stabilisation property $\mathbf{F}\,\psi'$, then under all possible executions a state satisfying ψ' will be reached within a *finite* number of computational steps. Hence, only a *limited* number of processes can be actively involved in a computation reaching ψ'. Let c be this number, then an instance of size $c+1$ is obviously a cutoff. In order to determine the maximum number of processes that can be involved in reaching ψ', we strengthen the partial stabilisation formula as follows: We replace $\mathbf{F}\,\psi'$ (which is equivalent to $true\,\mathbf{U}\,\psi'$) by $\varphi[1]\,\mathbf{U}\,\psi'$. If we can prove the stronger formula $\varphi[1]\,\mathbf{U}\,\psi'$ for a fixed instance of size $c+1$ this tells us that $\mathbf{F}\,\psi'$ holds *and* there will be always at least one process in its initial region *until* ψ' holds. We can conclude that c is the maximum number of processes that can be involved in a computation reaching ψ', and since $\mathbf{F}\,\psi'$ holds for a system with $c+1$ processes we can transfer this result to any larger instance as well.

In comparison to existing techniques, e.g., [4,7,9] that detect cutoffs based on an analysis of the local state space of processes, we follow a different approach: We integrate cutoff detection into the verification task, i.e., we strengthen the property of interest such that we will only obtain a *true* result if we are using an admissible cutoff *and* the property of interest holds for the cutoff instance.

The following procedure illustrates how we iteratively search for a provable partial stabilisation property:

for $c = 1$ **to** ∞ **do**
    for $d = 1$ **to** c **do**
        if $Sys(c+1), \varphi_g \wedge \varphi[c+1] \models (\varphi[1]) \, \mathbf{U} \, ((\mathbf{G}\,\phi)[d] \wedge \varphi_g \wedge \varphi[c+1-d])$
        then
            return
            $\forall n > c : Sys(n), \varphi_g \wedge \varphi[n] \models \mathbf{F} \, ((\mathbf{G}\,\phi)[d] \wedge \varphi_g \wedge \varphi[n-d])$

For our example the procedure terminates for $c = 2$ and $d = 1$. Hence, we get

$$\forall n > 2 : Sys(n), \varphi_g \wedge \varphi[n] \models \mathbf{F} \, ((\mathbf{G}\,terminated)[1] \wedge \varphi_g \wedge \varphi[n-1])$$

This result points at a CSA with one terminated process to be summarised and $n-1$ concrete processes. Since the number of concrete processes would be still parameterised, the application of CSA would so far not give us a finite abstraction. However, we will now see that partial stabilisation results can be easily expanded such that they point at expedient CSAs. In expanding the result we already make use of the conditional spotlight principle: We need to show that the partial stabilisation property Ψ' also holds when we extend $Sys(n)$ by an approximative component. In the same manner we have proven Ψ' for all instances of $Sys(n)$ via the cutoff theorem, we can also show the following:

$$\forall n > 2 : Sys(n) \parallel P^{\perp}_{\mathbf{G}\,terminated}, \varphi_g \wedge \varphi[n] \models \mathbf{F}\left((\mathbf{G}\,terminated)[1] \wedge \varphi_g \wedge \varphi[n-1]\right)$$

If partial stabilisation Ψ' has been proven for both, systems *with* and *without* an approximative component then we can apply the following theorem that gives us the expanded partial stabilisation result:

Theorem 3 (Expanding Partial Stabilisation Results). *Let $Sys(n)$ be a system with initialisation predicate $\varphi_g \wedge \varphi[n]$. Let $c, d \in \mathbb{N}$ be fixed with $d \leq c$ and ϕ be temporal operator-free LTL formula. Then the following holds:*

$$\forall n > c : \left[Sys(n), \varphi_g \wedge \varphi[n] \models \mathbf{F}\left((\mathbf{G}\,\phi)[d] \wedge \varphi_g \wedge \varphi[n-d]\right)\right]$$
$$\wedge \; \forall n > c : \left[Sys(n) \parallel P^{\perp}_{\mathbf{G}\,\phi}, \varphi_g \wedge \varphi[n] \models \mathbf{F}\left((\mathbf{G}\,\phi)[d] \wedge \varphi_g \wedge \varphi[n-d]\right)\right]$$
$$\Rightarrow \forall n > c : \left[Sys(n), \varphi_g \wedge \varphi[n] \models \mathbf{F}\left((\mathbf{G}\,\phi)[n-f] \wedge \varphi_g \wedge \varphi[f]\right)\right]$$

where $f = (n \mod d) + c + 1 - d$ (which also means $1 \leq f \leq c$).

Proof. *See* http://www.cs.up.ac.za/cs/ntimm/proofs.pdf

In the proof we make use of the fact that $Sys(n)$ will eventually reach a configuration corresponding to $Sys(n-d) \parallel P^{\perp}_{\mathbf{G}\,\phi}$, which will in turn reach a configuration corresponding to $Sys(n-d-d) \parallel P^{\perp}_{\mathbf{G}\,\phi}$ and so on, until we reach a configuration where the number of non-stabilised processes is f with $1 \leq f \leq c$ and the number of stabilised processes is $n - f$ which is a multiple of d. Thus, from Theorem 3 we get that partial stabilisation of d processes implies partial stabilisation of $n - f$ processes. For our running example we get $f = 2$, i.e.,

$$\forall n > 2 : \left[Sys(n), \varphi_g \wedge \varphi[n] \models \mathbf{F}\left(\underbrace{(\mathbf{G}\,terminated)[n-2]}_{P^{\perp}_{\mathbf{G}\,\phi}} \wedge \underbrace{\varphi_g \wedge \varphi[2]}_{Sys(2),\varphi_g \wedge \varphi[2]}\right)\right]$$

The expanded result points at a CSA where we summarise the parameterised number of stabilised processes in the approximative component. Via CSA we now can check for full stabilisation $\mathbf{F}\left((\mathbf{G}\,leader)[1] \wedge (\mathbf{G}\,terminated)[n-1]\right)$. Since the stabilisation of $n - 2$ processes in *terminated* is part of the already proven assumption, it only remains to show that

$$Sys(2) \parallel P^{\perp}_{\mathbf{G}\,\phi}, \varphi_g \wedge \varphi[2] \models \mathbf{F}\left((\mathbf{G}\,leader)[1] \wedge (\mathbf{G}\,terminated)[1]\right)$$

holds. Checking this decidable task yields *true* and the CSA theorem from Sect. 3 allows us to conclude that also

$$\forall n > 2 : \left[Sys(n), \varphi_g \wedge \varphi[n] \models \mathbf{F}\left((\mathbf{G}\,leader)[1] \wedge (\mathbf{G}\,terminated)[n-1]\right)\right]$$

holds, which successfully completes our parameterised verification task. For other verification tasks f (which is defined as $(n \mod d)+c+1-d$) may be not distinct but restricted to values from the typically very small set $\{1, \ldots, c\}$. This reflects the fact that the extent of partial stabilisation may depend on the instance size n. In this case we have to check for full stabilisation via CSA for all $f \in \{1, \ldots, c\}$.

In summary, our technique for parameterised verification of stabilisation works as follows: Given a system $Sys(n)$ and a stabilisation property $\mathbf{F}\,\psi$, we systematically search for a corresponding partial stabilisation property $\mathbf{F}\,\psi'$ that can be proven for both $Sys(n)$ and $Sys(n) \parallel P_{G\,\phi}^{\perp}$ via our cutoff technique with property strengthening (Theorem 2). Next, we apply stabilisation expansion (Theorem 3) which yields an expanded property $\mathbf{F}\,\psi''$ that also holds for $Sys(n)$. Finally, we use ψ'' as the assumption for CSA, which gives us a finite abstraction on which we can check $\mathbf{F}\,\psi$. Theorem 1 allows us to transfer the result to all instances of $Sys(n)$ that are greater than the cutoff. Since we deal with an undecidable problem, our approach is incomplete in the sense that the search for a partial stabilisation property might not terminate or CSA-based model checking might return *unknown*. However, in preliminary experiments we were able to successfully verify several example systems implementing leader election.

5   Related Work

Our technique is related to a number of existing approaches to parameterised verification. The cutoff concept was introduced in [4] where it was shown that for the verification of certain properties there exist cutoffs that are polynomial in the number of local states of processes. Other cutoff approaches impose restrictions on the communication scheme, e.g., only lock-based communication [7], and thus do not support the verification of systems with shared-variable, concurrency. [8] introduces dynamic cutoff detection during verification. The approach has no restrictions on communication but is limited to safety properties. To the best of our knowledge, we are the first to integrate cutoff detection into the verification task by strengthening the property to be checked with a cutoff condition. Verification of stabilisation has been considered in [6, 10, 11]. [6] presents a semi-automatic strategy for stabilisation checking that requires a user-provided function on states measuring the progress of computation towards stabilisation. In [10] an approach to the verification of convergence in self-stabilising protocols is proposed. It is based on the derivation of convergence proofs. Convergence is a necessary but not sufficient condition for stabilisation. In [11] a verification technique for stabilisation in population protocols is presented. The technique is based on modelling the possible actions of the protocol whereas actual processes are not part of the model. All these approaches for stabilisation checking perform verification on the basis of an algorithmic description of a protocol. In contrast, we focus on the verification of systems that *implement* protocols in a C-like language. Since the implementation of a protocol may introduce errors that are not present in the algorithmic description, a distinct verification of implementations is indispensable. (Unconditional) spotlight abstraction was introduced in [12, 14].

While the original technique is not capable of verifying stabilisation, our extension to CSA has closed this gap. Another related approach is conditional model checking [1]. Here properties are checked under conditions that restrict which part of the model is explored. In contrast, we use conditions in order to abstract away processes while preserving relevant information about their behaviour.

6 Conclusion and Outlook

We introduced an automatic technique for parameterised verification of stabilisation, which is a vital property in many safety-critical systems. Our technique reduces parameterised verification to a finite number of abstraction-based model checking runs. One of our key concepts is *incremental verification* by first proving partial stabilisation, and then checking for full stabilisation under the assumption of partial stabilisation. The approach profits from the fact that proving partial stabilisation naturally requires smaller cutoffs and thus less computational effort than directly proving full stabilisation. Our conditional spotlight abstraction allows us to exploit already proven properties in order to construct a small abstract model that still preserves relevant information about the system. Stabilisation cutoff detection and CSA are not limited to stabilisation checking. The cutoff approach also works for arbitrary properties of the form $\mathbf{F}\,\psi$. CSA can also be used for other forms of conditional verification. Moreover, our approach can be generalised to the verification of systems with different classes of uniform processes (class-wise symmetric systems) and to systems extended by individual processes like daemons modelling potential faults. We implemented our technique on top of our 3-valued model checker [13] with strong fairness. Preliminary experiments show promising performance results. With our tool we could verify stabilisation of several leader election protocols implemented as parameterised systems. An experimental evaluation based on wireless sensor networks is in preparation.

Acknowledgements. We thank Mike Poppleton for fruitful discussions in the context of this paper.

References

1. Beyer, D., Henzinger, T.A., Keremoglu, M.E., Wendler, P.: Conditional model checking: a technique to pass information between verifiers. In: Tracz, W., Robillard, M.P., Bultan, T. (eds.) 20th ACM SIGSOFT Symposium on the Foundations of Software Engineering (FSE-20), SIGSOFT/FSE 2012, Cary. 11–16 November 2012, pp. 57:1–57:11. ACM (2012). http://doi.acm.org/10.1145/2393596.2393664
2. Bruns, G., Godefroid, P.: Model checking partial state spaces with 3-valued temporal logics. In: Halbwachs, N., Peled, D. (eds.) CAV 1999. LNCS, vol. 1633, pp. 274–287. Springer, Heidelberg (1999). doi:10.1007/3-540-48683-6_25
3. Clarke, E., Kroening, D., Sharygina, N., Yorav, K.: SATABS: SAT-based predicate abstraction for ANSI-C. In: Halbwachs, N., Zuck, L.D. (eds.) TACAS 2005. LNCS, vol. 3440, pp. 570–574. Springer, Heidelberg (2005). doi:10.1007/978-3-540-31980-1_40

4. Emerson, E.A., Kahlon, V.: Reducing model checking of the many to the few. In: McAllester, D. (ed.) CADE 2000. LNCS (LNAI), vol. 1831, pp. 236–254. Springer, Heidelberg (2000). doi:10.1007/10721959_19

5. Fitting, M.: Kleene's three valued logics and their children. Fundamenta Informaticae **20**(1/2/3), 113–131 (1994). http://dx.doi.org/10.3233/FI-1994-201234

6. Ghosh, R., Mitra, S.: A strategy for automatic verification of stabilization of distributed algorithms. In: Graf, S., Viswanathan, M. (eds.) FORTE 2015. LNCS, vol. 9039, pp. 35–49. Springer, Heidelberg (2015). doi:10.1007/978-3-319-19195-9_3

7. Kahlon, V., Ivančić, F., Gupta, A.: Reasoning about threads communicating via locks. In: Etessami, K., Rajamani, S.K. (eds.) CAV 2005. LNCS, vol. 3576, pp. 505–518. Springer, Heidelberg (2005). doi:10.1007/11513988_49

8. Kaiser, A., Kroening, D., Wahl, T.: Dynamic cutoff detection in parameterized concurrent programs. In: Touili, T., Cook, B., Jackson, P. (eds.) CAV 2010. LNCS, vol. 6174, pp. 645–659. Springer, Heidelberg (2010). doi:10.1007/978-3-642-14295-6_55

9. Kouvaros, P., Lomuscio, A.: A cutoff technique for the verification of parameterised interpreted systems with parameterised environments. In: Rossi, F. (ed.) Proceedings of the 23rd International Joint Conference on Artificial Intelligence, IJCAI 2013, Beijing, 3–9 August 2013, pp. 2013–2019. IJCAI/AAAI (2013). http://www.aaai.org/ocs/index.php/IJCAI/IJCAI13/paper/view/6919

10. Oehlerking, J., Dhama, A., Theel, O.: Towards automatic convergence verification of self-stabilizing algorithms. In: Tixeuil, S., Herman, T. (eds.) SSS 2005. LNCS, vol. 3764, pp. 198–213. Springer, Heidelberg (2005). doi:10.1007/11577327_14

11. Pang, J., Luo, Z., Deng, Y.: On automatic verification of self-stabilizing population protocols. Front. Comput. Sci. China **2**(4), 357–367 (2008). http://dx.doi.org/10.1007/s11704-008-0040-9

12. Schrieb, J., Wehrheim, H., Wonisch, D.: Three-valued spotlight abstractions. In: Cavalcanti, A., Dams, D.R. (eds.) FM 2009. LNCS, vol. 5850, pp. 106–122. Springer, Heidelberg (2009). doi:10.1007/978-3-642-05089-3_8

13. Timm, N., Gruner, S., Harvey, M.: A bounded model checker for three-valued abstractions of concurrent software systems. In: Ribeiro, L., Lecomte, T. (eds.) SBMF 2016. LNCS, vol. 10090, pp. 199–216. Springer, Heidelberg (2016). doi:10.1007/978-3-319-49815-7_12

14. Timm, N., Wehrheim, H.: On symmetries and spotlights – verifying parameterised systems. In: Dong, J.S., Zhu, H. (eds.) ICFEM 2010. LNCS, vol. 6447, pp. 534–548. Springer, Heidelberg (2010). doi:10.1007/978-3-642-16901-4_35

Author Index

Printed in the United States
By Bookmasters